Brazil

modern architectures in history

This international series examines the forms and consequences of modern architecture. Modernist visions and revisions are explored in their national context against a backdrop of aesthetic currents, economic developments, political trends and social movements. Written by experts in the architectures of the respective countries, the series provides a fresh, critical reassessment of Modernism's positive and negative effects, as well as the place of architectural design in twentieth-century history and culture.

Series editor: Vivian Constantinopoulos

Already published:

Britain
Alan Powers

Finland
Roger Connah

USA
Gwendolyn Wright

Forthcoming:

Austria
Liane Lefaivre

France
Jean-Louis Cohen

Germany
Iain Boyd Whyte

Greece
Alexander Tzonis and Alkistis Rodi

India
Peter Scriver

Italy
Diane Ghirardo

Japan
Botond Bognar

Netherlands
Nancy Stieber

Spain
David Cohn

Switzerland
Stanislaus Von Moos

Turkey
Sibel Bozdogan and Esra Akcan

Brazil

modern architectures in history

Richard J. Williams

REAKTION BOOKS

Published by Reaktion Books Ltd
33 Great Sutton Street
London EC1V 0DX, UK

www.reaktionbooks.co.uk

First published 2009

The publishers gratefully acknowledge support for the publication of this book by the
Graham Foundation for Advanced Studies in the Fine Arts

Printed and bound in Great Britain by MPG Books Ltd, Bodmin, Cornwall

British Library Cataloguing in Publication Data
Williams, Richard J., 1967–
    Brazil. – (Modern architectures in history)
    1. Architecture – Brazil – 20th century
    I. Title
    720.9'81'09045

ISBN: 978 1 86189 400 7

Contents

Introduction

Ever since its discovery by the Portuguese in 1500, Brazil has been a mythic as well as a real place. Its empty centre in particular has been an imaginative space as much as a real one, filled with all manner of fantasies. For Brazilians themselves in the 1950s, it was the site of the construction of a new capital – a central episode in this book – an act that realized a long-held desire to unify the nation and open up commercial development of the country's supposed vast mineral wealth.[1] For the foreign visitor, Brazil was for centuries an emptiness that was known to exist, but about which almost nothing could be verified. It could be imaginatively filled with the fears and desires repressed from bourgeois European civilization: sexual licence, nudity, violence, lawlessness, tropical disease, shamanist magic and dangerous animals. Arthur Conan Doyle provided the popular blueprint for this imagination of Brazil in *The Lost World* (1912), which describes an expedition to a plateau so remote from evolutionary processes that it is still populated by dinosaurs.[2] Something of this exoticism persists when it comes to architecture. Brazil always seems to represent the exotic or the erotic;[3] things are invariably possible there that are not elsewhere; the normal rules and conventions are suspended, at least discursively; it is the perennial exception.

However, for the middle part of the twentieth century (usually 1930–60, for reasons that will become clear), Brazil was an exemplar of modern development. During this period, it would be no exaggeration to say that Brazil was the most modern country in the world. That is not to say the most developed (it was not) or the most socially advanced (it was in most respects little changed from the colonial period), but that it was the country that had bought into the idea of modernity most comprehensively, and it wished to remake itself in that image. The place of architecture in this scheme was crucial. For many outside the country, Brazil represented the pinnacle of what could be achieved with modern architecture given enthusiasm and the absence of the restraints of the Old World. When the Austrian poet Stefan Zweig arrived there in 1941, he dashed off a memoir of his stay called *The Land of the Future*.[4] It was

Lúcio Costa, Oscar Niemeyer and others, MES building, Rio de Janeiro, 1936–43.

written, probably, as part of a bargain with the regime of President Vargas to let him stay, and is a eulogy from start to finish: everything about the place is energetic, exotic, exciting – but not enough to restore the poet's mental equilibrium, it should be said. He and his wife committed suicide in Petropolis in 1942, apparently in despair at the state of the Europe they had left behind.

Zweig may have been under pressure from the Vargas regime to say good things, but equally, by 1942, there was plenty to say. As Zweig found, much about the country was self-consciously modern. It had an unusually well-developed air transport network. Foreign visitors increasingly flew around it by aeroplane rather than travel by land or water. It had a wealth of new infrastructural projects. It had (as we would call it now) a booming leisure industry centred on the developing resort-city of Copacabana, the equal in sophistication to anything found in Europe. And it had, above all, a remarkably modern architectural culture that had appeared out of nowhere, and was now doing things with concrete and plate glass that were as advanced as anything anywhere.

One of the principal motivations for representatives of the Museum of Modern Art in New York to visit Brazil the year after Zweig's book was published was to see for themselves the new technology of the *brise-soleil* of which they had heard in respect of the new building of the Ministry of Education and Health (Ministério de Educação e Saúde, or MES) in Rio de Janeiro. As MOMA's Philip Goodwin made clear in the catalogue *Brazil Builds*, the treatment of the façade on modern buildings such as the MES and its near neighbour, the Associação Brasileira da Imprensa (ABI), was unusual, and far in advance of anything they had encountered in the United States.[5] They went to observe and learn. Similarly, when the anthropologist Claude Lévi-Strauss visited Brazil for the first time in 1936, he found in São Paulo a city as self-consciously modern as any in the world.[6] Indeed, up until the inauguration of Brasília in April 1960, Brazil was understood as a country that, whatever its limitations, was modernizing fast, and could leapfrog development in more advanced nations.

The Ministry of Education and Health

The architectural emblem of this process is unquestionably the MES. The result of an architectural competition initiated by the energetic 36-year-old minister of culture, Gustavo Capanema, it marked the beginning of the Brazilian state's long-standing engagement with Modernism. Designed in 1936 by a team consisting of Lúcio Costa, Carlos Leão, Jorge Moreira, Oscar Niemeyer, Affonso Reidy and Ernani Vasconcelos,

Lucio Costa, Oscar Niemeyer and others, MES building, Rio de Janeiro, 1936–43.

with the involvement of a painter, Cândido Portinari, and a landscape architect, Roberto Burle Marx, on the exterior, the building indexed the best young architectural talent available in Rio. But it was the involvement of Le Corbusier that attracted particular comment outside Brazil. Invited by the team, Le Corbusier arrived in June 1936, and spent four weeks on the project, during which he worked most closely with Niemeyer. Niemeyer became Le Corbusier's de facto interpreter, translating the Swiss architect's ideas for the rest of the team, and it

Cândido Portinari, *azulejos* on the MES building.

was his involvement on this project that kick-started his remarkable seventy-year career.[7]

Formally, the MES was an eleven-storey slab on pilotis, set back from the busy Rua da Imprensa in the centre of Rio. Its north-eastern face was marked by a deeply sculptural use of *brises-soleil*, the south-western face by plate glass. The small park at ground level, landscaped by Roberto Burle Marx, was dotted with Modernist sculptures, while the walls in the shady area under the pilotis sported a cubist design in blue Portuguese-style tiles (*azulejos*) by Cândido Portinari. It was not just a building therefore, but a showcase of Modernist visual culture, all the more remarkable for Rio, a city then still making itself in the image of Second Empire Paris. The biggest, boldest exercise yet in architectural Modernism, as word seeped out, it became a worldwide architectural sensation. The initial reaction was uncertain, the architectural historian Yves Bruand has written, with the American journal *Architectural Record* giving it a somewhat uncomprehending treatment in 1943.[8] But the same year Philip Goodwin provided a rave review in the catalogue *Brazil Builds*. It was, he wrote, 'no merely skin-deep beauty', but a 'fresh and careful study of the complicated needs of the modern office building'. The system of *brises-soleil* was 'startling', the first of its kind in the world.[9] In 1943 the *New York Times* declared the MES 'the most advanced architectural structure in the world'.[10] In 1947 the French journal *L'Architecture d'aujourd'hui* devoted six pages to the MES in a special issue on new architecture in Brazil. By this stage, as Bruand has described, the MES had been published in all the major journals worldwide, and had been almost universally praised. Furthermore, it had come to embody a new national sentiment: everything the Brazilian government wished to communicate about its modernizing intentions was materialized in this building.[11] The only discordant note in the early years was provided by the Swiss architect-critic Max Bill, who in 1953 complained about the MES's highly decorative façade, its *azulejos* in particular: a 'dangerously academic' building, he thought. But it is his puritanical brand of Modernism, not the MES, that now seems out of step.[12]

Brazil's Modernisms

In standard architectural histories, Modernism is a set of precise values, with clearly defined historical limits. For Kenneth Frampton, Modernism's origins lay in the latter part of the nineteenth century, in the various flourishings of Art Nouveau, for example, and the work of William Morris. Modernism came into being in the first two decades of the twentieth century through Le Corbusier and his followers, and the Bauhaus, then passed through the polarized sensibilities of Brutalism and Miesian neo-classicism. It is underpinned throughout by the certainty that architecture and human behaviour are linked, and the resultant belief that architecture can and should change human society. It often declares itself to be inevitable, the logical result of developments in the human and natural sciences.[13] Most importantly, the historians of Modernism write, it is *over*.

In Anglophone histories of Modernism, the date of the end is often astonishingly precise. Charles Jencks's notorious statement that it ended with the demolition of the Pruitt-Igoe public housing project in St Louis on 16 March 1972 is clearly rhetorical. But for others, Modernism's end is not much less precise; few writers in English assume it persisted any longer than the early 1970s.[14]

Marcelo and Milton
Roberto, ABI building,
Rio de Janeiro, 1936–9.

Such a history is misleading when applied to Brazil, a country that has
never had any popular reaction against Modernism. In Brazil, Modernism
is, and has been since the 1930s, the default style for buildings of any size.
In terms of brute output, the moment at which in the international
journals Modernism was passing through its greatest crisis – 1968 to 1972
– was in Brazil probably its apogee, when its great cities became mega-
lopoli, built up in the Modernist style, albeit a loosely interpreted version
of it. If we are to take Brazilian Modernism seriously, we need therefore a
different historical structure, crucially one that understands it not as a
tendency of the historical past, but as something that continues into the

present. This has not only to do with the particular critical understanding of Modernism in Brazil, but also – perhaps uniquely – at the time of writing the living presence of architects of the Modernist generation who have continued to work in the same idiom into the twenty-first century, principally Oscar Niemeyer and Paulo Mendes da Rocha. The book's timeframe therefore extends into the present.

At the other end of the timeframe is February 1922, when a remarkable arts festival, the *Semana de Arte Moderna* (Modern Art Week), took place in São Paulo's Municipal Theatre. Organized principally by a painter, Emilio di Cavalcanti, and a poet, Mário de Andrade, it marks the first attempt to introduce Modernist culture to Brazil, and – most importantly – to establish the nature of Brazil's potential contribution to it. In terms of architecture, the real starting point is 1927, when the Russian émigré architect and polemicist Gregori Warchavchik started work on a Modernist house for himself and his wife in the São Paulo suburb of Vila Mariana. Completed in 1928, the house is a tour de force, integrating the latest European practice with local materials and methods.

A year later, 1929, Le Corbusier first visited Rio de Janeiro. The conditions he found were not promising. As fascinating as Brazil was for him, it was also at that moment an isolated and provincial culture, only 17 million in population, mostly rural, and socially backward. What high culture existed was imported from Europe. As Lauro Cavalcanti has noted, the fact that Le Corbusier spoke only French on his Rio visits – apparently without interpretation – meant that his audience was limited to a highly educated, middle class. It seems that the audience for his 1929 talks in Rio numbered as few as ten, mostly the architects (Costa, Niemeyer, et al.) with whom he would go on to collaborate.[15] Even then, Costa recalled dropping in on one of the lectures and leaving again, not really having paid much attention.[16] In the mid-1920s there were only eleven subscriptions in the whole of Brazil to *L'Esprit nouveau*, edited by Le Corbusier and Amédée Ozenfant, a journal usually considered vital for the development of Modernism. The great Brazilian historian Sérgio Buarque de Holanda complained that Brazil's culture was just 'grafted' from elsewhere: 'this means that a false tradition has arisen which doesn't stop short of prolonging foreign traditions . . . what we need to is to find our own way'.[17]

Le Corbusier's visit – discussed in more detail in chapter Two – is nevertheless important in developing a dialogue between Brazil and Europe on the topic of modern architecture, and, moreover, providing Le Corbusier with a great deal of imaginative material. The crucial design output of this visit is perhaps the plan for Rio de Janeiro. Here a series of sketches re-imagine the city as a serpentine megastructure, curving along

Gregori Warchavchik,
house, São Paulo,
1928. The house is
now badly decayed.

Le Corbusier, plan for
Rio de Janeiro, 1929.

Lúcio Costa and
Oscar Niemeyer,
Brazilian Pavilion,
New York World's
Fair, 1939, sketch.

the coast, providing its citizens with both beach and mountain scenery and a new transport infrastructure. It is pure fantasy, and never worked up into anything concrete, but has echoes in housing projects done later by Affonso Reidy, including the iconic Pedregulho (1947).

From this point on, a series of significant moments can be delineated, in which Brazil became progressively more central to a global history of Modernism. The most important of these is the sensational MES, already mentioned. But before the MES's completion there had already been the equally sensational Brazilian pavilion for the New York World's Fair by Costa and Niemeyer in 1939. This brought Brazilian design to an American audience for the first time, and created for that public a profoundly erotic image of leisure, luxury and natural abundance that was hard to resist. The pavilion also made clear the country's immense scale; by means of a giant map of Brazil on which the US was super-imposed, Brazil was shown to be rather bigger in land area than the main part of the host nation. In 1942 Niemeyer's widely reported designs for the luxury housing development at Pampulha and the exhibition *Brazil Builds* (1943) at MOMA in New York were again vital in disseminating the developments in Brazil to the wider world. Niemeyer's conspicuous involvement on the design for the United Nations headquarters building during the years 1947–50, under the leadership of the American architect

Wallace K. Harrison, made Brazilian modern architecture in effect the image of world government – indeed modern government in general, thinking of Harrison's later design for Albany civic centre in upstate New York. At the same time, the São Paulo Bienal, an event of remarkable bravura founded by the Italian-Brazilian industrialist Ciccillo Matarazzo, turned early 1950s Brazil into a clearing house of global visual culture. In its first manifestation in 1951, the Bienal managed to borrow, quite remarkably, Picasso's famous *Guernica* from the Museum of Modern Art in New York.[18] Finally, the adventure of Brasília during 1957–60, the biggest single building project in world history up to that point, showed the ambitions of Brazilian Modernism to be unsurpassed. The heroic period of Brazilian Modernism belongs not just to Brazil, but also to world history. The listing of Brasília as a UNESCO World Heritage Site in 1987 is important confirmation.

Brasília is where many histories of Brazilian Modernism stop. As the Brazilian critic Ruth Verde Zein has put it, because of the military coup in 1964, and the subsequent close identification of the capital with the new regime, Modernism and authoritarian politics became closely linked in the minds of many in the mostly liberal or left-leaning intelligentsia. It became easier to say that, in terms of architecture at least, 'after Brasília nothing happened', and this is certainly the impression given by many histories of the topic, both domestic and foreign. It was a process aided by the exile or imprisonment of most of the crucial figures of Brazilian Modernism, from Niemeyer to Mendes da Rocha.[19]

But an enormous amount happened after Brasília, not least because under the military Brazil underwent an unprecedented period of economic growth, the so-called economic miracle during which many large infrastructural projects were realized: the BR 230 Trans-Amazonian highway (1972), the Ilha Solteira hydroelectric scheme of the Paraná River (1973) and the São Paulo metro (1974) are representative examples. My extended history of Modernism therefore looks at the 1960s and '70s in some detail. Crucial moments include the radical architectures of Vilanova Artigas and his disciples, the Grupo Arquitetura Nova; the para-architectural activities of artists such as Hélio Oiticica, and their sublimation of the aesthetics of the *favela*; the enormous growth of São Paulo and the extraordinary landscape produced by the 'miracle'; the continued work of Modernists such as Niemeyer and Mendes da Rocha; in recent years, the revised concept of Modernism in the work of Ruy Ohtake and others; and the continuation of the liberal character of Modernist urbanism in the work of Jaime Lerner in Curitiba. This is a history that continues up to the present day and explicitly does not identify familiar points of 'rupture' in the discourse about Modernism.

Such ideological rupture is, in any case, hard to find in Brazil. It is significant that one the main sources for the death of Modernism, Jane Jacobs's *Death and Life of Great American Cities*, was not published in Portuguese until 2000.[20] This could be regarded as evidence of a provincial and backward architectural culture. I would argue otherwise – that Modernism was simply more embedded in Brazilian culture than elsewhere. It was, and many ways still is, the default architectural culture, defining the country much better than the few remaining examples of Portuguese colonial building.

The Brazilian architect best-known outside Brazil, Oscar Niemeyer, dominates all existing accounts of Brazilian Modernism, unsurprising given the number and quality of his buildings and his major presence in Brazil as a cultural figure. But his work is concentrated in a few places, and is dominated by a few prestigious building types. A study of Niemeyer has little to say about the explosive growth of Brazil's cities during the late 1960s and early 1970s, about the vast commercial development of São Paulo, about radical attempts to rethink architecture and the role of architects in the 1960s, or about the astringent, moralizing strand of Brutalism that is still visible in the work of Mendes da Rocha, or the continuing presence of the *favela* in all big Brazilian cities. This book therefore employs an expanded definition of Modernism to the one normally employed. I am not concerned here only with a small number of critically validated Modernist buildings by Niemeyer and a few others, concentrated in a limited historical period, but rather Modernism as a field of action, containing multiple critical ideas, architectures of varying and often degraded quality, and activities (such as art) on the periphery of architecture but still nonetheless important to its understanding of itself. This expanded view of Modernism provides a framework that allows us, as we shall see, to talk about such things as the extraordinary, but critically devalued landscape of São Paulo, the reiteration of Modernism in architecture in recent years and the luxury developments along the oceanfront in such places as Rio de Janeiro. It also provides many opportunities to talk about questions of poverty in architecture, questions that are usually ignored or devalued.

By traditional standards, Brazil's Modernism is of a decidedly impure kind. This has long been recognized, but more usually described as a fault. In architectural discourse, perhaps the best-known statement about it is by the Bauhaus-trained architect Max Bill. We have already seen his opinion of the MES. Even worse was what he had seen in São Paulo. Bill was incandescent. In the city he had found modern architecture sunk to the depths, a riot of anti-social waste lacking any sense of responsibility towards the business occupant or his customers . . . thick pilotis, thin pilotis, pilotis of whimsical shapes lacking any structural rhyme or reason, disposed all over the place.[21]

It was 'jungle growth', he concluded in a curiously neo-colonialist aside, not architecture. Bill's understanding of Modernism is a fundamentally rational project in which form is ultimately determined by function or need. It has little room for flights of fancy, for decoration, for individualism, for anything, in fact, that cannot be rationally justified. It barely needs to be said that Bill's formulation rules out not only the street that caused him so much displeasure, but also most of Brazil's Modernist buildings.

Bill's Modernism is univalent, and in a curious way apolitical in that it attempts to stand outside worldly affairs. By contrast, Modernism in Brazil is polyvalent and highly politicized, with each strand in effect a representation of a distinct worldview. Not all of these worldviews overlap, either chronologically or ideologically, and for these reasons normative Euro-American understandings of Modernism do not work. In the past this was understood as a problem, or a weakness, inside as well as outside Brazil – there was, as it were, an intellectual conspiracy to keep Brazil provincial. More recently, a revisionist approach has become apparent, not least because the multivalency of the Modernist project in Brazil has provided contemporary architects with models for its continuation in the present. The exhibition *Entrar e Sair da Modernidade* (Getting In and Out of Modernity), held at the Museu de Arte de São Paulo (MASP) in 2008, is a good example of the revisionist approach in practice. Its curator, Teixeira Coelho, wrote:

> The Modern is not one but several. All of them, plus the reflection on the whole, form Modernity. The artists of the time did not all line up along the same perspective. Some of them decided to enter this Modernity; others, at some moment tried not to get in, or get out of it – at the same time pretending by doing that, in certain cases, to be more modern than the rest or to be really modern.[22]

Coelho was writing with regard to art, but the argument he makes works equally well for architecture and urbanism. For this reason, the book has been organized around a set of distinct politics. There is a broad chronology, but this chronology does not itself describe a coherent narrative because, frankly, there is none to be described. If there is a story here, it is that the mutability of Modernism in Brazil is what has allowed it to persist, in marked contrast to the situation elsewhere, in which it has ossified or died. Modernism in Brazil remains alive because of its capacity to change. Some of this mutability can be seen here in the topics of the chapters: the politics of historical identity, the politics of Eros, the politics of industrial progress, the politics of poverty, the politics of social liberation, the politics of spectacle, the politics of public space, and, finally, the politics around the legacy of Brazil's Modernist architecture. All these categories have clear representation in architecture, as we shall see. They show that we are not dealing with a single, monolithic Modernism, but multiple, overlapping and often contradictory Modernisms. The traditional view of Brazil's modern architecture, dominated by the so-called *Carioca* school around Niemeyer, is therefore just one strand among many.

Political Contexts

These distinct notions of politics are nevertheless fragments of a broader history. The period 1929 to the present is characterized by a number of major transitions, from dictatorship to democracy and back again, periods of economic despair, and equally periods in which to some – such as Stefan Zweig – Brazil appeared to be on the point of becoming a world power. The crucial ideas are, first, Brazil as a country with a colonial history. The Portuguese lost control of the country in a military coup in 1889, but this came after decades of weakness: for example, a bizarre period from 1808 to 1821 found Rio temporarily as the centre of the Portuguese empire after Portugal itself was lost to Napoleon.[23] All attempts at political and cultural modernization in the twentieth century were in one way or another attempts to establish a post-colonial identity, the chief example of this being Brasília, whose inland location was a figuration of this desire, a turning away from the cities of the coast, founded by Europeans and looking towards Europe, towards the uninhabited interior.

The second context is dictatorship, of one kind or another. During the twentieth century Brazil passed through two periods of dictatorship. The first was the relatively benign, technocratic, modernizing *Estado Novo* (New State) under Getúlio Vargas (1930–45). Adapting imagery and ideas from Italian fascism, this was a period of nationalism and modernization, but not especially of political repression. The second period was military rule from 1964 to 1985, which had an entirely different character. This was first of all a state of emergency brought about by a coup, which itself occurred because of an unstable economy and a

Tanks in Rio de Janeiro, the day after the 1964 coup.

20

weak democracy. Initially relatively benign, the regime hardened in the late 1960s and early 1970s, the so-called *anos de chumbo* (years of lead). During 1969–74, under Emilio Medici, Brazil's government had much of the same character as the military regimes in Argentina and Chile: political dissent was not tolerated; opposition figures were 'disappeared' by the authorities; torture was institutionalized; and Brazil cooperated with other South American military regimes in Operação Condor (Operation Condor), a coordinated attempt to rid the continent of left-wing opposition.[24] The repression in Brazil never reached the same levels as seen in other countries – its 'disappeared' numbered in the hundreds rather than the thousands, as in Argentina and Chile – but the methods and principles were the same. Architects had particular reasons to fear the military. After 1964 a number of prominent architects were banned from teaching, while the eminent and successful Vilanova Artigas was imprisoned for his political views in 1967, and his architect pupils Sérgio Ferro and Rodrigo Lefèvre were jailed in 1969 for political activities.[25]

The third political context, vital for the development of Modernist architecture, is the experiment in democracy after the Estado Novo, especially during the presidency of the populist Juscelino Kubitschek. 'JK' was an immensely popular and charismatic figure who promised 'fifty years' progress in five.[26] The use of the acronym JK is contemporaneous with his period in office, although to an Anglophone readership in retrospect it recalls the convention of referring to the American president John F. Kennedy by (almost identical) initials. And it has to be said that JK's status in Brazil has something of JFK's in the US – a youngish, highly attractive figure who spoke a modernizing language, and who was anxious to advance his country's reputation abroad. There is also in both cases the sense of a career cut short by circumstances – JFK's by assassination, JK's by the Brazilian constitution's then rule that no president serve more than one term. JK's project was more importantly cut short by the coup of 1964 and his subsequent exile. His influence on Brazilian public life was finally cut short in 1976 by a fatal car crash in the state of Rio de Janeiro, which – like JFK's assassination – has never been definitively explained.

The fourth context would be the economic liberalization after the *abertura* (opening) in 1985. Since then, Brazil's economy has become increasingly open to foreign investment, and as a consequence increasingly resembles the economies of the developed world. After appalling economic instability during the 1970s, with long periods of hyperinflation, Brazil has achieved over a decade of low inflation, stability and growth, sluggish at first, but increasingly rapid at the time of writing, averaging 5 per cent per year.[27] The two main political figures of this period have been Fernando Henrique Cardoso (1994–2002) and Luís Inácio da Silva, better known as Lula (2002–). The country has been as stable as it has ever been as a democracy, with no likelihood, at the time of writing, of any return to authoritarian government.

Brazil's Geography

The architecture this book describes is concentrated in a few places, mainly big cities: Rio de Janeiro, São Paulo, Brasília, with the occasional excursion to Belo Horizonte, Curitiba, Recife. But by and large this is a history of the metropolitan centres, because this is where the architecture is. It would not be right to attempt another history; the story of Modernism in Brazil is the story of the cities. Among those cities, Brasília and São Paulo are pre-eminent in representing what a modern Brazilian city ought to look like. Both are showcases of Modernism, albeit in different ways. Looking at a map of Brazil, it will become clear too that the triangle described by Rio de Janeiro, São Paulo and Brasília is extremely small by comparison with the area of the whole country, which slightly exceeds that of the continental United States. My emphasis might seem to some the equivalent of describing American architecture only in terms of the corridor between Boston and Washington, DC, ignoring everything further west. That argument makes sense up to a point. But the differences between the two cases are greater than their similarities. The US, despite the pre-eminence of New York and Los Angeles, has a much more even pattern of development, and, as has been well documented, its identity has been only partly constructed in cities or places that resemble them.[28] In Brazil by contrast, a few cities dominate life to a remarkable degree. Chief among these is São Paulo, a megalopolis of 17.9 million. The city is pre-eminent in the Brazilian economy, accounting for up to 40 per cent of the country's Gross Domestic Product (GDP).[29] Rio is the next largest city, with a metropolitan population of around 10 million; Belo Horizonte is third at 5 million; there are then a number of cities with populations in the 1–2 million range, Brasília included. But my emphasis is based on economic importance, and, flowing from that, the patronage of Modernism, and beyond that the critical discourse around these places or buildings. It is hard to argue against this triangle of wealth in Brazil's south-east; there is no other history of Modernism other than one focused on these cities.

That said, the modernization of Brazil and the architecture that went along with it were intimately bound up with a continental-scale vision of the country in which the cities and the land were very much part of the same system. Brasília is a case in point, as we shall see in chapter

BOA VISTA

MACAPÁ

MANAUS

BELÉM   SÃO LUÍS

FORTALEZA

TEREZINA

NATAL

JOÃO PESSÓA

RECIFE

MACEIÓ

ARACAJU

PORTO VELHO

RIO BRANCO

SÃO SALVADOR

CUIABÁ — 925

BRASÍLIA

GOIÂNIA
125

VITÓRIA

BELO
HORIZONTE

RIO DE JANEIRO

SÃO PAULO

CURITIBA

FLORIANÓPOLIS

PÔRTO ALEGRE

2 490

1 940

1 770

1 995

1 290

660

575

1 750

1 685

1 620

1 455

1 270

1 030

1 920

2 280

725

940

890

940

1 240

1 110

650

A map with Brasília
commanding the
centre.

Three; the vision of the city was not simply that of a showcase capital built in the Modernist style, but also a means of opening up the interior of the country for development. A famous map was produced at the time of Brasília's realization to show the distances between the new capital and other parts of the country. The rhetoric of the map was clear enough: the entire country had been now reorientated around the capital, and goods, information and services were now meant to circulate in new ways. The sketch map was in effect made real by a programme of highway building, connecting the capital with the major cities. During the period of military rule, the growth of São Paulo was connected with continuing infrastructural projects, especially hydroelectric schemes to provide power for its industries; to put it another way, the city of São Paulo became a *representation* of the modernity achieved elsewhere in the country. A further point to make here would be the continuing imaginative presence of the rural parts of Brazil within the cities. Unlike the cities of the developed world, which often exist in opposition to the land, in Brazil the extent and recentness of rural migration to the cities, particularly from the north-east, means that rural cultures have a significant presence – see the Feira do Nordeste in Rio de Janeiro, held in the (Modernist) Campo de São Cristovão; the cities continue to be poles of migration from rural areas, and are, as a consequence, clearing houses of those cultures. Brasília's extraordinary central bus station (discussed in detail in chapter Three) is one architectural figure of this developmental progress. Located at the symbolic heart of both the city and of the country, it is not just the centre of the city's commuter traffic, but also the figuration of the traffic of internal migration. Migrants arrive here from all over the country, and many of them go on to do business in the lively street market that surrounds it. More generally, the remote and undeveloped regions of Brazil, Amazonas and the *sertão* of the north-east, continue to have an important imaginative presence in the culture of the country. The cities, and the Modernist buildings they contain, therefore exist in an important relation to the land. Their size alone is one indicator of this; their enormous growth, to a size unprecedented in Europe, is a function of the size of the country and the amount of migration it sustains.

Brazil's geography is important here in a national context, but it is also important at an urban level – at the level of human geography. In this book, I understand Brazil as having a certain geographical shape, one dominated by cities in the south-east but imaginatively connected with rural places elsewhere. At the level of urban geography, the cities themselves are often highly distinctive. These are places that are on the one hand often rather seductive – through climate and physical geography, they may have, like Rio and Recife, outstanding beaches, on which a life of leisure may be played out; or they may, like Brasília, simply have a pleasant climate that lends itself to a life lived out of doors. The best Modernist buildings, from Niemeyer's Casa das Canoas to Artigas's Faculty of Architecture and Urbanism, have celebrated these natural facts.

But the cities can be exceptionally fearful places too. The beach at Copacabana, one of the most successful urban projects of the landscape architect Roberto Burle Marx, is delightful, but also dangerous, a place of robberies and muggings and prostitution on an epic scale, which one visits only after taking a number of precautions. More seriously perhaps is the effect of the fear of crime on the design of residential buildings, which can resemble prisons, surrounded by security grilles at ground-floor level and with security posts manned by private guards. The tendency for middle-class Brazilians to live behind walls in *condominios fechados* (gated

Security measures in Jardins, São Paulo. Security fence with barbed wire, CCTV, entryphone and concierge.

communities) is highly developed. As the anthropologist Teresa Caldeira has described, for the middle class, the city is increasingly a 'city of walls', defending its residents from everything that is outside.[30] There are good reasons for this: Brazilian cities remain among the world's most dangerous, with rates of murder and assault that approach or sometimes exceed those found in conditions of war – and the term 'civil war' has been often deployed. Armed attacks on tourist buses travelling from Rio's Tom Jobin international airport in the early 2000s required a federal response involving the army; in May 2006 a series of attacks on police stations coordinated from prison by a criminal gang, the Primeiro Comando da Capital (PCC, or First Capital Command), effectively shut down the entire city of São Paulo for two days.[31] Rates of violence in some cities, notably São Paulo, had decreased markedly at the time of writing. But profound cultures of fear persist in urban Brazil, and their effect on the look and inhabitation of the built environment remains strong.[32]

Modernist architecture exists in an uneasy relation with this culture, as we shall see throughout the book. Modernism's rhetoric invariably includes some notion of freedom played out in architectural space. At the MES, for example, the entire ground level is in effect an urban square, open to all: the use of pilotis sees to that. It is easy to see that this is as much rhetorical as practical, communicating an idea of openness, a useful idea in respect of the identity that the government might wish to promote. Or Brasília, whose superb residential areas on the south wing are in effect an urban park, delightfully planted, through which anyone is, in theory at least, free to wander at will. These places, however, are undoubtedly the exception rather than the rule. It is far more normal to see Modernist buildings with security measures fitted retrospectively, negating whatever sense of free space they may once have had. Modernism's values consist of free and public space above all; the reality of Brazil is of spaces that are increasingly privatized. It is rare to see examples of Modernist architecture in anything other than some sort of reserve, barricaded from the outside world. Functionally speaking, Brazilian Modernism is almost never now a truly public architecture, whatever its original intentions. The country's origins were originally southern European, and it has had continuous immigration from that region and other parts of the Mediterranean, where traditions of public culture are strong. But to assume that Brazil shares these traditions would be misleading, for its own public traditions are weak. This is not a country of the public square; it has a poorly developed sense of civic life. Its traditions much better resemble those of the United States. Any consideration of Modernist architecture needs to recognize that. Modernism's tendency to invoke the Mediterranean city works well in Brazil in terms of climate. In most other respects it is a fantasy.

Intellectual Contexts

Brazil's Modernism exists in two related intellectual contexts, the exceptionally vibrant intellectual life it developed in the first half of the twentieth century – a context that fed directly into architecture – and the foreign architectural criticism produced in response to Brazil's modern architecture. The local contexts first: the flowering of Modernism that occurred in the 1930s was part of a more general development of an intellectual culture, a scene consisting of a number of well-connected, middle- or upper-class, generally Francophile individuals, whose knowledge of developments in Europe was good. They were also – probably for the first time – committed to Brazil and concerned to explicate it, or represent it in terms of a relationship of equals with the rest of the world. This is in other words a post-colonial milieu, which regards Brazil not as some second-rate colony, always late to developments in Europe, but as a place under development that in fact in some ways may be culturally in advance of things in the Old World.

Among the principal figures in this milieu are the poet Mário de Andrade, the historian Sérgio Buarque de Holanda, whose *Raizes do Brasil* (*Roots of Brazil*, 1936) was one of the first attempts to write a post-colonial history of Brazil, and Gilberto Freyre, a sociologist. Freyre's work on race, sexuality and Brazilian identity is particularly relevant here. His major work, *Casa Grande e Senzala* (in English, 'Big House and Slave Hut', but published as *The Masters and the Slaves*), describes the origins of urban Brazil and the complex relations between the rural aristocracy and its imported slave labour.[33] Freyre's thesis, both here and throughout his work on Brazil, appears both archaic and extremely modern: he argues that Brazil, unlike the United States, developed a much more fluid approach to race through its peculiar interpretation of slavery; slaves in Brazil were not simply bodies, but also central to the sexual lives of their masters. Slavery occupied an intimate place in the lives of the colonists, inseparable from 'sensuality' and 'polygamy'. Slavery was in the special circumstances of Brazil, the 'complement of the harem'.[34] Such intimate relations were, as Freyre recognized, fundamentally exploitative. But they were characterized by an indifference to colour, and in many cases a preference by the Portuguese for the other, which made for a situation very different from that found in the US. Freyre's optimistic conclusion was that Brazil was, uniquely, a racial democracy in which differences of skin colour were of little consequence.

Freyre's optimism can be easily criticized. In crude economic terms, Brazil is no more a racial democracy than the United States, with success closely associated with pale skin. But the Freyre myth is nevertheless vital in the construction of a modern Brazil, and still widely believed. Most importantly, the concept of a racial democracy underpins the work of the Modernist architects discussed here: at Brasília, for example, as Niemeyer wrote, the idea was a city of 'free men' with access to the best living conditions regardless of racial or social origins – as we shall see, an idea built into the city fabric in the planning of its residential buildings. Freyre's beliefs were widely shared. The fact that they can be easily disproved is less relevant here than their importance as a belief system; for someone like Niemeyer, an atheist, they came to stand in for religious belief. The musician Caetano Veloso, himself one of Brazil's more important contemporary cultural figures, has said – invoking Freyre – that he believes in the 'myth of Brazil', a phrasing that leaves open to question the objective truth of Freyre's ideas, but also allows them a continued presence.[35]

A very different generation of intellectuals in the 1960s and '70s underwrites the later forms of architecture I discuss. Informed by Marxism, the work of Paulo Freire, a sociologist, or Augusto Boal, a radical playwright, or Glauber Rocha, a film-maker, understands Brazil as an essentially poor society that must be recognized as such.[36] Such writers stood in opposition to the utopianism of the earlier generation and its projects such as Brasília, which they regarded as facile and self-serving. In place of grand utopian projects erected in the name of those in power, they proposed engagement with the poor and dispossessed in the form of cultural acts that would leave no material monument, but (they hoped) would quietly revolutionize Brazilian culture. In Boal's tough and radical work, which has been widely performed outside Brazil, theatre becomes a tool for the resolution of conflict in real-life situations. The 'theatre of the oppressed' sets out to empower those without power, and to discover tactics of influencing the world around them. In Boal's worldview, culture is imagined in terms of processes rather than monuments, and, critically, it identifies with those without power – the poor, the marginalized, the dispossessed. As we shall see, this vein of Brazil's intellectual culture became important for some forms of Modernist architecture in the 1960s.

Brazil Now

If during the years 1930–60 Brazil held a pre-eminent position in the field of architecture, it is equally true that post-1960 it faded. It is a commonplace in international architectural discourse that after Brasília 'nothing happened', in the words of Zein;[37] it is equally a commonplace inside Brazil that architecture post-1960 is clouded by shame and doubt, a function of a political situation that placed many if not most architects under suspicion. That some of Brazil's architecture can and should be recovered is one of the projects of this book. But equally, its disappearance from the international architectural scene was real, and there is no doubt that for much of the second half of the twentieth century in architectural terms Brazil was a peripheral place, largely forgotten. Since the late 1990s, that has undoubtedly changed. As Fernando Luiz Lara, a Brazilian critic, has noted, Brazil has suddenly returned to the pages of international journals.[38] Citing the Avery Index of journal publications, he describes how there were 404 articles on Brazil during the 1990s, almost as many as during the previous 90 years. The same index would show continued growth and interest through the first decade of the twenty-first century, with such events as Niemeyer's Serpentine Gallery Pavilion in London in 2003 (his first building in England, and his first in Europe for two decades) and Paulo Mendes da Rocha's receipt of the Pritzker Prize for architecture in 2006 causing minor sensations. The choice of Niemeyer, already awarded a RIBA Gold Medal in 1999, to address the annual conference of that organization in 2007 (albeit by a TV link from Rio, and via an interpreter) was further confirmation of the changed status of Brazilian architecture in the world.[39] With the possible exception of Mendes da Rocha, Brazilian architects were not, for the most part, building abroad. But the project of Brazilian Modernism can certainly be said to have been rehabilitated internationally, up to and including the somewhat toxic and controversial project of Brasília.

Why and how this happened has two likely causes. First is the return of architectural Modernism itself during the 1990s in the developed world after a period of stylistic eclecticism. Modernism is undoubtedly back in fashion, especially in the Anglophone world, if not as a mode for domestic architecture, then certainly as the mode for public buildings. But its return has seen it stripped of any social project; it is pure style, mostly for privileged clients, a means of connoting fashionableness through slick surfaces. Its crucial manifestations in (say) the City of London in the early 2000s have been spectacular formal exercises first and foremost. Their emphasis on form, surface and spectacle above all else strongly recalls Niemeyer's work, and it has been no surprise to find Norman Foster, Zaha Hadid and others cite him as a crucial reference point for their work.[40] Niemeyer, in other words, has legitimized an architecture of formal experiment forty years after his greatest period; he has been a useful precedent. It is instructive, however, that the revival of Niemeyer's reputation has had no place for the architect's uncompromising politics. The revived Niemeyer has been stripped of his communism.

The second cause is less concrete, perhaps. The first great period of interest in Brazil coincided with its emergence in the world as both an economic power and a democracy. The 'disappearance' of Brazil from international discourse coincides, arguably, with the period of military rule, when from 1964 onwards Brazil and Brazilian culture became inward-looking and xenophobic. The revival of Brazil in architectural terms is coincident with the return to democracy, but more than that, its entry into a globalized world of trade and the consolidation of its economy, particularly under Cardoso and Lula. But further, we might say that Brazil once again has started to represent a kind of future. It is big, and growing, and it has interests in areas of strategic, but often overlooked importance in the contemporary world. It is, and has long been, the world's leading producer of bioethanol, and since the 1970s has run much of its private cars on this fuel. It grows soya in immense quantities, most of which it sells to the Chinese. It has lots of oil, most of it recently discovered. It builds more than 2.9 million cars annually, equal to production in France, and comfortably exceeding that of the UK and Spain.[41] Its aerospace industry is the third largest in the world, and dominates the world market for airliners of up to 100 seats.[42] There are few areas of the contemporary world in which Brazil does not have some strategic interest.

On top of this, Brazil's experience of modernization during the past century has been an unusually self-conscious one; its economy and political life may be relatively undeveloped, but its intellectual culture has in many respects been as advanced as any in the developed world. The production of a new capital city and the explosion of São Paulo were accompanied by abundant discussion and analysis in a relatively free and vibrant media; academic life too remained relatively open, even vibrant, even during the most repressive years of the military period. Free and open discussion was for the most part possible, and the outlets for discussion abundant. There is an immense amount of material to work with. The revival of the reputation of Brazil's Modernism has been accompanied by a remarkable growth in the number of architecture schools: there were 42 schools at the end of the 1980s, and more than 120 now, a threefold increase that contrasts sharply with the situation in the developed world where contraction, not expansion, is the more familiar scenario.[43] Brazil and its architecture are of global, not local significance, as this book aims to make clear.

chapter one

The Politics of the Past

In the Introduction, I described Brazil's Modernism as polyvalent, plural and often frankly contradictory. Nowhere are these qualities more apparent than in the relationship of Modernism to the past. Brazil's official view of itself is, to appropriate Stefan Zweig's description, 'the land of the future'. It has been the land of the future for the best part of a century, and this idea has become something like an article of faith. The building of the new capital, Brasília, is its principal material manifestation, but at first sight almost all the built environment of Brazil seems to be modern. Unlike the United States, or Britain, or even much of continental Europe, there is seemingly little appetite for an architecture of historical pastiche; neo-colonial styles are relatively rare. Commenting on this peculiar attitude to the modern, the architectural historian Adrian Forty has described a country in which 'the old does not exist . . . newness of things is valued, and "oldness" is not easily distinguished from dilapidation'.[1] Forty's remarks here recall Claude Lévi-Strauss's account of 1930s São Paulo, in which the French anthropologist describes a city maniacally building the future, but leaving a trail of devastation in its wake. Things are either brand new or in a state of ruin. The 'old', that category so familiar and so vital in Europe, seemingly has no place.[2]

This is a familiar idea – in fact, in the Anglophone literature about Brazilian architecture, it is more or less the only idea available to describe the country's relation with its past. However, it is not quite right. The 'land of the future' certainly continues to exist, but equally there are, and have always been, vitally important discourses of architecture that stress a remarkable degree of continuity between Modernism and the past. In these discourses, the architectures of the past and of the future are thought to exist in a condition of mutual reinforcement, the past (for example) nourishing the present, or providing it with an agreeable context.

An early example of this tendency is the house that Gregori Warchavchik built for himself and his wife (1927–8, cited in the Introduction). As

Lúcio Costa, Museum of the Missions, São Miguel das Missões, 1937.

much as this house broke with tradition, it also made explicit reference to the local context: its tiled roof, whitewashed façade and extensive veranda clearly refer to the vernacular architecture of the *casa grande*, of which more later. But Warchavchik is an isolated case. The crucial ideas in this context come from an institution, SPHAN (Sociedade do Patrimônio Histórico e Artístico Nacional, or Society of National Historical and Artistic Heritage), created in 1937, and in which Lúcio Costa was closely involved at the same time as designing the sensational MES. SPHAN was an organization that understood the codification and protection of the past as integral to the Modernist project. In short, Brazil's Modernism coexists with the desire to preserve the past; not only that, but its processes of modernization and preservation were often to be found in the hands of the same people. Modernization and historic preservation were not ranged against each other like implacable enemies as they so often are in Europe. Rather, in certain crucial contexts, they were regarded (and regard themselves) as coterminous. The shared enemy of both was unrestricted commercial development – hence Costa's well-known essay of 1951, 'Muita Construção, Alguma Arquitetura e um Milagre' (With so much construction, any architecture is a miracle).[3]

As Lauro Cavalcanti has written, 'Lúcio Costa and Oscar Niemeyer planned the capital of the future at the same time as they remodelled the face of the symbolic capital of our colonial past.'[4] In the European tradition, this is an unfamiliar conception of the modern, which is generally more ruthless with the past. What it does resemble, however, is the British approach to Modernism seen in the circle around the *Architectural Review* in the 1930s. In this case, the same advocates of European Modernism – such as Nikolaus Pevsner – were also advocates of the English tradition of the Picturesque.[5] The difference in Brazil is that such a vision was not marginal, in the true sense avant-garde, as it was in Britain. Instead, it was de facto government policy.

Brazil's Different Pasts

However, as at the *Architectural Review* in England, SPHAN served up a highly idiosyncratic version of the past. SPHAN, much influenced by Costa, has always emphasized the architecture of the Portuguese colonial period, representing it as the one true historical architecture. Its principal sites of the Baroque, now protected under the aegis of IPHAN (Instituto do Patrimônio Historíco e Artístico Nacional, the successor to SPHAN) or UNESCO, or both, include the colonial churches of Rio de Janeiro; most of the former capital of Minas Gerais, Ouro Prêto; the historic centre of

Salvador da Bahía in the north-east; the eighteenth-century centre of Olinda in the state of Pernambuco; and the missionary towns of the far south-east of Brazil. Among these, Ouro Prêto is probably pre-eminent in that it represents the most intact, and therefore immersive, colonial environment in Brazil. Its hilly landscape is dominated by churches, which are variations on the same theme: they are stone-built with (normally) twin façade towers and an elongated plan; they have highly sculptural stone doorways and occasional blue *azulejos*, but are otherwise unadorned; they have small window openings; and they are well adapted to a climate with both strong sun and high rainfall. Domestic colonial Brazilian architecture is similarly plain, with intermittent decoration to give relief. Stone is the most common building material; walls are thick and ceilings are high. Brazilian colonial urbanism follows the Portuguese pattern, and is notably less formal and more picturesque than that found in Spain or Spanish America; its towns were formed for trading and developed organically. This narrative explains most substantive building in Brazil from the moment the Portuguese arrived in 1520 to its constitution as a republic in 1889.

But it does not by any means explain everything. There is a history of pre-colonial indigenous building that is rarely part of any architectural discourse. And there were other European presences besides the Portuguese. In 1816 the Portuguese emperor João vi brought a number of significant French artists to Brazil, including the architect Grandjean de Montigny, who designed the first significant French-style building in Brazil, the Escola de Belas Artes in Rio de Janeiro – thus began a significant period of French influence. This piece of restrained Neoclassicism was the model for a small number of semi-public buildings in the middle of the nineteenth century: the Imperial Palace in the summer retreat of Petrópolis, for example (1845–62). But this influence was limited to the royal sphere. The years immediately after the formation of the republic (1889) saw far more dramatic changes in Brazil's built environment, especially in the big commercial centres. This period, at least the appearance of the Vargas regime in 1930, is characterized by architectural eclecticism, planning on a grand scale and giganticism in architecture to match a booming economy. In architectural terms all this signified a literal turning away from Portugal. Rio was the centre of this process, which saw it partially reinvented as a subtropical Paris with vast Second Empire public buildings, formal parks and boulevards. This process was planned as early as 1871, and finally begun in 1903 under Francisco Pereira Passos, Rio's municipal prefect. The crucial work was the creation of the Avenida Rio Branco, a major boulevard cutting straight and level, north–south across the old centre of the city.

Francisco de Paula Ramos de Azevedo, Teatro Municipal, São Paulo, 1903–11. A Second Empire public building in São Paulo, contemporary with similar exercises in Rio and Manaus.

This unmistakable piece of Haussmannization was accompanied by some flamboyant public buildings built in Rio in the Second Empire style, including the Biblioteca Nacional (1910) and the Museo Nacional de Belas Artes (1908). However, the Teatro Municipal (Francisco de Oliveira Passos, 1909) stands out, an extraordinary confection of marble, onyx, bronze and mirrors, based on Charles Garnier's Paris Opéra, with all materials imported from Europe. Its highly ornate main façade has a ceremonial stair leading to a triple porticoed entrance, with Corinthian columns, pilasters, balustrades, stained glass and twin domes, the whole pile topped by figurines representing *Comedy* and *Tragedy*, and, at the very summit, a giant sculpted eagle. The excess of Rio's theatre was matched only by the Teatro Amazonas in Manaus, completed by Celestial Sacardim in 1896, again from substantially imported materials.

The Haussmannization of Rio had echoes in most other large Brazilian cities. Rio experimented further with this mode in the years 1926–30 with a megalomaniac scheme under the Frenchman Alfred Agache, which saw little realized apart from the creation of the gargantuan Avenida Presidente Vargas (for more on Agache, see chapter Seven). The first decades of the twentieth century are in some ways better characterized by the internationalization of Brazil's trade and its representation in increasingly eclectic private buildings. The Rio suburb of Santa Teresa is (as Norma Evenson has described) an assortment of 'Gothic Revival, Swiss Cottage Style, Second Empire and Art Nouveau'.[6] Similar eclecticism was clearly visible at the same time in São Paulo, especially along the newly created Avenida Paulista. Here it was common to see villas in the English half-timbered style too. English influence was more publicly manifest in the city's Luz railway station (Charles Henry Driver, 1896–1901), whose clock tower disconcertingly cites the Palace of Westminster. The city's real innovation in the early twentieth century was, however, the skyscraper, which in the form of the Prédio Martinelli (1929), an inflated Renaissance *palazzo*, was as eclectic as anything found in New York.

But the richness of early twentieth-century architecture in Brazil has been consistently devalued in favour of that of the colonial period. This is both a problem and a paradox. Many of the most admired structures of the colonial period were openly a means of maintaining a feudal slave

Charles Henry Driver,
Luz railway station,
São Paulo, 1897–1900.
Big Ben meets
Portuguese Baroque.

Francisco Marcelino
de Sousa Aguiar,
Biblioteca Nacional,
Rio de Janeiro,
1905–10.

society, yet their advocates were in most other respects politically progressive. One of the few architects to recognize the difficulty was Henrique Mindlin (1911–1971). For him, colonial architecture was

> severe, solid, unadorned. It expressed the severe and clear-cut social structure: the supremacy of man, the almost oriental segregation of woman, and the whole system of the exploitation of the Negro and the Indian.[7]

Mindlin's own work, especially the ABI, has something of this colonial character. The austerity and whiteness of its façade, the way (unlike its near neighbour, the MES) it affirms the existing street grid, its clearly hierarchical internal organization and its clear demarcation of private and public spaces mark it out as a building that confirms the past rather than wishes to sweep it away. And yet Mindlin's remarks, made in 1956, twenty years after the completion of the ABI, indicate a residual uneasiness about this relation with the past, a sense that affirming the colonial past in terms of architecture amounted to affirming a way of life that

Cândido Portinari, tiles on Pampulha church, Belo Horizonte, 1943.

Eclectic style villa, Avenida Paulista, São Paulo, c. 1905. In the background is Ohtake's Berrini 500 building, under construction.

could not and should not persist. Mindlin did not resolve this, and neither did Costa or Niemeyer, the other significant figures in this chapter. The contradiction did not get addressed properly until the work of the Paulista school – for more on that, see chapter Four.

The accommodation of the past is manifest in a wide range of modern buildings in Brazil. It informed the use of such details as *azulejos* on the MES and Niemeyer's church at Pampulha by Cândido Portinari. It is manifest on the content and imagery of these works, heavy on Old Testament subject matter and informed as much by El Greco as they were by the latest developments in Paris. The techniques used to shade and ventilate such buildings also derive from historical – especially colonial – practice. It informs a huge number of private houses. But most significantly here, it results in some unusually sophisticated Modernist buildings by Costa and his circle that, although small in number and small in scale, were disproportionately important in articulating an idea of what it meant to be modern in Brazil. Occupying sensitive natural or historical sites, and making use of traditional materials and technologies, they prefigure what Kenneth Frampton would call, half a century later, 'critical regionalism': a modern architecture sensitive to place and context, tough, pragmatic and local, resistant to both capital and internationalism.[8] It is by any standards prescient work.

Lúcio Costa and SPHAN

But first we should look more closely at the intellectual context that makes possible this sophisticated and nuanced engagement with the past. One figure in particular stands out, Lúcio Costa (1902–1998), born in Toulon (France) and educated in Newcastle, Montreux and finally Rio de Janeiro, where he graduated as an architect in 1924 from the Escola de Belas Artes. Costa soon established a partnership with Warchavchik, and in 1930, only six years after graduating, became the director of the Escola de Belas Artes. His reign there was controversial, and he was forced to resign after only a year. Like Gilberto Freyre, the sociologist whose work was introduced in the last chapter, Costa came from a privileged background, and was both well educated and travelled by the time he began to have influence. Also like Freyre, he combined progressive political views with a fundamentally conservative approach to culture. His future Brazil had a strong connection with the society and architecture of the colonial past, while at the same time being a declaration of a break with it. This curious, even paradoxical, position explains much of the character of Brazilian Modernism.

The year before the foundation of SPHAN, Costa had published what amounted to a manifesto of modern architecture, 'Razões da Nova Arquitetura' (Roots of Modern Architecture) in the journal *Revista da Directoria de Engenharia da PDF*.[9] It is a long and difficult article, simultaneously high-flown and circumlocutory, with a somewhat solipsistic character, too: as much as he was writing for an audience, Costa was also writing to himself, clarifying his own change of position as regards the modern: from being closely identified with neo-classicism, Costa now positions himself as a Modernist. But his understanding of Modernism is based explicitly on an understanding of what might be useful from the historical past.

The argument is principally that architectural tradition is not invested in surfaces, but rather in traditions of building, wherever they may be found. He had not realized, he wrote later, that 'the real tradition was right there, two steps away, with our contemporary master-builders . . . it is enough to make up all that lost time by extending a hand to the master-builders, always so scorned, to the old *portuga* of 1910 because, say what you like, it was he, alone, who was guarding tradition'.[10] Benzaquen de Araújo uses Costa's term 'saúde plástica' to indicate an ideal relation between past and present. This concept, 'plastic health' loosely translated,

40

indicates a way of thinking that describes a close, and essentially Modernist, relation between form and function; aesthetics cannot exist alone, but must be accompanied by an interest in the 'primordial' activity of construction. Costa argues therefore that 'popular' architecture is more interesting than 'erudite'; it is not affected or pretentious; it wears no make-up; it is primarily communicated through the skills of craftsmen without formal education. This 'honest' and 'sober' architecture survived a long time in Brazil, he argues, right up until the middle of the nineteenth century. This architecture describes a 'saúde plástica perfeita'.[11] This perfect historic architecture is manifest in certain specific kinds of construction: *pau-a-pique* (wattle and daub), whitewashed walls, tiled roofs, *azulejos*, local stone, local wood. Costa rejects an architecture of surfaces, an impractical architecture where things will not work: 'conservatory neo-colonial, with verandas where a chair won't fit, lanterns that won't light, roofs won't cover anything, flower-stands in inaccessible places, props that won't hold up any floor . . . everything in architecture must have a reason to exist, and exercise a function'.[12]

All this leads Costa to a surprising re-evaluation of Portuguese Baroque, an architecture that by contrast to its Italian or Austrian counterparts is remarkably little concerned with surface. The surprise is not

Igreja de Nossa Senhora da Glória do Outeiro, Rio de Janeiro, 1714–39.

about form, in this case, but the fact that it is a form irrevocably linked with the colonial period. The intellectual context, whether Freyre or Sérgio Buarque de Holanda, is preoccupied with *post*-colonial values. Yet the valuation of the Baroque is a crucial element in Costa's architectural theory. He drags it into the orbit of the modern, praising some surprising things. It has, he declares, 'composure, even dignity', even in its most 'delirious' moments.

Costa's worldview was articulated through the government agency SPHAN. Its creation in 1937 was an act of the minister of culture Gustavo Capanema, who was anxious that Brazil's history was being lost. He charged Rodrigo Melo de Andrade to set it up at precisely the same moment as he was developing the radical new building to house his department. On SPHAN's legal creation in November, it was charged with identifying and preserving historic monuments, giving them legal protection by inscribing them in one of four *livros de tombo*. As Lauro Cavalcanti has described, it was 'integral to the project of modernization' and was charged with the 'construction of symbolic national capital'.[13] Under the directorship of Andrade, the architectural nucleus of SPHAN in the late 1930s was Costa, Niemeyer and Carlos Leão, all of whom were simultaneously involved in the construction of MES. SPHAN became crucial in facilitating, but also controlling, the relationship between modern buildings and historic sites. SPHAN, dominated by Modernists, could establish the relation with the site and the appropriate form of the new building without capitulating to archaic forms of architecture. From the beginning, however, it identified Portuguese colonial as the only historic architecture worth preserving, an attitude that has led to the destruction or abandonment of vast numbers of buildings by Italian, German and other immigrants. SPHAN's view of the past was therefore highly selective.

Freyre and the Casa Grande

One of the crucial intellectual sources for this unusual attitude to the past was the sociologist Gilberto Freyre. As Cavalcanti notes, Freyre's work was integral to the development of a concept of a modern Brazilian identity. His great idea was racial democracy: that is, Brazil as a racial democracy at a time of ubiquitous racism. Brazil's race relations, he argued, were uniquely liberal, in spite of, or in some ways because of, its long history of slavery. The crucial work in Freyre's œuvre, and the best known outside Brazil, is *Casa Grande e Senzala*, already cited in the Introduction. Translated as *The Masters and the Slaves*, the book describes a social system and a mode of development based on a rural plantation economy dedicated to the production of sugar and coffee. The central architectural figure of this way of life is the *casa grande* (big house). The *casa grande* is the centre of everything:

> an entire economic, social and political system; a system of labour; a system of transport; a system of religion; a system of sexual and family life; a system of bodily and household hygiene; and a system of politics . . . a fortress, a bank, a cemetery, a hospital, a school and a house of charity giving shelter to the aged, the widow and the orphan.[14]

The *casa grande* was 'the complete and sincere expression of the absorptive patriarchalism of colonial times'.[15] It had a particular form: a long, low building, often built into the side of a hill to provide shelter from the wind. There was invariably a long veranda at first-floor level, which defines the public face of the building. From here, the planter and his family had a clear and powerful view of the land under their control. Inside there was a clear hierarchy of rooms, with private functions well hidden: unmarried daughters would be kept at the centre of the complex, almost entirely shielded from public view. Meanwhile, public rooms were built on an enormous, and sometimes opulent, scale. There would invariably be vast dining rooms and kitchens, rooms that, in the same way as the dining halls of the English country house, supposed a big passing population, an ever-present crowd beyond the immediate family of the planter and their staff.

The *casa grande* is in a basic sense Portuguese, but becomes powerfully identified with the new nation, ultimately as 'Brazilian as a jungle plant'. It is also, as Freyre argues, representative of a powerful and successful form of civilization. It is the image of nothing less than 'the most stable type of civilization to be found in Hispanic America'. This was (quite unlike the situation found in Spanish-speaking America) a society identified by essentially rural values, a situation that persisted until well into the twentieth century. It was the *casa grande* presiding over the plantation that represented Brazil, not the church watching over the city. As Freyre notes, in architectural terms, the *casa grande* in many ways 'supplants' the church. Not only was it socially and structurally more important, but it also provided an architectural vocabulary for it; in the north-east, the church takes on the form of the *casa grande*, appropriating its terraces and verandas, suppressing its more obviously ecclesiastical features.[16] The 'arrogant solidity of form' that Freyre describes in the *casa grande* is the expression of a society profoundly at ease with itself and its hierarchies. This just happens to be a feudal and rural one.

Freyre's affection for the *casa grande* was shared by many important Brazilian intellectuals of the 1930s, almost all of whom can be identified with the left. Among them was Costa, who included it among the types of buildings of the historical past that he wished to defend. Like Freyre, he moves into a wistful, nostalgic mode when describing the *casa grande*. Quoted by Freyre in the English preface to *Casa Grande e Senzala*, he declares: 'How one meets oneself there . . . and how one remembers things one never knew but which were there all the while; I do not know how to put it – it would take a Proust to explain it.'[17] For both Freyre and Costa it was an 'honest' form, a true expression of a national identity, an expression of continuity with the past. It was the exact equivalent of the Georgian townhouse in British architectural discourse at the same time: an acceptable historical building that could be adapted or appropriated for modern design. Neither Costa nor Freyre entirely forgot the fact that the *casa grande* was the representation of a feudal system based on slavery, which materialized innumerable cruelties. Freyre's problem was the amelioration of this cruel fact. The solution was the fantasy of racial democracy. Freyre argued that what appeared on the surface to be cruel and unequal was underneath more complex, with means of communication – principally sex – between master and slave that suggest a far more permeable and mobile system than might otherwise be imagined. The frank miscegenation represented by Brazil's population – in stark contrast to the cult of segregation in the United States – was Freyre's principal evidence. That this mixing may arise from rape, sexual bondage, prostitution and other forms of non-consensual sex is never fully accounted for. The important thing is the creation of a myth of freedom. Costa admits that the *casa grande* is dependent on slave labour, but when he refers to the *casa grande*'s 'terrace from which the planter with his gaze could take in the entire organism of rural life', his sympathies are with the planter. Given his patrician views and bourgeois upbringing, however, it is hard to imagine him thinking in any other way.

Freyre's advocacy of the *casa grande* remained with him throughout his career. A critique of Brasília published in 1960 (*Brasil, Brasis, Brasília*) complained of the defiantly urban sensibility of the new capital, proposing instead a mode of settlement derived from the plantation.[18]

Now in all of this there is an understanding that traditional Brazilian society was facilitated by slavery. The slave, as Costa noted later, was the antecedent of mechanized labour; the slave was 'the sewer, running water hot and cold, light switch, the doorbell'.[19] But there is nevertheless a powerful romanticization of the society and life of the *casa grande*, a romanticization that is made from the point of view of the privileged class. This is seen generally in the nostalgia in Freyre's writing for a pre-industrial society, and the accompanying mythification of class and race relations, and in specifically architectural terms in the forms of certain modern buildings. The architects (in every sense) of the Modern Movement in Brazil therefore came from the privileged classes, and retained – albeit in modified form – much sympathy with the values of the class from which they came. Hence the curious paradox of Modernist buildings being designed for a future classless society, yet deploying the vocabulary and reference points of the elite. It is Brazil's manifestation of a similar paradox seen in Modernist architecture from the Soviet Union to Britain.

The Grande Hotel, Ouro Prêto (1940)

These ideas of Costa and Freyre, with all their manifest contradictions, were played out with remarkable clarity in a handful of small buildings. Chief among these is the Grande Hotel in Ouro Prêto, whose name belies its small scale. It was designed by Oscar Niemeyer in 1938–9, with the well-documented involvement of SPHAN, and it was completed in 1940. The government of the state of Minas Gerais, of which the town is the old capital, first looked at building a new hotel on 1938, to capitalize on the city's touristic potential, and considered a number of designs. Niemeyer's eventual design, illustrated here, is a four-storey building built into the side of a hill near the Casa dos Contos, the old treasury building. It contains 44 rooms, including 17 curiously shaped duplexes, their two floors linked by a spiral staircase. Offices and kitchens occupy the ground floor, with a restaurant and public rooms on the floor above.[20] It is horizontal in plan, and is defined by a veranda extending the width of the building. Each bedroom looks out onto the terrace, all of which overlook the town. The first two floors are mostly unimpeded public spaces. In common with the surrounding buildings, the building has a red tiled roof, whitewashed walls and stone from the nearby Pico

Oscar Niemeyer, Grande Hotel in Ouro Prêto, 1940; perspective sketch of interior.

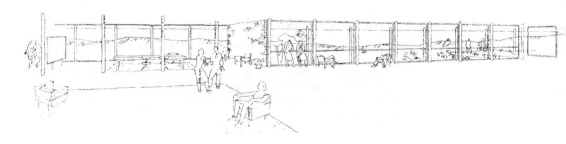

Oscar Niemeyer, Grande Hotel in Ouro Prêto, 1940. The view shows why Niemeyer originally wanted a grass-covered roof.

do Itacolomí. There is wooden trellis dividing up the first-floor veranda; there are *azulejos* in the public rooms. In terms of materials the only outstanding concession to modernity is the use of opaque glass on the terrace. It is nevertheless a modern building, however much the exterior fits in with the surroundings. Its horizontal façade has no equivalent in the town; it has a concrete frame; it has pilotis reaching up to the third floor; its duplex apartments and spiral staircases have no historic precedent here.

The insertion of this modern building into a historic landscape was fraught and SPHAN was involved from the start. Its director, Andrade, approached the architect Carlos Leão to produce a design. Leão's design, for the same small, sloping, site as that originally built on, was a heavy-handed symmetrical neoclassical building of four storeys, with a grand ceremonial staircase leading up to the main entrance. It employed the same tiles and stone as the neighbouring buildings, and its squat window openings alluded to the solidity of the surrounding architecture. In its symmetry, proportions and solidity, it resembled the public buildings of the Praça Tiradentes, the city's central square. Its location, an awkward,

Oscar Niemeyer,
Grande Hotel in Ouro
Prêto, 1940.

narrow site halfway down the steep Rua São Rocha Lagoa, was quite different. Leão's design seems meant for a more open and central location; its grandeur is misplaced here. Andrade's initial response, however, seems to have been favourable.[21]

At this point Costa became involved. Writing to Andrade from New York, where he was busy building the Brazil Pavilion for the 1939 World's Fair (see chapter Two), he politely expressed alarm that Leão's design was a capitulation to neo-classicism, a style that Costa himself had recently abandoned, but which still had numerous influential adherents.

Costa wondered if the project marked a 'rejection' of the Modernism with which he was himself now increasingly identified. He encouraged Andrade to commission a further study with Oscar Niemeyer as the architect; Andrade agreed.[22]

Niemeyer's design was an uncompromisingly Modernist horizontal block, whose potentially tense relationship with the site was ameliorated by the use of a flat grass roof. This, Niemeyer argued, would make for a building that when seen from above (thinking of the vertiginous landscape of the town) would be hard to separate from the surroundings. Costa was not so sure, and argued for tiles; Andrade agreed and advocated a pitched roof too. The columns on the new design were also designed to be spaced so as to make a visual connection with the *pau-a-pique* construction of the surrounding buildings. Costa thus won over the traditionalists. His argument was that Niemeyer's scheme, whatever its incorporation of historic elements, had 'beauty and truth'. Good architecture, he argued, would sit well in any combination, 'regardless of its age or style'; neoclassical buildings were only convincing with a great deal of artifice, and in any case they ran the risk of confusing the visitor to Ouro Prêto, who might mistake the neoclassical for the authentic. Better a building that was unambiguously modern.[23] In a rare judgement on taste, Costa stated that only 'new money' wanted pseudo-authenticity. Only those with really poor taste would want to hide the modern; one who really likes old furniture has no objection to placing a modern telephone or fan on it. The result, in the Grande Hotel, was a building that refused to confuse past and present, making them distinct and legible, without creating a building that failed to fit in with its surroundings.[24]

As a composition, the building was well regarded. Describing the building in 1981, Bruand wrote:

> The inclination of the roof, the repetition of a uniform motif on the main floor integrates itself magnificently with the simplicity and lack of pretension of the old buildings . . . far from being a pastiche, the building maintains its contemporary personality, and offers a play of plastic form, resulting from the use of contemporary technology . . . the solution adopted deserves the greatest praise for preserving the integrity of the monumental city.[25]

However, the emphasis on what might be termed the sculptural aspects of the building is made at the cost of the building's practicality; in other words, the concern for surface effect overrides the expected Modernist preoccupations of light and space. Bruand wrote of the disastrous quality of the rooms: their 'total' discomfort, their claustrophobic form 'like narrow corridors', their scale 'visibly sacrificed' to the overall visual effect.[26] Access to the upper floors is via a spiral staircase, which is 'impractical and dangerous' for the old and children, and robs each apartment of valuable living space.[27] The relationship to mainstream Modernism is therefore a curious one: as Bruand puts it, Niemeyer's interest here in the work of Le Corbusier extends only so far as it allows him 'new possibilities of formal expression'.[28] Functionalism is not a priority here. Bruand's assessment tallies with the architect's own views of the project, which are couched in purely aesthetic terms. He is bothered about the quality of the construction (poor), but more about the later additions to the ground floor, which have taken away from the original design, in which the public spaces were imagined as free-flowing; the pilotis are now hemmed in, he complains. But worse, the hotel has been disfigured by the addition of terrible furniture. Niemeyer complained to Israel Pinheiro (director of NOVACAP, the company responsible for the construction of Brasília) in the mid-1950s about it, offering to waive the fee for a government building in order to pay for restoration work, but to no avail. Niemeyer's views locate the building in the realm of art, a singular vision that cannot be altered.[29]

The Grande Hotel at Ouro Prêto identifies a number of crucial differences between Brazilian and other Modernisms. There is the emphasis on history and historical context – a surprise for those who expect Zweig's 'land of the future' to wish simply to erase the past. There is the use of local materials in order to fit in with a particular context, fourteen years before Le Corbusier tried the same thing in his Maisons Jaoul (1954–6). And in ideological terms there is also the sense that this is not just an isolated project, but a central one. It occurred at a crucial stage in Niemeyer's career; he was appointed to the job in place of Leão, and what he designed had the blessing of Costa and SPHAN, set up to define for the first time Brazil's built heritage.

Brazil Builds and History

The Grande Hotel at Ouro Prêto was a small building in a remote location. Part of the reason it assumed such importance was its presence in a remarkable exhibition held at the Museum of Modern Art in New York in 1943: *Brazil Builds: Architecture New and Old, 1642–1942*. Curated by the museum's co-director Philip Goodwin, himself an architect, with photographs by G. E. Kidder-Smith, it was vital in reinforcing the idea of Brazil as a modern nation, and the architectural careers of Costa and Niemeyer in particular.[30] Its impact in Brazil was considerable, too,

MOMA, *Brazil Builds*, cover, 1943.

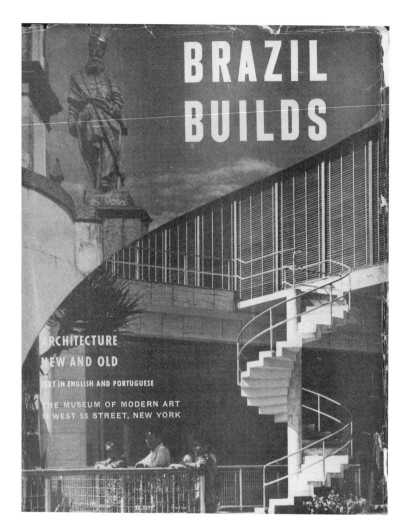

aided by the production of the catalogue in a bilingual edition (the Portuguese title was *Construção Brasileira*). For the Modernist critic Mário de Andrade, writing in 1943, the importance of the exhibition could not be overstated:

> I believe it is one of the richest gestures the USA has yet made in relation to us, the Brazilians. It gives us confidence, diminishes the disastrous inferiority complex that we have, gives us consciousness of our normality, and makes us realize that we have modern architecture of the most advanced kind in the world.[31]

Luis Nunes, Olinda
water tower, 1937.
Reproduced in
Brazil Builds.

In terms of its impact, *Brazil Builds* was a critical event of the same order
as the realization of Brasília.[32]

With good reason, the critics of the exhibition, both at the time of its
production and subsequently, have tended to emphasize the remarkable
new architecture produced by Niemeyer and his circle. This interpretation has tended to overshadow the fact that the exhibition was as much
an argument about the past as the new. Specifically, it juxtaposes
Brazilian architecture of the early colonial period with the contemporary, making a series of highly rhetorical comparisons through the
medium of photography.

There is a particularly suggestive spread on page 158 of the catalogue.
It depicts a Modernist water tower in the colonial city of Olinda in the
state of Pernambuco, north-eastern Brazil. Now a de facto suburb of the

adjoining, much larger, city of Recife, it is of similar historical impor-tance to Ouro Prêto, and is another UNESCO World Heritage Site. Kidder-Smith's photograph, taken in 1942, depicts the Alto da Sé, the town's central square, which occupies a distinctive site at the highest point of the town. There are spectacular views of Recife and the Atlantic coast from here. The photograph depicts the tower, built in 1937 by the radical young Recife architect Luis Nunes, rising to six storeys above the square. An exceedingly plain building, it is built of *cambogé* or pierced concrete blocks. The ground floor is left open (for dancing, apparently) with the upper storeys raised up on pilotis. Although made of concrete, in image, Kidder-Smith emphasizes its graph-paper-like qualities; its construction notwithstanding, it resembles early Mies buildings in its formal restraint. Kidder-Smith's photograph has it in bright sunshine, and it has perhaps burnt out slightly too, so any details are removed. The photograph depicts it surrounded by a group of colonial buildings – to the right, the squat, Baroque Igreja da Sé, to the left a large house. There is a mature tree on the far right framing the church. The building itself is uncompromising and plain, daringly brutal, as Lauro Cavalcanti has described. It does not seek any 'structural similarity nor dialectical rela-tion between future and past'. It is a 'monolith, announcing new times'.[33]

Yet this is not precisely what is communicated by the image. Nunes's tower is framed picturesquely by the surroundings. It rises above them, but its delicacy and purity mean that it does not dominate them; indeed, the church and the tower have equal billing, more or less. And there is a formal comparison too, the verticals of the church tower emphasized by the water tower, while the white line of the third floor is continued by the projecting cornice of the house. Investigate further and other compar-isons begin to suggest themselves. As Goodwin notes – in fact it is the only thing he says about it – the tower is highly illusionistic, its utili-tarian appearance disguising the fact that only a part of it is used as a storage tank. And in the image, its scale is quite uncertain. By burning out the details, Kidder-Smith plays up the fact that it could read as a 30-storey slab block. These things suggest a connection with the Baroque, which is illusionistic if nothing else. In other words, the dialectic between past and present is strongly here in the *image*, whatever the aims of the architect.

Brazil Builds presents colonial architecture as a kind of proto-Modernism: austere, site-specific, using local materials and techniques, fit for purpose. Hence – consistent with Costa and Freyre – the enthusiasm for the *casa grande*, the form most amenable to this Modernist revision-ism. The Fazenda Vassouras, in the state of Rio de Janeiro, is a simple square mass on a huge monumental terrace, barely decorated outside, but housing some spectacularly florid interiors. The Fazenda Colubandê, in

Fazenda Vassouras,
from *Brazil Builds*.

Fazenda Colubandê,
from *Brazil Builds*.

São Gonçalo, state of Rio de Janeiro, is an austere, horizontal building, with a grand terrace affording a splendid view – a prototype Grande Hotel.[34] The Fazenda Garcia, near Petrópolis in the mountains in the state of Rio de Janeiro, is a simple house built into a steep forest hillside, almost inseparable from its forest surroundings.[35] Besides the *fazendas*, there are discussions of forts and industrial buildings, and a great many colonial

churches. Lúcio Costa's Museum of the Missions, in São Miguel das Missões in the far southern state of Rio Grande do Sul, built in 1937 from the ruins of an eighteenth-century church, is represented, notably, within the *historic* part of the catalogue: a 'simple, glass-walled building' that 'provides a pleasantly non-competitive background for the brilliantly arranged sculpture'.[36] In each case, however, historic buildings are selected to represent the Modernist argument; the colonial is powerfully represented as a prototype Modern, austere, simple, logical and sculptural.

However, Brazil's historic architecture can only be understood as a precursor of Modernism if it is also *primitive*. *Brazil Builds* demands that it be primitive in order to be authentic, drawing on by then well-established models in other areas of the visual arts. In painting and sculpture, primitivism was, by 1943, ubiquitous, and MOMA had played a large part in its propagation. MOMA's landmark exhibition *Cubism and Abstract Art* (1936) was the first large-scale attempt to codify abstraction in art, and it did so by referring to so-called primitive art from sub-Saharan Africa. The exhibition catalogue, written by the museum's young director, Alfred H.

54

Barr, included a famous diagram that showed a direct lineage to 'primitive' work.[37] The cult of primitivism is equally well represented in *Brazil Builds*. Its historic buildings are those that are easily recuperated into a primitivist paradigm: without exception, they are simple, robust and austere, just like the Modernist buildings they supposedly prefigure.

Goodwin's view is notably inclusive. But it also clearly *excludes* much from its understanding of Modernism. It disparages most of the contemporary fabric of Brazil's big cities. It has little to say about São Paulo, for example, then overtaking Rio as the country's largest commercial and cultural capital. It ignores the gargantuan Edifício Martinelli in that city, a skyscraper the equal of anything in New York, built in 1929 in the style of an over-scaled Renaissance *palazzo*. In Rio, Goodwin can complain only about the modern development along the Avenida Rio Branco, for example, development that turned a small colonial town into a version of Second Empire Paris, complete with the technological infrastructure (the paved roads, the street lighting, the trams, the elevators) that made such a vision of modernity possible. Neither does he say anything about Belo Horizonte, a new city designed from scratch by the planner Aarão Reis between 1893 and 1897, whose vast grid and ambition already strongly recalled Chicago. The extraordinary and now justly celebrated Teatro Amazonas in Manaus is dismissed as 'academic correctness' and 'sterility'; it is not 'living, breathing architecture'.[38]

The Architectural Legacy

The work of Costa, Freyre and MOMA amounts to a coherent intellectual attempt to project the past into the present, with the Grande Hotel at Ouro Prêto perhaps its most highly developed manifestation. In terms of architecture, the Grande Hotel produced several significant derivatives, two of which are worth describing in detail. First is Costa's own Park Hotel, in the Parque São Clemente at Novo Friburgo, a mountain resort town in the state of Rio de Janeiro (1940–44). In Cavalcanti's view, this is no less than 'Costa's masterpiece'.[39] In appearance, the Park Hotel is at first sight strikingly similar to Niemeyer's Grande Hotel. Like the Grande Hotel, it is a horizontal block set into a hillside on a narrow, steeply sloping site. It is relatively small, just ten rooms; it is four storeys in height; it has clearly demarcated public and private sides: the private side is defined by a balcony running the entire length of the structure, and providing access to the private rooms; the more public functions of the hotel are located on the ground floor of the building. From the private side, it is (like the Grande Hotel) a building that fits seamlessly into its context. For the inexpert, it is hard to distinguish from historic

Lucio Costa, Park
Hotel, Novo Friburgo,
1940–44.

buildings. It makes much use of historic materials and techniques. The architect Henrique Mindlin draws attention to its 'open work panels of hollow tiles or pre-cast concrete . . . trellises or jalousies – sometimes revivals of old designs, like the *muxarabis* . . . balustrades are used almost in their original form, or occasionally on a more magnified scale for more obvious and emphatic architectural accent'.[40] He praises the 'fusion with the environment, embodying an emotional relationship with the past yet free of any slavish urge to copy or imitate and hence leaving the way clear for the adoption of characteristic contemporary solutions'. The construction is 'extremely rustic'; the materials and construction use local techniques.[41] It is an example of the past being evoked in an 'abstract' rather than 'figurative' way; it is not a copy of an old building, but rather one that evokes comparison with one.

It is worth noting, however, that the construction itself is not primitive, having many similarities with more explicitly modern buildings. It was constructed on pilotis and has a trapezoidal section; the wooden structure, using rough tree-trunks, had certain advantages: cost (the construction materials were practically free), an appearance of rustic

56

simplicity greatly appealing to the hotel's clientele, and respect for an environmentally sensitive site. Furthermore, formally this is a knowing, learned building, Bruand wrote: there is a 'sound sense of proportion based on the application of a classical model . . . apparent simplicity an expression of sober refinement'. The historic and modern elements are simultaneously revealed and concealed – the pilotis, for example, are not all exposed; there are walls of unadorned stone. Some elements can only be modern, such as the horizontal windows on the rear façade, but at the same time some elements can only be colonial.[42] It is a superficially simple exercise, but in reality much more knowing and sophisticated than it originally appears.

The second case is Niemeyer's so-called Catetinho ('little *Catete*'), named after the president's palace in Rio de Janeiro. This house for President Kubitschek was designed and constructed by Niemeyer in ten days in November 1956 from locally available materials. It is celebrated as the 'first' building in Brasília, although that honour should really go to the *favela* of the Cidade Livre. Simple and rustic in appearance, it is located 26 kilometres from the city centre at the far end of the south end of the city,

just beyond the airport, in what is still virgin forest. At the time of its construction, the plan of the city had yet to be determined; all that existed was a site. Exceedingly simple and rustic in appearance, it consists of two floors, and from a distance seems to reiterate the basic plan of the hotels in Ouro Prêto and Novo Friburgo. Situated in a small clearing in the forest, it is two storeys in height, made almost entirely of wood, held up by a series of pilotis, with a projecting balcony along the length of the façade. The principal rooms, including the president's bedroom and rooms for guests, are found on this floor. Meant originally as a temporary structure, it was declared a national monument in 1960, and has been kept as a museum ever since.[43] It was cheap to build, and the cash to build it was supplied by ten friends of the president. He liked to cultivate an image of simplicity, and the Catetinho supplied an appropriate architectural representation. At the same time, it conformed to Modernist architectural principles. It was a politically expedient compromise, but also an agreeable building.

There are a few other structures built on similar principles. There is a country house for Hildebrando Accioly near Petrópolis by Francisco Bolonha from 1950, and a resort complex by the Roberto brothers from 1944, both large-scale exercises in Costa-style Modernism. For Bruand, the latter was a real triumph: 'a perfect example of the application of the

58

theories of Lúcio Costa . . . here the synthesis between local tradition and the modern spirit reaches the high point of perfection'.[44] But the real legacy is perhaps simply in the legitimacy Costa's theories gave to the use of historic elements in otherwise Modernist buildings. The best-known examples include the use of *azulejos* at the MES, and at the buildings in Pampulha, and the traditional Portuguese tiling of pavements in otherwise Modernist urban schemes, such as the Avenida Atlântica in Copacabana. Perhaps the most extensive application of Costa's ideas can be found in high-class domestic architecture. Many of Niemeyer's early buildings reference colonial methods and styles: see the monopitch tiled roof and whitewashed walls of his Cavalcanti House in Gavea, Rio (1940), or his own house in the same location (1942). Costa's houses do much the same: see his Casa Hungria Machado in Leblon (1942) or a very late exercise in the same style, Residência Helena Costa in Rio (1980–84), which is almost indistinguishable from the colonial vernacular. For the critic Maria Alice Junqueira Bastos, this is a vital building representative of Frampton's global concept of critical regionalism. In the 1950s and '60s the Italian-born architect Lina Bo Bardi built numerous houses for wealthy clients that referenced the local vernacular, especially the forms of the rural north-east. Like Costa's work, her houses could approach the condition of the vernacular to the point at which they are inseparable from it. Her Casa de Valéria P. Cirrel (1958) in Morumbi, São Paulo, is a particularly striking example. And at the same time, the Paulista architect Vilanova Artigas built much that referenced the historical past, often in a polemical way. His rather ironic Casa Elza Berquó (1968) in São Paulo has a concrete roof held up with an unadorned tree-trunk, a reference to Brazil's condition of underdevelopment as much as its traditional forms of building.

Much more recently, Paulo Mendes da Rocha has built a chapel that is legibly a reprise of Costa's Museum of the Missions of 1937. Built for the artist Francisco Brennand on his sprawling estate in Recife, the chapel is a new structure in the ruins of an old building. It is modern while making abundant reference to the past. It uses the forms of colonial buildings to moderate the tropical climate, while, like Costa, Mendes da Rocha is unfazed that this structure reiterates the forms and rituals of colonial Brazil. Brennand's estate, on the outskirts of one of Brazil's most unequal cities, is the direct continuation of the colonial *fazenda*, continuously inhabited by his family since the eighteenth century. Brennand's income derives from the international art market, in which he has made a substantial career. But everything else about the estate speaks of the persistence of colonial values, with the artist as benign patriarch ruling over what is in effect a mini-state. Mendes da Rocha's

Paulo Mendes da Rocha, chapel for Francisco Brennand, 2006.

work is simply the latest manifestation of a complex and ambiguous tradition of Modernism in Brazil, in which the past and the future are kept simultaneously in play.[45]

The same attitude towards the past is manifest in the continued activity of IPHAN, an organization that has operated with notable consistency since its foundation as SPHAN. Andrade remained director from 1937 to 1967, to be succeeded by Costa, who had already spent most of his working life with the organization. Continuing the tradition, on his retirement Costa handed over the directorship of the organization to his granddaughter, Maria Elisa Costa. According to IPHAN itself, 20,000 buildings are now protected (*tombados*, to use the organization's terminology), along with 83 towns and cities, and more than 12,000 archaeological sites. The emphasis on Portuguese colonial architecture, a peculiarity of Costa, continues. Among the most remarkable of the protected sites is the capital, Brasília, whose realization had been in large part the responsibility of Costa himself. The act of *tombamento* preserves the city's now historic buildings, while the integrity of the plan is looked after by UNESCO: World Heritage Status was awarded in 1987 (for more, see

Paulo Mendes da
Rocha, chapel for
Francisco Brennand,
2006, detail.

chapter Three). The Brasília episode makes clear the curiously close relationship between Modernist and historic architecture. The ferocity of
development in Brazil's large cities suggests a widespread indifference
to the past. But this coexists with an anxiety to bring those officially
validated kinds of Modernism within the historical frame as soon as
possible. Brasília was barely 30 years old when it was inscribed in the
livro de tombo. Its historicization, you might say, has been pursued with
the vigour of the true Modernist.

chapter two

The Politics of Eros

The desire to assimilate the architectural past into the present described in chapter One was motivated in no small part by the erotic.[1] One motivation was certainly – as with Costa – the desire for cultural continuity between past and present, as a part of an ultimately conservative worldview. But both Costa, and (particularly) Freyre found an erotic nostalgia in the *casa grande*, a longing for a slow, sensuous way of living in which nature was beautiful and abundant, as was sex; indeed, for contemporary readers of *Casa Grande e Senzala*, it is the frankness of Freyre's account of the sexual life of the *fazenda* that stands out as most prescient.[2] While conscious of the power exercised in sexual relations between owners and slaves, he describes a sexual landscape of apparently far greater range and licence than that possible in the world of the urban *bourgeois* of the early twentieth century. There is in Freyre and his circle a nostalgia for an erotic life they knew of by rumour or hearsay, but in all probability had never experienced themselves. This nostalgia has a large amount of fantasy (after all, sex in the *fazenda*, as Freyre himself acknowledges, could be a vehicle for oppression as much as pleasure), but, nevertheless, it is a vital part of Brazil's self-perception. Specifically from the point of view of architecture, the erotic is an integral part of early Modernism in Brazil. It is sometimes more explicit than others; sometimes the erotic is manifest in sublimation of the realm of the senses, sometimes in the provision of spaces in which flirtation may be positively encouraged, sometimes by designing buildings that allude specifically to sex. But it is, arguably, always there, above all in Niemeyer's work. Sex is central to his visual repertoire, from the comparison he has repeatedly made between the female form in his curvaceous architecture, to the women sunbathers who populate his architectural sketches, to the photographs of female nudes that decorate his desk.[3] This chapter explores these manifestations of the erotic in Brazil's Modernist architecture, centred on the architecture and architectural discourse of the 1940s, but also showing how they persist into the present day.

Oscar Niemeyer,
Casa do Baile,
Pampulha, 1940.

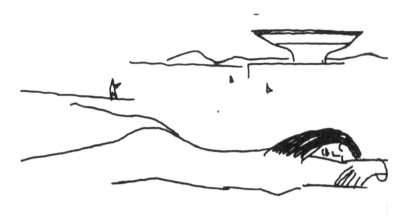

Oscar Niemeyer,
sketch of Museu de
Arte Contemporânea,
Niteroí, c. 1996.

Niemeyer's small architectural office can be found on the Avenida Atlântica, the great boulevard that defines Copacabana's beach. There is in all probability no better-known beach in the world, its fame a product of such films as *Flying Down to Rio* (Thornton Freeland, 1932), starring Fred Astaire and Ginger Rogers, where Copacabana is represented as the apogee of urban eroticism. In thinking about the erotics of modern architecture, the beach is surely the best place to start. It is a landscape of vital importance, defining an ideal of sociability that architects have frequently tried to emulate or represent. Until the eighteenth century, beaches were generally perceived – where they were perceived at all – as places of labour. In art they are littered with the debris of fishing, not leisure.[4] But global exploration from the sixteenth century onwards began to produce images of beaches that contain recognizably modern, and particularly erotic, elements. In accounts of first contact with indigenous peoples the beach can become an erotically charged space, a space in which suddenly, after months or years of voyaging, immense sexual possibilities could be released. In relation to Brazil, there are numerous, fascinating accounts of first contact in which the beach is the spatial frame. In one report to the Portuguese king Dom João II in 1500, Vasco da Gama described landfall in Brazil and contact with a deputation of Tupi Indians. The Indians caused a sensation, particularly the girls, who were 'very young and very pretty, with very dark hair, long over their shoulders and their privy parts, so high, so closed, and so free from hair that we felt no shame in looking at them very well'. The explorers, greatly impressed, compared them favourably with Portuguese women.[5]

It is too much of an intellectual leap to declare da Gama's encounter with the Tupi as the beginning of the modern conception of the beach. The modern beach, however, embodies something of the mythology of first contact: it remains a place where convention is (conventionally) abandoned, and where erotic possibilities open up. Brazil has a particularly strong relationship with the beach. Most of its population is still found on the coast, and the beach has become central to the country's urban life, providing a space equivalent in symbolic function to the civic squares of European cities. Stefan Zweig said as much in 1942, when describing the life of the poor in Rio. The climate was accommodating, the food was cheap, and above all the spectacular beaches provided a place for them to go. This 'super-Nice, super Miami, possibly the most beautiful strand in the world' (as he put it) was therefore also the embodiment of a different kind of civil society.[6] The symbolic centrality of the beach in Brazilian cities marks a significant difference between the western European and North American understanding of the beach. For Europeans, the beach is typically a place of periodic escape and disengagement *from* the city; for Brazilians, the beach is integral to it. The contemporary Brazilian novelist Ruy Castro provides an up-to-date commentary on the place of the beach in the Brazilian city. Europeans and North Americans, he observes,

> take a trip to the beach as if they were going to a hotel in the mountains or another country. In Rio people just go to the beach, like going to the cinema, the shops or the bank – because it's there 24 hours a day, all year round, and with an entire city round it, all its services fully available. . . . it's a whole culture. You go to the beach to read the paper, meet friends, play foot-volleyball, get to know people, get the latest gossip, and even, sometimes, to talk business. It's a space as natural as a town square, a restaurant or an office.[7]

But both Zweig and Castro are also preoccupied with the eroticism of the beaches. For Zweig, writing in the late 1930s, the beach is the place where dress codes relax, a place 'devoted exclusively to luxury and sport, to the enjoyment of body and eye'.[8] For contemporary commentators like Castro, the eroticism of the beach has come to subsume everything else. Copacabana (along with its prolongation, Ipanema) is the only place in a metropolitan city where it is entirely acceptable for diners to enter an expensive restaurant almost naked, in 'bathing costume, no shirt, in sandals or barefoot, with the vestiges of the Atlantic ocean still on their bodies . . . Cariocas' familiarity with their own bodies must have no parallel in any other metropolitan city.'[9] Castro goes on to describe the casual eroticism of the beach: Carioca women weaving their way in bikinis through crowds of men on their way to the office, the constant and all-pervasive ogling of bodies, a system of visual pleasure (an 'art form' in Castro's words) in which the one doing the looking and the recipient of the gaze are both knowing participants.[10] So, in summary, in myth Rio's beaches are suffused with the eroticism one might expect: they frame an eroticized social life.

It is a myth that is attractive and useful for both Brazilians and visitors, not least architects. But it *is* a myth: the eroticism has nothing much natural about it, and is the result of a lot of hard work. For Regina Guerrero, a former editor of both *Vogue* and *Elle* in Brazil, the beach is eroticized to the point where any semblance of normality has disappeared. A disillusioned and disenfranchised populace has become fixated on the body to the exclusion of everything else. A beautiful body, regardless of the social or economic cost, has become a matter of survival: 'our unique motivation is sexuality, beauty, health, form, and depending where one is, eternal youth . . . getting old, fat, or letting oneself go, it's suicide. All doors close, those of work as well as those of love.'[11]

Architecture on the Beach

Le Corbusier visited Brazil twice before the Second World War, visits that were of signal importance in the architect's own career, but also of importance more widely in advancing an erotic conception of modern architecture. Kenneth Frampton wrote of the first visit (1929, organized through contacts of the French poet Blaise Cendrars) in particular as a 'personal epiphany' for the architect, and (later) probably the happiest time of his life.[12] It also seems to have been an erotic epiphany, since Le

Le Corbusier, sketch of Josephine Baker, 1929.

Le Corbusier, sketch from a 1929 visit to Rio de Janeiro.

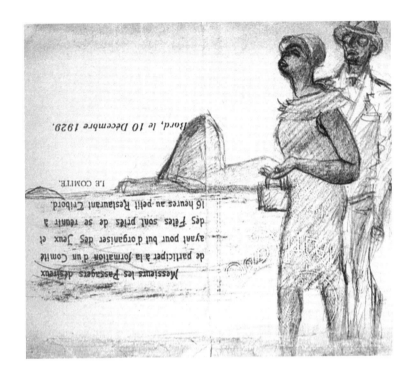

Corbusier seems to have enjoyed a 'close relationship' (as Frampton coyly puts it) with the African-American jazz singer Josephine Baker, whom he met *en voyage* to Rio, and who is the subject of a number of drawings. The architect sketched incessantly during both these early visits. Architecture in fact makes up only a small fraction of his output, which mostly concerns the natural landscape of Rio and its pneumatic female inhabitants. There are numerous letters and other bits of correspondence, and other, longer accounts of the city and its life that made their way into the public speeches he gave at the time.[13] It is in sum a major body of work.

The impressions gathered in the visit of 1929 inform the major imaginative work of the period, the re-planning of Rio as a sinuous megastructure, curving its way between mountain and sea. But this plan exists in only the sketchiest of forms, and Le Corbusier's imaginative investment in recording the erotics of the beach as it already exists is, in some ways, greater. The small sketch illustrated here is a piece of ephemera, but seen through an erotic lens, a highly significant image. It was executed in coloured crayon on a card from the steamer *Lutetia*, on board which Le Corbusier sailed with Josephine Baker from Buenos Aires northwards to

Brazil. The text on the card (in French) concerns the formation of a club on board to organize games and other entertainments. Le Corbusier inverts the card so the text reads upside down, and draws himself and Baker on, or close to, the beach at Flamengo, a well-to-do southern suburb of Rio, located between the commercial centre of the city and Copacabana – the architect stayed at the recently built Hotel Glória, and, it is recorded, swam at least once off the beach outside the hotel (a photograph exists of him standing by the sea wall overlooking the beach, dressed in one of the hotel's dressing gowns). His drawing places him and Baker on the right-hand side of the image. Dressed in a white suit he stands close behind her. She wears a sleeveless green dress, her chin lifted slightly, her eyes apparently closed as if in ecstasy at the beauty of the situation. In the background the great priapic form of the Sugar Loaf rises, an indicator, perhaps, of the architect's state of mind.

The sketch relates closely to a series of slightly later erotic sketches of *mulatas*, mostly unclothed, by which Le Corbusier was clearly fascinated. They are big women, large-hipped and muscular, buttocks and breasts highly pronounced, the opposite in every way from Le Corbusier himself, a pale, angular, awkward-looking European male. Look at these sketches side by side with the Baker sketch and the connection is clear enough,

Le Corbusier, sketch of apartment interior, Rio de Janeiro, 1942.

Baker as quasi-*mulata*, a safe form of exoticism, temporarily within the architect's orbit.

The second image, or more correctly set of images, dates from 1942 (that is, six years after Le Corbusier's last visit to Rio) and depicts the Sugar Loaf progressively recuperated as image. In the first, a series of lines delineates the mountain, the beach towards Flamengo and the sea; the second adds a palm tree on the left-hand side of the image, rendering it picturesque; the third places a man in a comfortable chair before the scene; the fourth image finally domesticates it entirely, placing a frame around the scene. Suddenly everything is clear: the Modernist house is a frame for the view; the window, as Beatriz Colomina puts it in her commentary on these images, 'is a gigantic screen'.[14] The architect makes clear that the relationship between the house and the view is a new and unconventional one. The house is not *in* the view, but a means of possessing the view. Nature is now a part of the 'lease' as Le Corbusier puts it, 'the pact with nature has been sealed'.[15]

For both the architect and for Colomina in her much later commentary, the act of framing nature in this way is an erotic one. For Le Corbusier, nature's forms and the forms of the *mulatas* (and Josephine Baker) were inseparable, and his architectural responses to the scene in Rio de Janeiro were about preserving the erotics of the site as far as possible. So the mega-structure that insinuates its way between the port and Copacabana is first and foremost a means of representing the erotic experience of nature. Its sinuous form simultaneously represents the geography of the city's coastline and the bodies of its female inhabitants. Le Corbusier's plan was never built, but its representation of the erotics of Rio had important consequences for subsequent modern architecture in Brazil.

The Brazilian Pavilion at the New York World's Fair

The first large-scale exercise of this erotically charged Modernist architecture materialized outside Brazil, however, in the form of the Brazilian Pavilion at the New York World's Fair of 1939–40. This, the first complete collaboration between Niemeyer and Costa, was located in the section of the fair given over to national pavilions. The two architects arrived in New York in 1938 and took up space in the office of Wallace Harrison, who would later coordinate the work with Niemeyer on the headquarters building for the United Nations.

The building itself, built in just five months, was a small, three-storey structure built on an L-plan, framing a small lake to the rear.[16] Raised partly on pilotis, and with an unusual *brise-soleil* on the front façade like a miniature version of the system used on the MES, the pavilion was

Costa and Niemeyer,
Brazilian Pavilion,
New York World's
Fair, 1939.

Brazilian Pavilion,
interior.

dominated by a wide, curving pedestrian ramp that scooped up visitors to the first floor. From here, they passed through a generous, curving entrance hall with a small bar serving coffee, to a series of stands showing off Brazilian commercial products: coffee, nuts, chocolate, tobacco, cotton and palm oil. Elsewhere, there was a formal exhibition hall with paintings by Portinari, a magnificent curving bar specializing in *caipirinhas* and a circular dance-hall.[17]

All the pavilions' purposes were propagandistic, namely the promotion of trade and culture and good relations with the United States. But the Brazilian Pavilion represented this soft diplomacy brief with an exuberant and decidedly erotic building. It was full of curves, up to that point unimaginable in a Modernist building, certainly in New York (the near-contemporary MOMA by Philip Goodwin and Edward Stone was a piece of graph paper by contrast,

rectilinear and more or less two-dimensional). It was profoundly conscious of the *body* of the visitor, leading him or her around the building, and providing invitations to pause or linger. In this regard, it encouraged visitors to look at each *other* as much as the products on display: the sinuous mezzanine above the main hall provided a voyeuristic pause in the programme for the visitor to look down at others, unseen.

Brazilian Pavilion,
interior.

And it provided plenty of spaces for simple pleasures – the bar and dance floor were not secondary spaces, but central to the programme. The pavilion defined Brazil, in other words, as a sensuous place above all, responsible for the production of pleasurable goods for world-wide consumption (coffee, cigarettes, chocolate), and populated by a pleasure-seeking population. The pavilion's starting point may have been the Modernist language defined by Le Corbusier, but the sensuality of the programme as realized helped define a distinctive, and decidedly erotic, Brazilian form of Modernism.

Pampulha

Inside Brazil, the erotic potential of Modernism is manifest on a grand scale at Pampulha (1940–42), Niemeyer's first major solo commission. The project was a high-class housing estate built around an artificial lake, in an outer suburb of Belo Horizonte, Brazil's third largest city and the capital of the inland state of Minas Gerais. It was initiated by the governor of the state of Minas Gerais, Juscelino Kubitschek (later president of Brazil, 1957–61), who proposed it as both a significant extension to the city and a piece of real-estate development through a publicly funded scheme to prime a new area with infrastructure. Designed in 1940, the complex was largely completed by 1942, in time for it to be featured prominently in the MOMA exhibition *Brazil Builds*.[18]

Oscar Niemeyer, Casino, Pampulha, 1940.

Niemeyer's design for Pampulha had six principal elements: the lake with the dam, six kilometres or so in perimeter, a casino, a yacht club, a hotel, an open-air night club (the Casa do Baile, or House of Dance) and a church. There was also, close to the yacht club, a house for Kubitschek. All the buildings exploited the possibilities of reinforced concrete: hence the extraordinary asymmetrical double vaults of the church and the undulating form of the Casa do Baile, which echoed the form of the islet on which it was located. The casino too was a formal experiment as much as anything, elaborating the idea of the architectural promenade, and juxtaposing a variety of contrasting forms and surfaces (in the eyes of more than one observer, it also pushed taste to the limit).[19] The result there drew in certain historical models too – all the buildings made use of *azulejos* – and the boldness of the architecture, with its many decorative or non-functional elements, led to comparisons with the Baroque. The invocation of the Baroque is of itself an invocation of an erotic sensibility: a response to the purity of the classical mode, Baroque art is bodily if nothing else.

Azulejos on Niemeyer's Casino, Pampulha, 1940.

Casino, Pampulha, 1940.

The erotics of Pampulha, however, are most clearly represented in an unbuilt part of the scheme, the hotel. Designed along with the rest of the main buildings in 1940, in plan it recalls the two hotels discussed in chapter One, namely Costa's Park Hotel in Novo Friburgo and Niemeyer's own Grande Hotel at Ouro Prêto. Like those two buildings, this one is a low, horizontal structure raised on pilotis; two levels of bedrooms rise above. There is, on these upper floors, a slightly inclined glazed façade the width of the building, allowing all the bedrooms to enjoy views of the (spectacular) lake. The view takes in the Casa do Baile, which the hotel formally echoes. Some bedrooms on the eastern side of the building might also have had views across to the church of São Francisco. It is, like the earlier hotels, a building designed first and foremost to make as much use as possible of the site, sublimating the view. But it departs from the earlier hotels in the treatment of the ground floor, which is much larger and more elaborate than anything seen in the earlier schemes, a huge area with spectacular views both inside and outside. It is formally complex, a big roof resembling an artist's palette, holding in play a series of undulating colonnades. There is not a straight line in sight; the palette form is punctuated by holes, out of which sprout great palms, and it is hard to tell if you are inside or outside. It is a highly rhetorical space that makes a case for a decidedly irrational, anti-functional architecture, a departure from the Modernism of the northern Europeans.

The Pampulha hotel is also, unquestionably, a space organized primarily for pleasure. The curves alone suggest organic, bodily forms, but they are filled with spaces for all kinds of physical pleasures: dancing, sleeping, relaxing, flirting. The furniture is virtually all horizontal. Bar the inevitable Barcelona chairs, the terrace is scattered with chaises longues and easy chairs. The terrace merges imperceptibly with the beach; one is

Oscar Niemeyer, scheme for hotel, Pampulha, 1940, sketches.

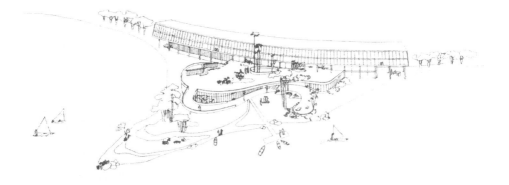

virtually commanded to lie down. And as Niemeyer draws it, it is a scene that is full of erotic activity. Le Corbusier's perspectives were – where they were populated at all – inhabited by tiny individual figures, alone with nature, nursing (as the philosopher Roger Scruton once put it) 'their inner solitude'.[20] Niemeyer's scene is inhabited only by couples, dancing, flirting, drinking, sunbathing. There is some attention to the last – a well-sculpted couple represent a new, modern beauty based on the simple enjoyment of the body. This is an image about sex, not callisthenics. Where for the Brazilians, Modernist building (through, for example, the opening up of indoor and outdoor spaces, the production of spaces in which the body might be exulted) opened up a realm of erotic possibilities, for the Europeans, it was, by contrast, often an architecture designed to keep them in check.

Sadly, the hotel was not built, but most of the rest of the scheme was. The Casino, however, completed in 1942, embodies much of the erotic programme of the hotel. Like the hotel it is mainly a linear building, against which there are curving contrasts. It has something to do with Le Corbusier's Villa Savoye, not so much in outward form (although both are largely rectangular pavilions on pilotis), but for the use of the architectural promenade. The visitor is taken on a defined route through the building, from the marbled exterior, dotted with busty sculptural nudes by August Zamoiski, through a dazzling double-height entrance hall in chrome and mirrors, up a ramp in marble, rising up and across the entrance space. The visitor finds the main hall of the Casino on the first floor. All through the promenade, views inside and outside mingle. One looks across the lake at the same time as one looks at the building inside, while the mirrors encourage one to look at both oneself and the other players. This is a space that frames an erotics of modern life. It puts bodies on display, and through the use of luxurious,

unusual or seductive materials, makes the visitor think in terms of the senses of both touch and sight.

The erotic potential of the Casino is reiterated in the much smaller Casa do Baile, a kind of outdoor nightclub. It takes up, in simplified form, the shapes of the hotel terrace, making a combination of a restaurant and a dance-hall, set directly across the lake from the more monumental Casino. Unlike the Casino, it is a calculatedly informal space, which confuses indoors and outdoors, private and public, providing a variety of spaces to frame a number of activities, from the public activity of dancing, to flirting, to (perhaps in the bushes by the lake) something more serious. The yacht club, a short distance from the Casino, is not legible in the same erotic way as these other spaces – it is a relatively formal building with a reverse-pitch roof that recalls Le Corbusier's Errazuriz House in Chile. The extraordinary church of São Francisco de Assis, however, with its bulging, asymmetrical vaults, and sudden vertical accents, is perhaps the most bodily space of all, a physical building that is much more easily legible as about the exultation of the body rather than the spirit. Niemeyer, an atheist, refused to build a confessional box, feeling that to do so would be to taint the activities his buildings framed around the rest of the lake with guilt.[21] This, combined (perhaps) with the unconventional forms of the church, led to a drawn-out controversy involving the established Church, which refused to consecrate it until 1959, sixteen years after its completion.

The unfortunate story of the church was replicated in almost every other aspect of the development. The Casino was rendered useless almost immediately it was finished after the Federal government in Rio passed a law forbidding gambling. It lay empty until late in the 1950s, when it became a gallery of modern art, a role that it performs – badly

Oscar Niemeyer, Church of São Francisco de Assis, Pampulha, 1940.

– to the present day. Its construction too lacked the sophistication of the design, a problem common to many of Niemeyer's buildings. Evenson reported a contemporary American architect's shock at the kitchen on the ground floor, an afterthought bodged by incompetent builders.[22] The Casa do Baile never became commercially viable. Designed for a mostly working-class clientele, it was simply in the wrong location, a low-density suburb for the wealthy, with only poor access by public transport. The yacht club was closed for years by an infestation of a water-borne parasite, only becoming safe for leisure use in the 1960s.[23]

These and other negative factors, including cracks in the lake dam and ongoing problems with the water supply, meant that the development entirely failed to become the commercial success that its backers envisaged. For years, its main buildings lay empty and abandoned, melancholy harbingers of an age of erotic liberation that never really came. The development looks marvellous now, although built at a low density and, like every other wealthy suburb in Brazil, patrolled by private security guards and almost entirely devoid of human life, so that it carries few, if any, of the erotic connotations it originally did. The original sketches and photographs nevertheless do still represent the original vision, and continue to represent a riposte to the puritanical and rationalist concept of modern architecture represented by the Europeans.

The Erotics of the Private Villa

The erotic programme described by Pampulha became part of fashionable architectural taste. In the private realm, Brazil's wealthy commissioned an enormous variety of modern houses from the 1930s onwards, many of which have since become iconic. The range, variety and quality of these houses is as high as anywhere in the same period. There was no systematic programme in Brazil, but the range and quality of the experiments bear comparison with the 34 Case Study Houses, built on the west coast of the United States between 1945 and 1966. As with the Case Study Houses, the best Brazilian houses often experimented with new forms of living, pulling out what were previously private functions – for example, sleeping and cooking – and making them central to the life of the house, rather than hiding them away. In Brazil, experimentation in housing tended to address questions of class. For the Paulista architect Vilanova Artigas, the private house was envisaged as an attack on class boundaries on the family level, by making domestic work a central part of the house's activity, rather than having it sequestered away somewhere private, as in the São Paulo house he built for himself in

Lina Bo Bardi,
private house,
São Paulo, 1952.

Lina Bo Bardi,
sketch of the interior
of the private house
in São Paulo.

Oscar Niemeyer, Casa das Canoas, Gavea, Rio de Janeiro, 1953.

1948–9. Joaquim Guedes's Casa da Cunha Lima (1958) does the same thing. For Lina Bo Bardi, the private house could be a means of developing a new, modern, sexual politics, providing, for example, a comfortable and appropriate frame for a professional woman to live alone. For Niemeyer, the private house is, inevitably, a way to try out a variety of new spaces to frame leisure and pleasure.

The most celebrated example is the architect's own Casa das Canoas (1952). For Lauro Cavalcanti, this is nothing less than 'one of the most beautiful modern houses in the world'. He continues:

> At the centre of the composition is a great rock, around which is developed the house and the pool . . . the flat roof links interior and exterior spaces, establishing a rich dialogue with the exuberant landscape of the Carioca sea and mountains. In this project Niemeyer resolves two of the great problems of glass houses: the invasion of sunlight and of the sight and sensation of excessive exposure to the night with an illuminated interior and dark exterior . . . bedrooms located in basement, protected from curious eyes, with access by means of a stair carved in the rock.[24]

Oscar Niemeyer, Casa das Canoas, Gavea, Rio de Janeiro, 1953. The kitchen seen from the garden.

In this account, Cavalcanti describes most of the significant elements of the building: an extraordinary site, high up above the city in the *mata atlântica*, with views of the surrounding mountains and sea; a building that plays constantly with ideas of public and private space, collapsing one into the other; a building that still provides areas of intimacy, hidden away from private view; a house that stages and spectacularizes the body, providing a grand terrace on which guests can see each other and be seen to the best effect; a great swimming pool, defining the entrance to the house from the rear – indeed the house, like the later, Californian archetype, seems to emerge from the pool. Perhaps Caval-canti could have also mentioned the sculptures littered about the place. In the architect's usual taste, these curvaceous nudes, all breasts and buttocks, make clear (if there was ever any doubt) that this house was meant to frame a liberated attitude to sex. During Kubitschek's presi-dency, the house was a critical part of Rio's cultural infrastructure, providing a regular setting for cocktails for visiting dignitaries and intellectuals. The erotic charge of the house was no doubt more imagi-nary than real, but equally, there is little doubt that it helped to contribute

August Zamoiski,
sculpture at Casa das
Canoas, 1953.

– along with the beaches and floorshows of Copacabana, and the genuinely uninhibited revelry of Carnival – to the myth of Brazil as an erotic
paradise. That erotic potential is well described by the architect Ernesto
Rogers, who recalled a visit to the house in the following terms:

> I doubt that I shall ever forget that scene: the sun was just dipping
> below the horizon, leaving us in a dark sea of orange, violet, green
> and indigo. The house repeated the themes of that orgiastic country-
> side (incense and the hum of insects); a vast rhapsody beginning

in the roof vibrated down the walls and their niches to finish in the pool, where the water, instead of being neatly dammed up, spread freely along the rocks in a kind of forest pool.[25]

The house in this scenario is far more than the European Modernists ever really envisaged. Far from a 'machine for living in', this is a riot of orgiastic pleasure.

The Erotics of the Apartment House

Brazil's experiments in Modernist apartment building can be read in the same way. In Le Corbusier's image of an ideal Rio apartment, the natural world is brought inside by means of a great glass curtain wall, which placed the resident of the interior in a voyeuristic role, the expanse of glass positively encouraging the outward gaze towards the beach. But it also implied an exhibitionistic role too; as much as it was possible to look out, it was also possible to look in. Corb famously disagreed with curtains, and any other means of maintaining privacy in a dense urban environment. Neither Le Corbusier nor his followers in Rio took up these suggestions until much later, but one architect who did was Àlvaro Vital Brazil in his highly regarded Edifício Esther (1934–6), for a long time the architect's home. The building also housed the headquarters of the Institute of Brazilian Architects (IAB) and the studio of another well-known Paulista modernist, Rino Levi. Located in the central Praça da República in São Paulo, its immediate environment in 1936 was a classic piece of late nineteenth-century urbanism, a collection of buildings in mostly Second Empire style and a lush public park, a piece of bourgeois European urbanism par excellence. Vital Brazil's block is a radical departure, being a slab of twelve storeys with extensive use of glass, a roof terrace for all the residents, visible from below, and a highly mobile façade, dominated by movable *brises-soleil*. It illustrates better than any other building of the time the exhibitionistic tendencies of Modernist architecture. Where the traditional residence places great store by the separation of private and public, its façade designed to repel the gaze from within, the Edifício Esther makes the façade into an ambiguous thing, half-glass, half-blind, constantly on the move, an architectural striptease simultaneously revealing and concealing its inhabitants. This might be implausible if it were not for the lengths to which Vital Brazil went to put leisure on display. On the most public part of the building, overlooking the squares, he inserts balconies and the

Àlvaro Vital Brazil, Edifício Esther, São Paulo, 1934–6.

Àlvaro Vital Brazil,
Edifício Esther,
sketch of terrace.

roof terrace, spaces that invite the display of the body. Finally, there are
the twin staircases at the sides of the building, elegant spiral stairs,
internal spaces openly on display through the glass. By contrast with the
nineteenth-century apartment house, a model of erotic propriety, the
Edifício Esther works hard to put its residents on display. Its present sad
condition communicates little of this, but early photographs do.

In the early years of the 1950s, Niemeyer experimented in a comparable way with the apartment façade in three vast large private multi-storey
housing projects in the centre of established cities. The complexes in Belo

Àlvaro Vital Brazil,
Edifício Esther, details.

Horizonte (1950) and São Paulo (Edifício Montreal, 1951, and Edifício Copan, 1953) deployed a unique rhetoric of curves and exaggerated *brises-soleil*, in which the latter element in effect described the outward form of the entire building. Both have something of the appearance of gigantic, but sinuous, venetian blinds. The façades of the Copan and the Montreal are distinct from that of their near neighbour in São Paulo, the Edifício Esther, but the effect is similar; the repeating, sinuous *brises-soleil* have the effect of both revealing and concealing the interior, setting up a teasing relationship with the passer-by: you can almost, but not

Oscar Niemeyer,
Edifício Copan,
São Paulo, 1951–3.

quite, see in, yet the drama of the façade invites the gaze. The curves in Niemeyer's personal iconography have erotic connotations, as we have already seen. But perhaps more important, especially in the case of the Copan, is the imagination of the building as more than simply housing, but also a leisure complex. Located a few hundred metres from the old commercial centre of São Paulo, the Copan contains a sizeable array of restaurants, bars, cinemas and shops, in which one may (theoretically) lose oneself in a frenzy of consumption. It is a profoundly individualistic place, designed to service the 2,000 or so flats, all built as *pieds-à-terre* for single adults. The building is clearly imagined as something like a giant singles bar. Its very form is a contrast with the upright, sober and restrained architecture of the surroundings, which both looks like, and is for, work. The Copan, by contrast, signals play, not least the play of the libido. Niemeyer's later work, as is well known, if anything exaggerated the erotic imagination of these buildings from the 1950s: his museums, galleries and pavilions of the 1990s and early 2000s deploy the inevitable curve, but are now overlaid or inset with the architect's sketches of young women.

The Edifício Esther and Niemeyer's 1950s blocks were private buildings for the well-to-do, located in the (then) exclusive parts of established cities. The erotic is also manifest – albeit less successfully – in Brazil's experiments in state housing. The 'Pedredulho', designed in 1947 by Niemeyer's contemporary and peer Affonso Reidy, is a good example. A multi-storey apartment complex built for low-ranking public sector workers, it is located in the poor northern Rio suburb of São Cristóvão. The project was superficially rational. The client was the state department of public housing (Departamento de Habitação Popular), and the form of the building was allegedly determined through interviews with 570 local families, enquiring about their needs and lifestyles. Like contemporary public housing projects in northern Europe, the Pedregulho was a total environment, a miniature welfare state in which all reasonable needs were catered for: it contained not only the 272 flats, but a

Affonso Reidy,
Pedregulho, Rio de
Janeiro, begun in
1947. Photo of 2004
showing the poor
state of the facade.

Pedregulho at
completion.

gym, a post office, a doctor's surgery, a crèche, a playground, a primary school, a swimming pool, a sports ground and a laundry. It was a clear response to the Athens Charter, the 1933 declaration of the Congrès International d'Architecture Moderne (CIAM), which separated human life into the functions of work, circulation, residence and leisure. It was also clearly a product of the more general Modernist belief that space should be essentially educative and moral in character, a means of framing, even inducing, a better way of living.[26]

At the same time, the project clearly derives from certain highly irrational sources. The serpentine form had a rational justification in terms of making the most efficient use of a hilly and awkward site – but much more clearly it is a reiteration of Le Corbusier's 1929 plan for Rio – that snake-like megastructure curving along the coast, an exultation of the body as much as anything else. Its curves have nothing rational about them; they evoke Le Corbusier's openly erotic response to Brazil.

The disjunction between this erotic aesthetic and the rationalist plan is represented by the building's functional failure. The crucial problem seems to have been the opposition between the needs and wants of the mostly poor inhabitants and the way those needs were imagined by the architects. The latter imagined a life of relative leisure, facilitated by relative automation, modern systems of social organization and so on; the building was light and spacious and accommodated most physical needs. The former just wanted a building that could frame the lives they already knew, lives largely defined by hard work, poverty and dependence on immediate family and friends. It was a contrast between two radically opposed conceptions of communal living: one in which pleasure and consumption took centre stage, and another predicated on work and material scarcity.

The disjunction between the two models was played out with ghastly clarity around the business of the laundry. Reidy built a communal facility, in which a bag system ensured anonymity, while a complex arrangement of codes provided security. Laundry was taken out of the hands of the residents themselves, and handed over to a centralized service, therefore freeing them up for other, supposedly more pleasurable, things. It was also a system designed with a clear aesthetic purpose – to eliminate unruly air-drying from the pristine façade of the building. But the residents mistrusted it from the start. The architects also completely failed to understand the social role of laundry. Residents socialized *through* the process of laundry, sharing the burden. Eliminating the traditional notion of laundry eliminated a crucial means of socialization.[27]

It did not help either that the building took fifteen years to complete. Residents ended up feeling like strangers in their own building. Le

Corbusier nevertheless thought it was brilliant. Writing on its completion in 1962 (a decade after the completion of his own iconic apartment house, the Unité d'Habitation in Marseilles), he declared: 'I never had the opportunity to realize a building so complete as you have done.'[28] The eroticism of the original plan, despite the failure, re-emerged in the 1998 movie *Central do Brasil*, in which the Pedregulho is in effect a character, a seedy ruin populated by prostitutes and child traffickers. The eroticism of the original plan is still clearly there, but made nightmarish, like the building that is the central character of J. G. Ballard's *High Rise*.[29]

Affonso Reidy,
Pedregulho, detail.

Affonso Reidy,
Conjunto Residencial
Marques de São
Vicente, Rio de
Janeiro, 1952. It is
very similar to the
Pedregulho, but far
better preserved.

In Brazil, the largest-scale exercise in public housing was the residential axis of Brasília, a project in which most of the principal Modernists,
including Niemeyer, were involved. Here too it is possible to speak of an
erotic sensibility determining the overall design, and, as at the Pedregulho,
such a sensibility resulted in a number of conflicts with actual use or
inhabitation. Like the Pedregulho, the blocks on the south wing were
envisaged as part of a more or less self-sufficient community organized
around leisure, especially to do with sports. The blocks contain large open
areas, swimming pools and tennis courts that put the residents on display.
James Holston, an American anthropologist, went further, arguing in 1989

that the blocks had been built with transparent façades as a means of breaking down class distinctions. Putting everyone and everything on display would have, it was thought, a levelling effect. Holston's classic account of the city produced disquiet among the residents of the super-blocks, almost exclusively middle-class people, whose norms of privacy and sexual propriety were violated by the transparency of the blocks, which they, in the end, managed to subvert by the expert placing of plants and furniture in prominent windows, blocking the curious gaze. In the early days, the threat of voyeurism was widely felt: Hoston reports that the transparent blocks were known as *televisões de candango* (*candango's* TV), a free *telenovela* with implicitly the same preoccupations of sex and money. Whether Brasília's super-blocks ever did function in this way is questionable: the blocks themselves use far less glass in the construction of the façade than Holston suggests, and further – unlike the Edifício Esther – they conspicuously lack balconies or terraces.[30]

City of Sex

For younger architects, even in Brazil, the erotic imagery of the modernists is no longer really tenable. For, as Niemeyer has continued to reiterate this archaic imagery, consciousness has developed about the darker side to Brazil's allegedly liberal sexuality. The creation of the spectacle of sexy bodies on the beach has deleterious health and social effects; the city of Rio de Janeiro has taken steps to attack the vast trade in child prostitution. Meanwhile, in terms of architecture, a new project was floated in 2006 that suggested the possibility of both a franker and a more realistic attitude to sex than that of the Modernists.

The so-called Cidade de Sexo, or 'City of Sex', was an interactive museum designed by a young Brazilian architect, Igor de Vetyemy. Vetyemy's idea was originally a student project, but it was floated as a serious proposition with backing from (among others) the British architect Nigel Coates. It was a minor controversy in the summer of 2006.[31] Judging by the plans on the architect's website, it would stretch out on stilts right across the Avenida Atlântica, almost as far as the beach, while the rear part would reach almost as far as the precipitous green hillside behind, the width of the entire *bairro*.[32] Vetyemy imagined it explicitly as a means of connecting the mountains with the beach. The location was the eastern side of the Avenida Princesa Isabel, a wide avenue with six lanes at right angles to the beach. The location of Copacabana's tallest building, the five-star Meridien, and adjoining the quiet neighbourhood of Leme, it is also a heavily trafficked zone of prostitution. The building's forms are hard to describe: in newspaper reports, it was variously a giant

Igor de Vetyemy,
Cidade de Sexo,
Rio de Janeiro,
proposed 2006.

phallus or a uterus. The entrance, a double tent halfway along Princesa Isabel, suggested breasts with well-defined nipples. The two great forms overhanging the Avenida Atlântica began as phalluses – but their positioning, one form crouched and leaning over another, combined with the placement of the stilts, read as intercourse *a tergo*, the position famously described by Sigmund Freud in his account of the primal scene.[33] The building would be formed from a steel frame, clad in white PVC panels. The cost, Vetyemy thought, would be in the region of R$260 million (US$160 million at the time of writing).[34]

In summary, all its forms alluded to sexual organs or sexual behaviour, without being absolutely explicit. As regards the contents, Vetyemy imagined a series of educational exhibits, but also a shop, a health centre, a strip club, a space for swingers and a 'capsule' (in one image, located far away from the beach among the greenery) in which new sexual possibilities could be explored. Vetyemy stated in an interview that the project was an attempt to deal with Rio's 'huge hypocrisy' regarding sex. People were 'terrified of talking about the idea, and only really discuss the negative things related to sex, like sexual tourism or child prostitution. I wanted to deal with it in a natural, official way.'[35] Official responses were likely to be unfavourable: the same report noted that the mayor at the time, Rosinha Matheus, had recently banned the sale of postcards of naked women as part of a more general set of policies to rid Rio of its sex tourism.[36]

The beach has always had an erotics, as I have shown throughout this chapter. It has always been the site of fantasy, a place in which normal behaviours are, if only temporarily, suspended. In Brazil, an entire urban civilization, as we have seen, has been built around this fantasy, in Niemeyer's work in particular, and its influence. But as we have seen, Niemeyer's vision – and that of colleagues and collaborators such as Burle Marx – is careless about its idea of freedom. It does not recognize, or perhaps cannot recognize, that what it sees as liberation is no more than a fantasy that requires domination: one person's sexual freedom is dependent on another's subjugation – the prostitution on the Avenida Atlântica is a case in point. Even the relatively innocent business of looking and being looked at – that activity celebrated by the novelist Castro – cannot happen without a great deal of what might be termed 'body work' in the case of one party, the female. Vetyemy's project is a different take on it all. Here, the erotics of the beach is made as explicit as it can be: there is a frankness about sex here that is not characteristic of the earlier projects, which are more about flirting. The frankness extends to a detailed level. Here sex is imagined not as something essentially valueless, available to all, universal – but as something that, like the body on which it depends, represents any number of identities. So sex in this museum, if we can call it that, seems to be codified, labelled, split up into different areas of activity. One may regard it academically, or one may participate, at various different levels. Sex here is made commodity in a way that exactly parallels its commodification outside on the Avenida Atlântica. Niemeyer and his circle pretended that such commodification did not exist, but ended up, by default, endorsing it. Vetyemy recognizes the reality of the situation. Such frankness, whether or not the museum gets built, suggests a less romantic, but more realistic, future.

chapter three

Brasília, or the Politics
of Progress

The desire to embody an idea of erotic liberation is one powerful motivation behind Brazil's Modernist architecture. No less powerful has been the desire to embody social and material progress, specifically through the building of new cities. Large-scale experiments of this nature had been carried out in Cidade de Minas, now Belo Horizonte, in the years 1893–7, and in Goiânia in the years 1937–42, both instances of the transference of a state capital to a new location. Both cities are now very large, five million and two million respectively, if their metropolitan areas are included.[1] But the best-known case, and by far the most important in respect of the development of Modernism, is certainly Brasília.

Inaugurated with great fanfare on 21 April 1960, Brasília was the signal achievement of the charismatic populist president Juscelino Kubitschek (1902–1976), whose period in office (1957–61) was a brief interlude of democracy in between periods of authoritarian populism and dictatorship. The city's inauguration was an event on a global scale. The pope offered a special Mass by radio; 150,000 people crowded into the city; and 38 tons of fireworks were detonated. The French minister of culture, André Malraux, called it the 'capital of hope'.[2] It was the culmination of an extraordinary adventure in which a new city of half a million was created from scratch, in a zone of unpromising upland scrub where few had even ventured, let alone set up home. Brasília is one of the twentieth century's great political adventures. It ranks among the single largest construction projects in human history, remarkable for a country that only thirty years previously was a largely rural oligarchy, with political traditions and physical infrastructure that had been little changed since the eighteenth century. Brasília was, quite rightly, fêted by the international architectural press. It appealed particularly to Europe, where for a large section of the architectural profession it represented everything that was desired but could not yet be achieved in a continent still suffering from the after-effects of the Second World War. Brasília may now seem to belong to the distant past, yet regardless of the

A worker shows his family the new city of Brasília on inauguration day, 1960, photographed by René Burri.

character of the buildings, the progressive vision it articulated prefigured that of the much later administration of Lula (2003–).

This progressive vision is brilliantly depicted in a photograph by the Swiss photographer René Burri, taken in the city shortly after its inauguration on 21 April 1960. It shows the twin towers of the Congresso Nacional (National Congress) from the Palácio do Planalto (the Presidential Palace) with the identical slabs of the Ministry buildings in the background. In the foreground stand a family of six, a couple in their thirties and their four young children. By the tone of their skin, their simple clothes and their deportment, they are readily identifiable as *nordestinos*, internal migrants from the poor north-eastern provinces of Brazil, present in the city to facilitate its construction. They look stiff and unnatural here, but the propagandistic message is simple – Brasília represents their future. They gaze in wonder at the Palácio do Planalto, as if the progressive quality of the buildings is a means of lifting them out of their own impoverished situation.

Brasília is certainly one of the most debated cities on earth, the object of architectural fascination in the 1950s, and then subsequently by anthropologists and sociologists who explored its lived reality, its class structure in particular. The architectural literature was always, and remains,

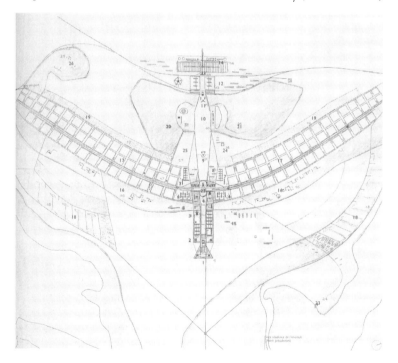

Lúcio Costa,
Pilot Plan for
Brasília, competition
entry, 1957.

Módulo, cover
depicting a model
of Niemeyer's Palácio
da Alvorada, then
under construction,
1957.

preoccupied with a small section of the city, the Plano Piloto, or Pilot Plan, an elegant sweep of a 14-kilometre Eixo Rodoviário (Highway Axis) bisected by a 5-kilometre Eixo Monumental (Monumental Axis). The plan is still startlingly clear from the air, resonating with primal imagery: it is a bird, an aeroplane, a tree, or the sign of the cross, depending on whose account you read. But within the Pilot Plan, it is only really the Eixo Monumental that has much of a presence in the architectural writing about the city. Running from the Praça dos Três Poderes (Square of the Three Powers) westwards to the army sector, it encompasses the city's main icons: the National Congress, the Ministries, the National Theatre and the cathedral, all designed by Oscar Niemeyer. Several of these buildings, the cathedral and the Palácio do Itamaraty, which houses the Ministry of Foreign Affairs, are widely regarded as the highpoints of Niemeyer's career, representing the culmination of his highly sculptural approach to the use of concrete. Their potential affect has also been widely discussed: Niemeyer himself widely encouraged surrealistic readings of these buildings in which a sense of 'surprise' or 'shock' was cultivated as a means of transporting the visitor beyond the everyday world, and accessing the Surrealist *merveilleux*.[3]

But the Eixo Monumental has also been described as an essentially conservative piece of work. Kenneth Frampton, an enthusiast for Niemeyer's early work, criticized his work at Brasília for being 'increasingly simplistic and monumental'. It seemed to be, he wrote, 'a return to Classical absolutes . . . the assertion of implacable form against remorseless nature', which is to say an ancient, and by implication discredited, mode of building a city.[4] It is a great symmetrical boulevard on an essentially neo-classical plan. Its buildings, even the most spectacular ones, appear simple in terms of design and construction; it is monumental in a way that is recognizable to anyone familiar with Western architectural traditions. The symmetry and whiteness of the palaces recall Greek temples. The Praça dos Três Poderes is the equivalent of a latter-day acropolis. The Eixo Monumental is in no way a popular space, but designed to represent and uphold authority. Progress is represented in these buildings in a general sense through the modernity of their materials (concrete,

Brasília, view from the
TV Tower looking east.

glass) and certain formal innovations (such as the inverted columns) whose unlikeliness is supposed to produce a sense of wonder. But the monuments of the Eixo Monumental are much more strongly representative of a call to order. The progressive project, the social and material modernization of Brazil, is represented somewhere else.

A particularly clear representation of the progressive project is the Estação Rodoviária (central bus station) designed and built by Lúcio Costa in 1960. Apart from the design of the Pilot Plan itself, it is one of only two major structures by him in the city, the other being the TV tower at the western end of the Eixo Monumental. The bus station is usually overlooked, literally, because in some senses it is actually subterranean. It is also a structure with little readily appreciable form, legible (depending on the viewpoint) as a giant parking garage for buses, a motorway underpass, an underground metro station, a row of informal kiosks selling newspapers and drinks, a street market, or – in the early morning or late afternoon – a kind of motorized ballet in which a gigantic number of buses simultaneously depart from the Pilot Plan for the satellite cities, bringing all traffic in the centre of the city to a temporary

98

standstill. The bus station at dusk is a sublime spectacle as vehicle lights and diesel fumes mix with the rich colours of the *Brasiliense* sunset.[5] It is the only part of the Pilot Plan with the density and richness of more traditional Brazilian cities. It was also, as James Holston noted, a space largely of the poor: only the poor really took the bus in the first place, so the bus station is in effect theirs, a poor space in the heart of (for Brazil) a wealthy metropolis, and a representation of the life of the peripheral satellite cities, themselves often poor, marginal and sometimes illegal.[6] There was for years as well a physical manifestation of the marginal by the bus station, a small *favela* just to its west, an irruption of the satellite city in the heart of the metropolis. Costa came to regard the *favela* approvingly, in spite of his overwhelming desire for order, as a representation of the true Brazilian nature of the capital: 'Brasília has a Brazilian heart', he said.[7]

But the anthropological interest in the bus station as a space of poverty obscures the fact that it is as good an image as any of the progress that the city as a whole was supposed to represent. It is less a building per se than a set of more or less motorized spaces. The pedestrian element, lively as it is, does not constitute a major part of its physical character. People go there to wait for buses, by and large; it is not a destination in its own right. It comprises a set of complex, overlapping spaces, built around a highway interchange at the very heart of the city. The location itself is curious. Costa did not put the political city at the centre – the Praça dos Três Poderes is the symbolic, but not the geographical, heart of the city. He could have put residence at the heart of the city, drawing on, for example, Le Corbusier's 1930s urbanism. Instead he put a transport hub, the centre of both the city's public transport network and its highway network. The images this produced were highly symbolic of the modernized condition of the city, its status as an image of modernity. The city is conceived of as fundamentally mobile; the spaces themselves are undemonstrative, flexible, designed for the rapid movement of people vehicles. And through this vast complex slices a four-lane motorway, facilitating car traffic at a then unheard-of 80 kilometres an hour. It is a building about movement and speed, connected to the modernized Brazil that the new capital was supposed to represent. In these ways, the bus station much better represents the idea of progress than the iconic buildings of the Eixo Monumental.

Brasília was not just an isolated project but representative of a wider campaign to modernize the country. Until the mid-1930s Brazil was mostly rural and its cities few and widely spread. Although growing, Brazilian cities lacked the infrastructure of their equivalents in the northern hemisphere, or, over the border in Argentina, Buenos Aires. The country's political institutions were weak. Power arguably still

resided in the country, based in widely spread and disconnected *fazendas*, each a power centre in its own right, but by any standards small, weak and dispersed. There was little if any national infrastructure – poor roads where they existed at all, weak rail links, mostly around São Paulo, and a poorly developed power-generation infrastructure that was, by the 1930s, starting to impede industrial development. Brazil's land surface remained for the most part unexplored, let alone developed. Civil society, of the kind found in Europe, the bourgeois public realm and its institutions and conventions, was largely absent. Culture was presumed to originate in Europe, and the political elite looked to Paris, rather than Rio or São Paulo, for its role models. In terms of population distribution and orientation, the Brazil of the 1930s was remarkably little changed from that of the sixteenth century. Brazil remained a 'crab civilization', to use the phrase coined by the sixteenth-century priest and first historian of Brazil, Frei Vicente do Salvador. It clung to the coast, looking outwards across the ocean towards Europe; it was post-colonial in name only, remaining a colonial society in function and structure.[8]

Lúcio Costa, bus
station / motorway
axis, Brasília,
c. 1957–60.

Getúlio Vargas's presidency of the 1930s set about changing that, instituting a policy of national development, in which infrastructure was improved and industry encouraged, based on an import-substitution model. Vargas's more visible achievements were widely praised in the MOMA exhibition *Brazil Builds.*[9] Less visible, but no less important, was the progress made on the country's power-generation infrastructure during this period. In 1930 the total potential power generation in Brazil was merely 350MW, mostly produced through simple hydroelectric schemes. In 1939 Vargas created the Conselho Nacional de Águas e Energia, later a government department, with a view to more coordinated development,

and shortly after the end of the Second World War, work was started on the first modern hydroelectric plant, Paulo Afonso I on the São Francisco river in the state of Bahía. Finally inaugurated in 1955, it had a generating capacity of 180MW, half the entire country's potential in the previous decade. Numerous similar schemes rapidly followed.[10] Kubitschek's presidency radically extended the developmentalist model, promising, with extraordinary bravura, fifty years' development in five.[11] It is hard to overstate the significance of this ambition: it meant nothing less than turning Brazil into an industrial, first-world nation in five years, a nation that would be, in theory, if not in economic reality, the equivalent of the United States. Brasília is the principal emblem of this process.

The crucial image of the development process was not in the first instance an image of the city, but the map reproduced on page 24. It depicts in schematic form an outline of Brazil with Brasília at the centre, linked by vectors to each of the 24 state capitals, each one accompanied by a figure representing the distance in kilometres. It was widely reproduced, appearing on school textbooks during the second half of the 1950s, used to advance the idea of development. It also decorates the back cover of Marcel Gautherot's early photographic survey of the city, one of the first to be published.[12] It is far less a depiction of reality than a depiction of a fantasy. The vectors to the big cities of the south-east – Rio, São Paulo, Belo Horizonte – correspond roughly to highways that originate at Costa's bus station, the

AO PRESIDENTE JUSCELINO KUBITSCHEK DE
OLIVEIRA, QUE DESBRAVOU O SERTAO E ERGUEU
BRASILIA COM AUDACIA, ENERGIA E CONFIANCA, A
HOMENAGEM DOS PIONEIROS QUE O AJUDARAM
NA GRANDE AVENTURA.

Portrait bust of
Juscelino Kubitschek,
on Oscar Niemeyer,
Museum of City,
Brasília, 1960.

symbolic heart of the city's highway network, and by the end of the 1950s actually existed, such that regular and reasonably quick inter-city bus services were possible. The same might be true, to a slightly lesser degree, of the cities of the north-east, with which the *planalto*, the central Brazilian high plain, had some historical connection. But the vectors to Rio Branco in the far west, Porto Velho, Manaus and Belém, the latter three in the Amazon basin, describe a fantasy of ground connections yet to be realized, if ever. The map resembles a vestigial, southern-hemisphere version of the United States' map of interstate highways, a scheme initiated in 1956 with the same integrationist and developmentalist motivation as that seen in Brazil. But the US map represents an integration that was in large part achieved; the Brazilian map represents an intention.

Brasília was the epicentre of the developmentalist process, becoming in thirty years the fourth largest city in population terms (metropolitan area), as well as one of the wealthiest.[13] The monuments of its centre, impressive though they are, are tiny by comparison with the desire to reorient the axis of the country's economy. Costa wrote that Brasília 'would not be the result of regional planning, but its cause . . . it would expand the real frontier of the country, not just the legal frontier . . . its nucleus would spread out like a drop of oil'.[14]

There were few exceptions, he continues, to the support given to the developmentalist ideology sketched out in the map – the extreme right, but few others. There seemed to be widespread acceptance of the need to modernize, a realization that society could no longer be organized on the lines of the isolated rural microcosm of the *fazenda*. Holanda cites the experience of the economic depression of the 1930s as critical in making a developmentalist worldview more plausible, for it was at this moment that it was realized that the country's weak infrastructure was impeding its ability to compete in international markets.[15] As a consequence, Vargas introduced major changes to what Holanda calls 'national space', particularly the building of new roads to bring the individual states under central control. The period also, paradoxically, exacerbated certain imbalances in the Brazilian economy. The emphasis on the south-east of the country – the Rio–São Paulo–Belo Horizonte triangle – entrenched the industrialization and wealth of these places to the detriment of the northeast; the ability of factories in the south-east to produce cheap manufactured goods, especially textiles, led directly to the decline of industry elsewhere.

But the process started in the 1930s led to a radical reordering of national space, whereby the country – via the colonial port-capital of Rio – no longer faced outwards, but inwards to the mineral wealth of the interior. A crucial international model for this process was the Tennessee Valley Authority (TVA) established in 1933 to regenerate a vast area of the United States through measures including flood control, modernization of agriculture, forestry and protection of the soil, and the generation of electricity. Brazil's strategies were similarly multi-dimensional, linking the cities to national space.[16] Power generation was a crucial developmentalist battleground. As Segawa has described, in the early 1950s about 80 per cent of Brazil's electricity supply was still in foreign hands (the British-owned Companhia Light e Power de São Paulo, popularly known as the 'Light', was a good example), a problem as operated in a low-tariff environment that discouraged investment in infrastructure.[17] A nationalist politics of energy developed at this point, shifting the balance towards the state to control infrastructure and generation, with private enterprise responsible for distribution. Numerous Brazilian electricity companies were established during this period. The burgeoning power infrastructure led to the specialization of

Panair do Brasil, advertisement, 1960.

a number of architects: Ícaro de Castro Mello and Hélio Pasta, for example, specialized in spectacular hydroelectric schemes, mostly in the state of São Paulo, schemes that ultimately served the broader economic shift away from imports and towards the production of manufactured goods rather than foodstuffs.[18]

The story of Brasília is intimately connected with the developmentalist agenda. Although an aspiration of Brazilian governments since at least 1891 and the first Republican constitution, it became a live issue in 1955 when Juscelino Kubitschek, campaigning for the presidency, was challenged on the stump about long-standing plans for a new capital. Without hesitating – or, he admitted later, thinking too hard about it – he said he would 'implement the constitution'.[19] In August 1956 the National Congress in Rio passed a law agreeing to the transfer of the new capital to Brasília, an act that met with remarkably little opposition, apart from the predictable complaints of Rio journalists.[20] The location of the new capital was the Planalto Central, an arid savannah at an elevation of 1,100 metres, with virtually no human habitation.

A design competition was held in September 1956, by which time Kubitschek had already decided that his friend Niemeyer would design the major public buildings. A design for the Palácio da Alvorada (the Palace of the Dawn, the president's official residence) was already well advanced and had been published in *L'Architecture d'aujourd'hui* and other international architectural journals.[21] Entries had to include a basic sketch of the city indicating the location of the principal elements of the urban infrastructure, the location and interrelation of diverse sectors, the distribution of open spaces and routes of communication, and also an explanatory commentary. There were 26 entries. The jurors were William Holford (UK), Stamo Papadaki (critic), Oscar Niemeyer, Paulo Antunes Ribeiro (Institute of Architects of Brazil), André Sive (France), Luiz Horta Barbosa (Society of Engineers of Rio de Janeiro) and Israel Pinheiro (NOVACAP).[22] The winning entry, by Lúcio Costa, was notoriously late, and slim – a hastily prepared set of sketches on file cards with a highly poetic text. But it impressed the international jurors, Holford in particular, with its literary qualities, and it had the vital support of Niemeyer, who was already in the frame to build most of the major public buildings.[23] The city was, in Costa's words, the capital of the 'autostrada and the park', combining the bucolic imagery of the English new towns with that of the automotive industry.[24] It is the latter that is really most important here. Up until JK's period in office, the car had had little impact on Brazil – he changed that, encouraging the development of the indigenous car industry. Brasília is as much a representation of that as anything.

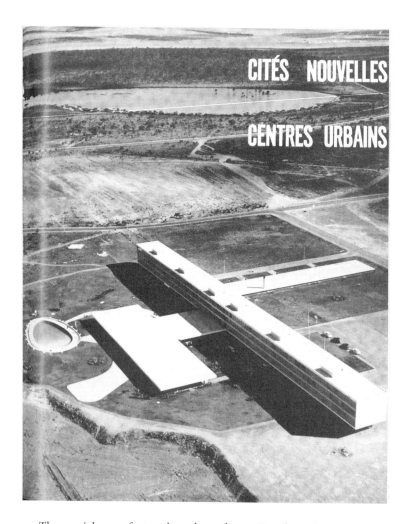

The crucial manufactured product of 1950s Brazil was the private car: during this decade, Ford, General Motors, Fiat and Volkswagen all set up factories in or near São Paulo; the industry quickly became one of Brazil's biggest and most strategic, serving not only an export market for Brazilian products, but also defining the look of new urbanization. The *fusca* or Volkswagen Beetle, which continued in production in Brazil long into the 1990s, became as iconic a vehicle for the country as Mexico, where in a slightly different variant it also continued. São Paulo at this time also became an image of that industry – a city that increasingly defined itself by the elements of a motorized culture, the high-rises and freeways and underpasses, rather than the historicist villas of the *bourgeoisie* that

*L'Architecture
d'aujourd'hui.*
National Congress,
1962.

overleaf:
Oscar Niemeyer,
National Congress,
1960.

Oscar Niemeyer,
National Congress,
1960.

Oscar Niemeyer,
Teatro Nacional,
Brasília, 1960.

they replaced. At the same time, Rio enthusiastically developed its waterfront around the suburb of Flamengo, just to the south of Centro. The Aterro do Flamengo was not, significantly, developed as a space of leisure, but principally a space of high-speed transit, although the land-scaping by Roberto Burle Marx is admittedly beautiful. But Brasília is the signal case of a Brazilian city built around automotive imagery. The Pilot Plan is designed around a motorway, the Eixo Rodoviário, in which motorized traffic dominates. Only rarely on this axis is there a

Lúcio Costa/
Oscar Niemeyer,
Praça dos Tres
Poderes, Brasília,
1960.

previous page:
Oscar Niemeyer,
Cathedral bell-tower,
Brasília, 1958–67.

Oscar Niemeyer,
Palácio do Itamaraty,
Brasília, 1958–67.

traffic light, such anachronisms having been largely abolished in favour of clover-leaf intersections. This was a design quirk of more rhetorical than rational importance since exit ramps are tortuously narrow as they spiral off the main highway, and often choked with illegally parked cars. However, they provide the impression, if not the function, of speed.

The rhetorical importance of automotive imagery has been continued into the present day with the ongoing battle about the nature of the Eixo Rodoviário. It has long been noted that the highway axis is dangerous. There are no crossings at highway level across the eight lanes of high-speed traffic (which, out of rush hour, move much faster than the legal 80 km/h), forcing residents to use the pedestrian subways, which are dirty and dangerous, or to run, illegally, across the highway, a common practice that still causes several deaths per week. Here the automotive aesthetic is upheld at the expense of quality of life.[25]

The Architecture of Progress

Brasília's other monuments to progress include the TV Tower, designed by Costa and among the earliest elements of the design. This largely steel structure crowns the top end of the Eixo Rodoviário, and lies close to the city's highest point. For years now it has defined an area of the city on which a relative freedom predominates. Unlike the formal spaces of the political city, such as the Praça dos Tres Poderes, which people visit largely out of a sense of obligation, the TV Tower is surrounded at ground level by a cluster of bars and barbecue stands, and a long-established market of handicrafts from north-eastern Brazil. This is a place, like the bus station, in which a relatively wide cross-section of the city gathers.

The tower itself is utilitarian. At ground level, there is some decoration, some ceramic tiles by Athos Bulcão and steel plates by Alexandre Wakenwith, but this is largely a structure defined by its function, and it is recognizably the same as the structure illustrated in Costa's sketch cards of the city for his competition entry. It is engineering as art. It is significant that the tallest building in the city is *not* part of the political city – it could easily have been the National Congress – but a symbol of the city's modernity and connectedness. Where the Congress draws on archaic imagery, the TV Tower is, through its function, contemporary, and it has remained so, now overlaid with the drums and dishes of cellphone networks. Something about the relative openness and informality of Burle Marx's landscaping, coupled with the architectural spectacle and the presence of little bars and stalls selling food, combines to produce a distinctly modern space of relaxation. This is not a civic square or a formal park – but the nearest thing the city has to a beach, in which informal sociality and sunbathing are the main activities.[26]

The sense of the possibility of a new kind of sociality, however, is most strongly suggested in the residential areas – it is here that the idea of social progress is most strongly played out. Here are Costa's initial thoughts about the residential zone in the Pilot Plan of 1957:

> The solution envisaged for the residential problem calls for a continuous sequence of large blocks set in double or single lines along both sides of the residential highway axis, each surrounded by bands of greenery planted with trees. In each block one particular type of tree would predominate, the ground would be carpeted with grass and, on the inner approaches, an additional curtain of bushes and plants would grow, the better to screen the contents of the blocks and make them appear on a second plane as though

merged into the scenery, whatever the observer's vantage point.
This layout has the double advantage of guaranteeing orderly
urbanization even where the density, type, pattern or architectonic
quality of the buildings varies, and of giving the inhabitants tree-
lined strips in which to walk or take leisure, other than the open
spaces foreseen within the blocks themselves . . . Within these
'superblocks' the residential buildings could be arranged in many
and varying manners, always provided that two general principles
are observed: uniform height regulations, possibly six stories
raised on pillars, and separation of motor and pedestrian traffic,
particularly on the approaches to the elementary school and
public facilities existing in each block.[27]

The residential areas are therefore imagined as a complete departure
from normal practice. As Holston wrote, they represented the 'death of
the street'; no longer would residential buildings define the street, but
would be set back from it, located in shared open space.[28] Drawing
strongly on Le Corbusier's urbanism of the 1920s (in particular the
Contemporary City for Three Million People), and Costa's own earlier
work in Rio de Janeiro at the Parque Guinle, the idea essentially reverses
the conventional city and turns it into a park. As built, this is best seen in
the south wing, where tree-lined boulevards stretch for 7 kilometres from

the entertainment district, parallel to the Eixo Rodoviário. The planting
may not have the sophistication that Costa originally intended (each
superquadra was to have been defined by a different tree), but it is certainly lush. There is clear separation of traffic and pedestrians. The
spaces between the blocks constitute semi-public areas, infrequently used
by visitors, it seems. There is in principle nothing to stop anyone from
enjoying them, although the presence of security guards in some of the
blocks discourages the visitor from lingering. But the structure of the
residential areas still permits more or less free circulation in a parkland
setting. The north wing, it should be said, does not work in the same way
because of the simple lack of planting and the modified design of some
of the blocks. But the principle remains the same, the city turned into a
park, with spaces of leisure replacing the street corner. Into this bucolic
setting are inserted crucial pieces of social infrastructure, schools and
sports facilities and churches and shopping areas, all in walking distance
of the blocks, shaded by trees.

Costa imaged each *superquadra* as a loose arrangement of six to eight
slabs, each no more than six storeys in height, most on pilotis, freeing up
space at ground level, as well as providing a covered place in which to sit.
While they all occupy space in much the same way, and are the same
size, they differ considerably in the treatment of the façade. This is
apparent right from the earliest parts of the development, and is if
anything exaggerated in the later north wing, in which the surfaces can
be highly, and quite eccentrically, differentiated. On the south wing, however, the *superquadras* have a number of important shared characteristics
beyond their height and the pilotis. They have clearly defined public and
private sides. The private side of each block covers the service functions
of each building – the kitchen, the smaller bedroom and the vestigial
copa, an area between the servant quarters and the kitchen forming a
liminal space between private and public worlds. In the *superquadra*
blocks this is represented not as a defined space as such, but a corridor
leading from the kitchen in which laundry might be hung, or tools be
kept. In several of the early blocks on the south wing, this private façade
manifests itself as a great, blank, perforated concrete wall, the perfora-
tions allowing a little light and air to penetrate, but otherwise ensuring
privacy.

By the standards of middle-class apartments in existing Brazilian
cities, the apartments of the Pilot Plan compare reasonably well; by the
standards of European social housing of the time they are extremely
generous. The influential Parker Morris report into housing standards
in Britain (1961 – more or less contemporary with the inauguration of
Brasília) recommended a minimum floor area of 72 square metres for a

LES SUPER QUADRAS   BRASILIA

dwelling for a family of four. The average floor area for an apartment in the Pilot Plan of Brasília is nearly 50 per cent larger, with an average of 101.94 square metres for the south wing, and 106.30 square metres for the equivalent on the north. These apartments afford a high degree of comfort and flexibility too: well over 60 per cent have three bedrooms, and over 7 per cent have four. These are by any standards good flats.[29] The outward migration to satellite cities seen in recent years has not been a function of any failure in the Pilot Plan, which is well liked. Rather it is the reverse; the success of the Pilot Plan has led to a sharp increase in housing values that has made it difficult for younger buyers to participate in the market.

The plan of the *superquadra* is of a life that is fundamentally *open*, a life lived less in the apartment per se, but in the dry, agreeable climate of the city, in the shade of the pilotis, in the green spaces, in the sports clubs and schools, in the open air. It is a healthy, sociable life in which the architecture itself helps to dissolve the boundaries between classes. This vision has a number of other elements. The *superquadras* are served by small shopping arcades on streets between the blocks running east–west. As Holston has described, these were originally built to face the *superquadras* themselves. This meant that access would be exclusively pedestrian, with the stores being serviced from the street side, the back as it were. In practice, the backs have been largely turned into fronts, creating in the process a series of short corridor streets. While they do not resemble what might be found in the dense, early twentieth-century landscape of Rio or São Paulo, they do now quite closely resemble the post-war suburban landscape found in parts of the US and Europe. This retreat from the progressive vision of the residential city is in some ways underlined by the residual conservatism of Costa's vision, in which a number of crucial elements from Brazil's past remain. Costa wanted a church at a strategic point in every *superquadra*. At 308 South, Niemeyer's Igrejinha remains a vital landmark in the city, the centrepiece to a development that now looks curiously traditional.

The Airport and the Hotel Nacional

Brasília's future was above all one based around mobility. Some of the clearest representations of this are found in the city's early hotels, where new ideas of movement and habitation were tried out. The Brasília Palace Hotel, close to Lake Paranoá and the Presidential Palace, is one good example. An elegant three-storey pavilion on pilotis, it was designed by Oscar Niemeyer.[30] It was one of the major poles of the city's social life in the early days, but was unfortunately destroyed in a fire in 1978.

South wing
superquadra blocks,
Brasília, c. 1957–60.
Note the greenery
in these images
from 2005.

South wing
superquadra blocks,
Brasília, c. 1957–60.

Much more durable has been the Hotel Nacional in the South Hotel Sector (SHS), a few minutes walk from the bus station, the centre of the city, and, from its eastern façade, commanding an impressive view of the Eixo Monumental. The hotel is at first sight not especially impressive. Designed by Nauro Esteves, it is an eleven-storey, mostly concrete, slab, with two-storey pilotis set on a level containing the entrance lobby and bar.[31] The dull exterior, however, conceals a spectacular double-height lobby faced entirely in black marble; it has both the right materials to moderate a hot climate and the glamour of a James Bond film set. The lobby opens out into an informal poolside bar area, defined on three sides by a small one-storey annexe. To the front of the hotel, adjoining the slab, is the hotel's real innovation, a concrete pergola, framing a short street with a handful of small storefronts containing offices of the main Brazilian and international airlines, travel and car rental agencies. This is partly functional – it is a building that makes for an easy transition from travel to hotel – but it is also rhetorical, putting at the heart of the city a de facto airport terminal. Air travel, symbolically vital to Brazil

120

Nauro Esteves, Hotel Nacional, Brasília, 1960.

from the 1930s onwards, produced numerous buildings in its image – the terminals at Santos Dumont in Rio, the Museum of Modern Art close by, the plan of Brasília itself. Here at the Hotel Nacional is a building that imagines itself as an outpost of the airport. When you step out of the lobby into the pergola, you are surrounded by the symbols of air travel. You are already in air space.[32]

The airport itself lies at the southern end of the Eixo Rodoviário, and was always symbolically vital to the city. Brasília's isolation meant that in the beginning equipment and materials needed to be brought in by air. Even when the city was inaugurated, air was for many the only feasible way of travelling to and from it. A widely circulated joke amongst officials sent from Rio during the early days was that the airport was their favourite building in the city, the site of their weekend departures home.[33] The present structure, the Presidente Juscelino Kubitschek International Airport, dates from 1965, and was built to a design by Tércio Fontana Pacheco, and has since been extensively modified and expanded, with a new terminal and runways; the expansion of the terminal was undertaken by Sérgio Parada. New circular buildings in *béton brut* (unfinished concrete) to handle passengers entering and leaving aircraft have been decorated by Athos Bulcão. The airport's outstanding feature, however, is its relation to its surroundings. The terminal building is defined by a giant steel canopy over the arrival and departures area. It remains open at both ground- and first-floor levels, making a large part of the terminal in effect an outdoor space. Passengers check in here, still in the city's comfortable outdoor climate; it is only once one has checked one's bags and passed through security that the building takes on the closed, secure quality of most airport interiors. Moving from the Hotel Nacional to the airport takes you from one of these spaces to another, and between them you move along a highway that itself, in form, describes the wings of an aeroplane. In this way the whole city is rendered symbolically as airspace.

Brasília after Brasília

Almost immediately on completion, Brasília's architectural imagery began to date. Moreover, its rhetoric of progress began to look suspect. In the decade after its inauguration, Brasília's construction began to appear shoddy, its failings as a social project became apparent, and from 1964 it became associated with a military regime that inadvertently had found in its epic open spaces a representation of authority. All this was widely reported in the international press. A good example of this critical representation of the city is the planner Colin Buchanan's short but pungent photo-essay of 1967 for the British RIBA Journal, 'The Moon's Backside' (the title is an apocryphal description of the city by Jean-Paul Sartre). Here Buchanan shows the city as a futuristic ruin; the floors of its marble museum are pools of stagnant water; raw sewage pours from newly built apartments; low-income housing flats look like prison cells; the Free City is a slum.[34] Such dystopian visions were already frequent in the press, and were an inspiration, perhaps, for the foreign anthropologists who began to visit the city in earnest at the end of the 1960s, in search, it seems, not of modernity, but of a return to a Hobbesian state of Nature. The anti-progressive project of such work is clear from the title of David Epstein's critique of the city of 1972, *Brasília, Plan and Reality*.[35] What followed was the effective disappearance of Brasília from architectural discourse, and its reappearance as de facto dystopia in discourses about social policy and urban planning.[36]

A powerful critique of progress started to appear inside Brazil too at the moment of Brasília's realization. In the field of architecture, by Vilanova Artigas, Lina Bo Bardi and later the Arquitetura Nova group, the cities in general were assumed to be ruinous by their nature, and large-scale progress in the present circumstances a myth (see chapter Four). Brasília's modernity therefore belonged by 1960 to a set of ideas that had already been superseded, in theory if not in practice. In particular, Brasília's allusions to cars and aircraft, to a world of speed and movement,

Colin Buchanan, 'The Moon's Backside', *RIBA Journal*, 1967.

looked suspect in a global context that was beginning to find such imagery militaristic. In the field of sociology, Gilberto Freyre produced a fascinating anti-progressive critique of Brasília in *Brasil, Brasis, Brasília*. He complained of the way the new capital invoked the rational, industrial world of modern Europe and the United States. His alternative was a *rurbano* ('rurban') sensibility, neither city nor country, but both, imbued with the gentleness and slow pace he perceived to be characteristic of the colonial period. Freyre argued that the new capital's leisure spaces were built in the same way as cities whose principal demands are work and not leisure; a traditional Brazilian way of organizing a settlement might be better adapted to the coming society of leisure.[37] This is classic Freyre. It is oddly blind to Brasília's actual qualities, which – looking at the spaces of the residential wings in particular – imagine a relative informality, with the life of the city organized around low-density open spaces, sports and socializing. Freyre's critique is nevertheless important, indicating that the developmentalist agenda of the government with its simplistic belief in material progress was not necessarily shared by the intelligentsia.

Brasília Now

Brasília still has the need to represent progress and development. It has done this in recent years by showing that it, and by extension the country, has bought into a global vision, in which goods, services and capital are shown to circulate freely regardless of political borders. This is a major shift of emphasis for a country that had experienced until the 1990s at least 50 years of nationalist politics of one kind or another, and in contrast to its easy-going, socially libertarian image had cultivated an inward-looking and often xenophobic outlook on the world.

In terms of architecture the effect on Brasília has been dramatic, but under-reported. The first way it has been represented is in terms of the proliferation of indoor retail malls, both inside and outside the Pilot Plan. Shopping – as it has anywhere else in the developed world – has become the defining activity for the middle classes. Emblematic of this process is perhaps Brasília Shopping, designed by the São Paulo-based architect Ruy Ohtake, best known for a series of graphic and colourful commercial buildings in his native city (see also chapter Six). Brasília Shopping is found in the Northern Hotel Sector (SHN), just to one side of the Eixo Monumental, between the bus station and the TV Tower – a strategic location. It is big by any standards, 105,000 square metres in total, including the offices. In form, it consists of two fourteen-storey towers, clad in navy-blue reflective glass. The towers themselves are fat but elliptical, like quartered cheeses. They are linked at the top by a tubular office section, which presents a circular aspect when seen straight on. The imagery is highly allusive without being specific. From the side, this is a giant, vaulted building that oddly recalls much poorer structures: the simple, low-cost housing built by the Arquitetura Nova group around São Paulo in the 1960s, for example. From either end, the circular form rising through the towers alludes – to anyone who knows Brasília – to the moment every year when the sun rises between the twin towers of the Congress building, a moment now freighted with mystical significance.[38]

Most visitors to the centre come to see only the first two storeys, the mall of 18,500 square metres, which forms a podium upon which the office towers are situated. The mall is impressively large, built around a central atrium, through which the building's vertiginous exterior can be glimpsed. It contains space for 180 shops distributed over the two floors; it is fully air-conditioned; it has a big food court; it is anchored by a major department store, Lojas Americanas, and a branch of McDonald's.[39] It is evidently successful, with 35,000 visitors per day, far in excess of any cultural or political institution in the city. And its visitors are from the wealthiest sector of the city's population: three-quarters, say the mall's owners, come from the two highest socio-economic groups (A and B), and the majority of them are young – more than half fall into the 23–40 age group.[40]

The centre is an isolated pavilion. Unlike the Ministry buildings on the Eixo Monumental, however, it makes no concession to landscaping in its surroundings. This may be a spectacular structure but it is, like any

Ruy Ohtake, Brasília
Shopping, 1991.

suburban shopping mall, fundamentally isolated from its surroundings at detail level, surrounded by acres of rather chaotically organized surface car parking. Neither does it make any concession to urbanism. In the Southern Hotel Sector, there are examples of early buildings that make important gestures towards place: the Hotel Nacional with its pergola is an urban place, of a kind. At Brasília Shopping there is nothing of this kind. Here the dark glass simply reflects the observer; there are no openings apart from the main ones; the relation to the surrounding street is brutal. One is either *in* or *out*.

It is all a marked contrast to the early public buildings of Brasília, which were always surrounded at ground level by a basic service. At Brasília Shopping, there is a more brutal separation between inside and outside on a model that, whatever the claims of the architect and the developer to respond to the forms of the city outside, has much less in common with Brasília than it does with suburban California or Florida. Indeed, it is the largely unconscious referencing of the world outside Brasília that probably contributes to its success. The socio-economic groups targeted by the development identify, it is certain, more readily with American forms of consumer capitalism than they do with the redistributive social engineering of Brasília's designers.

Brasília Shopping is one of a series of malls around the city that show how a Modernist or neo-Modernist vocabulary might be adapted to convey new meanings; although Ohtake can claim that his mall reiterates the forms of Niemeyer's architecture, it means something else entirely. The curious thing is that both the earlier and later architecture of the city are meant to convey ideas of progress. But the ideas of progress in each case could not be more different. A similar trans-

Águas Claras, 2005.

formation of the spirit of the city can be seen in the latest residential

Águas Claras,
central avenue
under construction,
2006.

development on the city's periphery, particularly in the spectacular suburb of Águas Claras, which in scale and ambition approaches the Pilot Plan.

The origins of Águas Claras lie in a masterplan commissioned by the Federal District in 1991 from a Brasília-based architect, Paulo Zimbres.[41] Zimbres had been asked to plan a dormitory suburb, but argued instead for the new settlement to be a dense piece of urbanism in the European tradition, drawing on the experience of the traditional city centres of Brazilian cities as well as European ones. He titled the plan, polemically, 'an exercise in urbanization in the Federal District'. Like the Pilot Plan, it was a plan on a grand scale, clear, legible and self-conscious. In it the city was laid out between two gently curving parallel boulevards 4.5 kilometres in length, with a heavy rail metro line running underground between them. The boulevards would have stores and cultural facilities at ground level, housing above; there were to be 45 new public squares, plus an 'ecology park', a network in other words of new public spaces making a coherent public realm. The plan's visual reference points include the Praça de Sé in central São Paulo, Curitiba, New York, Milan and Edinburgh, the last being the city where Zimbres had studied under Percy Johnson-Marshall between 1972 and 1974.[42]

The Portal das Andorinhas is one of the larger developments and lies on the south side of the city, just off the southern boulevard. Built by the Goiânia-based firm, MB Engenharia, it consists of four point blocks of seventeen to eighteen storeys, set in a gated compound, in which sport is well catered for.[43] There is a football pitch, two outdoor swimming pools, a tennis court, children's playgrounds, a sauna, two gyms, various indoor *salões de festas* (recreation rooms), barbecue areas and extensive gardens. The blocks have a somewhat garish decorative scheme – predominantly

MB Engenharia, Portal das Andorinhas, Águas Claras, c. 2004. 'To live well is to live in one of the ten marvels of Águas Claras'.

white, with thick bands of green, blue and red, a kind of bastard tartan. The individual apartments are big, more than 154 square metres, with two receptions, four bedrooms, no less than *five* bathrooms, a balcony and quarters for domestic staff. The literature is bullish: this is 'one of the ten wonders of Águas Claras'.[44]

Superficially, this development deploys the language of architectural Modernism. However, the decoration in this case is somewhat baroque. At roof level, the vertical bands continue *beyond* the roof line, turning in

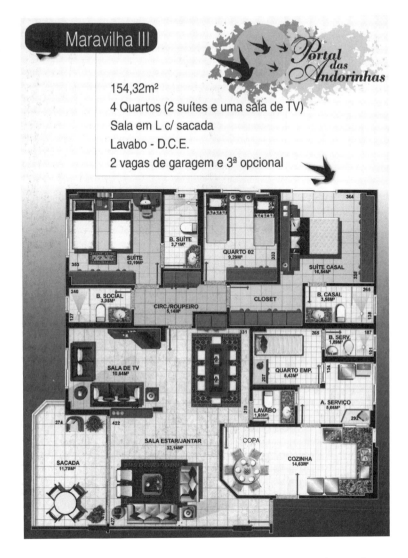

Maravilha III

Portal das Andorinhas

154,32m²
4 Quartos (2 suítes e uma sala de TV)
Sala em L c/ sacada
Lavabo - D.C.E.
2 vagas de garagem e 3ª opcional

the process a piece of two-dimensional patterning at once into a three-dimensional part of the structure, a *trompe l'œil* effect clearly forbidden by orthodox Modernism. But aside from that, the buildings, as far as we can tell, are surprisingly functional looking. There is little here that would identify them as of the early twenty-first century rather than of the early 1960s. And the background in this admittedly sketchy rendering fills in the urban landscape with a series of schematic slabs and towers, all very plain, all set in open parkland. The basic design language here, mediated through the low form of the rendering, is little removed from *Urbanisme*. The parallels with the Pilot Plan are clear.

The impression of continuity breaks down, however, at the level of detail – and the manner of its breaking down is revelatory of the break-down of Modernist principles, so that in practice this is not, whatever its outward appearance, an extension of the original Brasília as its designer wished, but rather an iteration of the gated communities or *condo-minios fechados* that now define the suburbs of Brazilian cities. At ground level, the development's four towers are surrounded by open space, but on closer inspection they are surrounded by a substantial wall, at least two metres in height. This is not then the city in the park of Le Corbusier's imagination, but something else, a camp perhaps.[45]

The metaphor might be profitably continued: in the Modernist imagination, the park had multiple, possibly unlimited uses. It stood precisely in contradistinction to the formalized, ritualized public spaces of the nineteenth-century European city, spaces that were consciously defined and limited as one of a battery of devices to control social life. The Modernist space could be defined precisely by its lack of definition. Here at the Portal das Andorinhas, all public space is named, and its purpose defined: here you play tennis, here football, there you drink a *caipirinha* or take a sauna. All activity is prescribed and regulated; a mass of petty rules no doubt will be, or already is, in operation to attempt to keep these activities within their correct bounds, with security guards, doormen and committees of residents to oversee their implementation. It is a place of numerous trivial kinds of authority, but authority nonetheless.

Finally, there is the question of class. Architectural Modernism in many of its iterations carried with it the desire for social levelling. This ideal clearly has no place in the marketing of the Portal das Andorinhas, whose landscaping, emphasis on security and leisure, not to mention price, all suggest – if not absolutely confirm – an appeal to class values.

But a class politics is seen more concretely in the physical layout of the individual apartments. In more established Brazilian cities, class was powerfully represented in the layout of apartments for the middle class. In early twentieth-century buildings, it is common to find substantial quarters for domestic staff, and elaborate circulation systems (including separate lift shafts) to ensure that contact between classes was kept to the minimum. Brasília did not abolish class distinctions by any means, but it did suppress its more baroque manifestations. Apartments in the Pilot Plan are suggestive of a more egalitarian way of living, even if such a transformation never really occurred.[46] Part of this was the de facto abolition of quarters for serving staff.[47] At Águas Claras, however, the servants' quarters – at least in this development – reappear with renewed vigour. Here in the Portal das Andorinhas there is a suite of reasonable rooms for domestic servants, 15 square metres in all, 30 if the kitchen is included; not only that, but this suite has its own entrance to the apartment, marking, in effect, a separate circulation system for domestic staff. The apartment therefore re-establishes all the traditional social hierarchies of the Brazilian middle-class dwelling, suppressed, if not abolished, by Brasília in 1960.

The realization of Águas Claras is therefore distinctly anti-utopian. Where the architectural vocabulary and the plan suggest a reinforcement of Modernism, the project utterly lacks the capital's utopian basis. The rhetoric of Brasília's authors was both liberatory and levelling, and the architecture was meant to bring about a social revolution. Águas Claras by contrast is a profoundly privatized space. Its housing is pitched squarely at the upper middle class; its blocks are closed at ground level; and its advertising rhetoric invokes internal security rather than public life. Águas Claras arguably represents the real future of the city better than the wealthy but now somewhat ossified Pilot Plan. Whatever notion of progress survives in the city – and Brasília's politicians still make great capital out of its representing the future of Brazil – it is a progress that is now irrevocably tied into a global, rather than a local, vision.

chapter four

The Aesthetics of Poverty

Brasília represents both the chief materialization of the developmentalist ideology in Brazil and its end. As we saw in chapter Three, the realization of the new capital city was accompanied by widespread professional anxiety about both its efficacy as a model and the nature of its imagery. Architectural responses were not slow to arrive – this chapter deals with some of them. The second half of the 1960s was a period of immense political and cultural turmoil in Brazil in which a remarkable number of architects found themselves in direct opposition to the government. Architects often profess radicalism, but act otherwise – their existence, after all, depends on their ability to acquiesce to a client. The situation described in this chapter finds architects, most unusually, matching radical thoughts with actions. The political background to this situation is complex. Juscelino Kubitschek's populist civilian government came to the end of its term in 1961, having achieved the construction of a new capital city, but also an economy with rampant inflation. A flamboyant right-winger, Jânio Quadros, was elected as president that year on an anti-corruption, anti-public spending ticket, only to be replaced in extra-ordinary circumstances the same year by a leftist, João Goulart. Goulart, always unpopular with the military, was deposed in a right-wing army coup, assisted by the United States, in 1964.[1] The political uncertainty of the early 1960s then gave way to a period of stability and renewed economic growth, with great implications for the appearance of Brazil's big cities. It was this period that saw, for example, São Paulo's Avenida Paulista come into being as a financial centre on a colossal scale: for more on this, see chapter Six. But it was also a period of increasing political repression. Along with all other political parties, the Brazilian Communist Party (PCdoB) was outlawed in mid-1964, and many of its most prominent members were harassed or imprisoned. The profession of architecture came under particular pressure, given that so many of its members (including Oscar Niemeyer and Lúcio Costa) were communists, and so much of its contemporary practice was bound up with notions of collective living. Some architects, including for a time Niemeyer, collaborated

Vilanova Artigas,
FAU-USP, São Paulo,
interior, 1961–9.

with the military, sometimes in spite of their politics – see, for example, Niemeyer's Quartel General do Exército (the Army Headquarters) in Brasília, completed in 1968. Others, such as the architects described in this chapter, tried to make their architectural practice into a form of political resistance, developing forms that they believed were, by their very nature, critical of authority. The idea of poverty assumed special importance here, becoming a field of action. For many on the left, architects or not, poverty became something with which to identify.

The late 1960s was nevertheless a rich period for left-wing culture in Brazil, the unhappy political situation producing an unprecedentedly rich variety of cultural responses, from architecture (Vilanova Artigas, Lina Bo Bardi, Arquitetura Nova) to theatre (Augusto Boal) and education (Paulo Freire). One of the crucial figures in this constellation was the young film director and theorist Glauber Rocha, widely regarded as a genius. His movies were difficult but arresting; shot in black and white on tiny budgets, they dealt with gigantic themes. *Terra em Transe* (Land in Trance) of 1967 is a good example, an uncompromising allegory of contemporary politics in Brazil. Abruptly shot and edited, and acted with peculiar intensity, it actively dispenses with the visual or narrative pleasures of mainstream cinema.[2] In 1965 Rocha published the article, 'A Estética da Fome' ('The Aesthetics of Hunger'), a short but powerful challenge to the modernizing culture of the authorities.[3] It draws attention to the things that the official discourses about Brazil would rather suppress, namely the country's underdeveloped economy and infrastructure. It also draws attention to those people (namely the poor) that

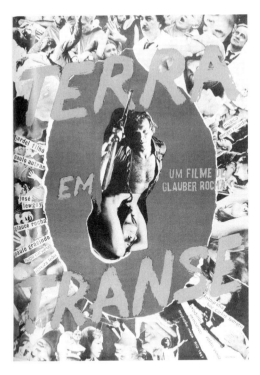

Glauber Rocha, *Terra em Transe* publicity poster, 1967.

the middle classes most fear. In it, Rocha described how Latin America existed in a colonial relation with the developed world, and how it was perceived by that world as poor or 'miserable', a fact that related to its economic condition – but which had also been cultivated by outsiders as part of a general taste for the primitive. This taste was not a result of any sympathy or understanding of actual conditions. If hunger produced for the European a 'strange tropical surrealism', which was highly attractive, for the Brazilian it was a 'national embarrassment'. He 'doesn't eat, but is embarrassed to admit it', wrote Rocha. 'Above all, he doesn't know where this hunger comes from.'[4]

The purpose of art in this context should be not to hide hunger or to distract the audience from it by technical or other means such as colour or narrative. Rather, the purpose of art should be to draw the audience's attention to its actual situation, to make it conscious of its poverty in order that it should be capable of revolutionary action. The art produced would be both 'miserable' and 'violent'.[5]

Although expressed within the context of film, Rocha's ideas are important here, since they explain how a culture might develop out of a context of scarcity rather than abundance. They also provide a sharp critique of the developmentalist culture long propagated by the ruling class of whichever political complexion. The impact of this kind of thinking on architecture was considerable. The most obvious and important manifestations of it lie in the so-called Paulista school, a loose grouping established in and around the Faculty of Architecture and Urbanism at the University of São Paulo (FAU-USP), in large part a response to the circle around Oscar Niemeyer in Rio.[6] The undoubted leader of the group was Vilanova Artigas (1915–1985), but other important figures included Carlos Millan, Paulo Mendes da Rocha, Fábio Penteado, Miguel Juliano, Julio Katinsky, Ruy Ohtake and Joaquim Guedes. The Italian-born, naturalized Brazilian architect Lina Bo Bardi (1914–1992) should also be included here, although she did not constitute part of the social and educational network around Artigas.

The work of these architects adapted and developed ideas expressed in Niemeyer's work, and that of other significant Carioca architects, especially Affonso Reidy, designer of the Pedregulho housing project and the Museu de Arte Moderna in Rio. But it also stood in critical relation to it. Its politics were further to the left; it was not often the subject of state patronage; and it had a greater concern for the construction process, both in terms of the materials used and in those doing the building. Its crucial buildings include the FAU-USP itself, designed by Artigas, and Bo Bardi's Museu de Arte de São Paulo. Both were completed in 1968, a critical year for Brazilian politics. Both were conceived as essentially public spaces, welcoming to all; both, in their materials and construction, invoked poverty. Bo Bardi referred to her work as 'poor architecture' in a way that invoked both Rocha's film theory and the contemporary Italian art movement Arte Povera.[7]

Much of what can be described as the Paulista School has also been described as a local variant of Brutalism. It is a term with a strange history. Brutalism was originally an insult thought up by Gunnar Asplund in Sweden to describe a variant of Modernism that favoured rough, untreated surfaces and a structural aesthetic – an aesthetic in other words quite different from that then favoured in Sweden with its domestic scale, simplicity and shallow-pitched roofs.[8] Brutalism then migrated to England, where, perversely, it got taken up as a term of approval by an argumentative group associated with the ICA in London, among them Peter and Alison Smithson and the critic Reyner Banham. This group responded to the possibilities suggested by Le Corbusier's recent architecture, in particular the Maisons Jaoul, Paris, and the Unité d'Habitation in Marseilles. What they got from those buildings was an interest in vernacular methods of construction, and *béton brut*. The significant buildings of English Brutalism include the Smithsons' projects for Sheffield and Robin Hood Gardens, and, later, the reconstruction of the South Bank and the Barbican arts centre.

For critics like Banham, what was most arresting about Brutalism was the novelty of its relationship with context. Instead of imagining an architecture in which the past had simply been erased, Brutalism assumed that the urban context already existed, but was in a state of ruin. Brutalist architecture overlaid the existing city, interacting with it in sometimes crude, sometimes poetic ways. The presence of the past in English Brutalism could produce effects that verged on science fiction. For example, Banham described the exhibition *This Is Tomorrow* (in which most of the Brutalists had participated) as 'homely junk excavated after an atomic holocaust'.[9] The great critic approved – the rough, provisional quality of the work was a form of realism, a coming to terms with the ruined condition of England immediately after the Second World War. But English Brutalism for the most part is conditioned by a touristic aesthetic. It might look tough, but was mostly appropriating a look in the same way that a sophisticated person might seek out a peasant cottage for a weekend retreat.

Something of this cultural tourism obtains in Brazil. Architectural cultures are, after all, international, and tend to have more that unites them than divides them. But it is surprising how much these cultures of Brutalism diverge, how superficially similar buildings such as Artigas's FAU-USP and the buildings of the South Bank Centre in London can represent radically opposing worldviews. In short, the Brazilian work was motivated by a radical politics much more than by style. For Artigas, to invoke poverty in architecture was to take a step towards the re-education of the political elite; the fortunate few who inhabited his private houses or who worked in his public buildings were in theory an avant-garde who would take the revolution forward. Similarly, the public spaces that were so prominent a feature of Lina Bo Bardi's architecture were in no sense decorative, but were meant to inculcate new forms of civic association: her SESC-Pompéia was, for example, 'a small socialist experiment'.[10]

Nevertheless, the two forms of Brutalism have some important things on common. Underlying both is an understanding of the existing built environment as essentially hard, with which an accommodation must be reached. In England, it was the ruined post-war landscape, whose reconstruction would take decades. In Brazil, it was São Paulo, where voracious development had produced strangely similar results. In both cases, there was a tendency towards inward-looking architecture, in which the building turned its back on the public realm and in effect offered a sanctuary from it. In the case of Brazil, as Guilherme Wisnik has described, the architecture from the outside might be a set of 'blind façades'. But inside, it might bring in some of the 'attributes of the external environment – water, gardens, and sunlight – thus internalizing a sense of the country's natural landscape'.[11] The peculiar attitude to context is one similarity. Another is a quasi-anthropological desire to preserve poor culture, in England the street life of London's East End, in Brazil the rural culture of the impoverished north-eastern states of Pernambuco and Bahia. Strongly a feature of Bo Bardi's work, it informs the imagination of the public spaces of her buildings.

These ideas have been little discussed in English, perhaps because of the unusual xenophobia of the architectural culture that produced them. The US-aided military coup made the Brazilian left as a result uniquely sensitive about foreign influence. Artigas had long complained about this, writing in 1953 of the São Paulo Bienal exhibition as simply a vehicle for imperialism. He also complained later about the tendency to discuss his work in the context of European Brutalism, which he thought was just an aesthetic exercise and little to do with his project. The Europeans were Surrealists at heart, he thought – they were interested in unexpected formal juxtapositions, but for aesthetic pleasure or effect.[12] Yet the ideas and buildings discussed here remain of vital importance, representing a corrective to the seductive vision of beaches and bodies of the Carioca school.

Artigas's Politics

The greatest figure in Paulista Brutalism is without question Vilanova Artigas, whose Faculty of Architecture and Urbanism was both his place of work and a monument to his ideas. He was, like Niemeyer, publicly a member of the PCdoB and, after 1964, suffered for it.[13] Artigas's architecture was underwritten by a xenophobia typical of the PCdoB of the 1950s, but which marks him out from the cosmopolitan Niemeyer. The clearest exposition of this is the polemic of 1951, 'A Bienal é contra os artistas brasileiros' ('The Biennial is against Brazilian Artists').[14] Alert to anything that might be a vehicle for American imperialism, he castigated the São Paulo Bienal, inaugurated in 1951 for representing a 'bourgeois, internationalist' conception of modern art that could only be harmful to Brazilian interests. Artigas went on: he was against 'abstraction' because it served only bourgeois interests. He thought modern art, and by extension modern architecture, no less than 'a weapon of oppression, a weapon of the dominant class, a weapon of the oppressors against the oppressed'. Cities run by the *bourgeoisie* were 'chaos'; books about urbanism were little more than 'a walk through slum tenements'. Invoking Friedrich Engels's work on nineteenth-century Manchester, he argued that planning was a sham, just a bourgeois attempt to hide the misery of the poor.[15]

At the same time as he criticized the US and its perceived imperialism, he enthused about the USSR's urban policies. It had, he claimed in his essay of 1952, 'Os caminhos da arquitetura moderna' ('The Paths of Modern Architecture'), produced 350 new cities in twenty years, and a Moscow 'as luxurious as New York'.[16] There were no slums in the USSR, he wrote, yet the *bourgeoisie* in the West attacked the USSR in the name of aesthetics:

> in the name of modern art, whose fundamental mission as we have
> seen has been to attack the working class and keep them in a state of

misery . . . in the name of this great mystification they attack communist architecture for being 'academic' because some of the buildings are built with columns, with balustrades, with cornices. Really they want to attack socialism and the proletarian revolution.[17]

Yet the Brazilian Communist Party, to which Artigas belonged, did not believe in working directly with or for the working class. Following Engels's century-old argument, the PCdoB held that to build for the proletariat was incorrect, since to make it more comfortable in its present circumstances lessened the chances of revolution. Instead, the PCdoB advocated revolution via a re-educated *bourgeoisie*. Artigas's villas, all built for a wealthy clientele, were meant to participate in this process. Austere and roughly finished, with the traces of their construction left bare, they were supposed to educate their inhabitants in the value of manual labour. In this way, a villa in an exclusive São Paulo suburb could be presented as a revolutionary project, a response to Brazil's condition of poverty.

In Artigas's worldview, certain kinds of construction were of themselves immoral, if, for example, they depended on materials that were scarce or abnormally expensive, or if the building process was unnecessarily labour-intensive. It was better to make use of whatever materials and techniques naturally abounded, and whose deployment was least likely to exploit those involved.

Artigas's xenophobia meant that he even regretted the influence of Le Corbusier in Brazil, describing him once as an 'imperialist . . . an ideologue of the ruling class, a fearless defender of the bourgeois order'.[18] Foreign influences were to be minimized, he argued, since Brazil was an exceptional case. Only Brazilians could understand the subtleties of their own situation, particularly its mechanisms of exploitation, and foreign influence meant the likelihood of American domination. But Artigas could argue for an internationalism of a different kind, drawing on his admiration for the Soviet experience. Architecture should be 'universal in content, national in form', he stated. He discussed the need for the 'decolonization of conscience' of architects, rather than banning outside influence.[19] Artigas's xenophobia was therefore qualified. It rejected the bastardized International Style that was coming to define the commercial buildings of São Paulo, since the adoption of this American style (with limited resources) served only to underline Brazil's peripheral and impoverished condition.

Artigas developed a distinctive programme of teaching at FAU-USP. Unlike the system in Rio, where architecture had always been based in the school of Fine Arts (of which Lúcio Costa had been briefly head), in São Paulo it was a product of the university's school of engineering.

Developing a model from the Bauhaus, Artigas reorganized teaching under three headings – 'history', 'techniques' and 'projects', none of which corresponded to a traditional drawing-based architectural education. A particular concern was the concept of *desenho*, which for Artigas represented an important conceptual problem. In English it translates as both 'design' and 'drawing', the former meaning carrying conceptual weight lacking in the latter. Artigas's use of the word *desenho* has something of this English meaning – he wanted to orient the practice of architecture away from the visual and towards a practice with greater organizational ambitions, and specifically the capacity to reorganize society. The architect, he argued in 1977, needed to be much more than someone who drew buildings; instead, he should someone capable of carrying out 'the most varied missions . . . from construction, through photography, and song, to the natural administrative and political roles'. The architect is envisioned here less as an artist than a social engineer. As Hugo Segawa has described, the architect in this scheme became a 'redeemer', a 'missionary', whose aim was to 'reformulate the world'.[20]

The Architecture of the Paulista School

Artigas's uncompromising political rhetoric achieved material form in most privileged spaces – private villas, sports clubs and university buildings – but their architectural programme can nearly always be read as an illustration of a rhetorical point. Interiors were kept as open as possible, in which (as Hugo Segawa has described) 'traditional hierarchies of use and sociality' were abolished, so that 'shared spaces were elevated in importance, while private areas were kept as compact as possible.'[21] There was also superficially less emphasis on luxury – these were tough and uncompromising spaces that made a point of revealing the amount of labour that had gone into their construction.[22]

The Casa Elza Berquó in São Paulo (1967) is a good example of Artigas's principles in built form. The origins of the house are themselves highly political. The military coup of 1964 landed Artigas in prison as a security risk, and although he was released after twelve days, he remained under suspicion by the authorities until 1966 when all charges against him were dropped. It was during this period of surveillance that he was offered the commission by Berquó and her husband Rubens Murilo Marques, both academics at the University of São Paulo. She was evidently an understanding client. When Artigas enquired if she was sure – did she really want him to design a house from his cell? – Berquó replied that she was quite happy to take him on as 'architect-prisoner'.[23] In the end, Artigas stayed out of jail, and the house was built as planned.

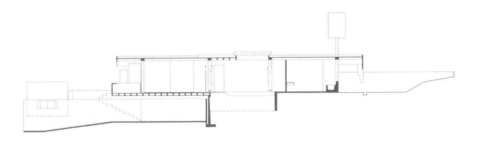

The house nevertheless has allegorical aspects that refer directly to its origins. The house itself comprises a concrete box, held up by nothing more than four tree trunks. Internally, a hole is cut in the roof allowing light to penetrate. In this light-filled space, defined horizontally by the four trunks, a small tropical garden flourishes. The weight of the roof and the unlikeliness of the trunks produced an allegorical contrast. Artigas's choice of deliberately poor materials to support the house's most fundamental structure was an ironic commentary on Brazil's development. He stated:

> this technology of reinforced concrete, which allows this splendid architecture to be made, is no more than an incurable stupidity in respect of the contemporary political situation.[24]

The Casa Berquó is an ironic commentary on Brazil's modernization: the modernity of its roof is supported by the oldest and crudest of building technologies, as if to say that Brazil's own modernity is no more than superficial, and that it is likely to collapse at any moment.[25] Aspects of this house, as contemporary photographs of it make clear, speak of a life of some luxury. It occupies a secluded plot, surrounded by the high fences and enormous trees typical of a high-end São Paulo suburb. The view of the rear of the house shows its cantilevered roof jutting out over a beautiful pool, like a tiled version of a Color Field painting, while the casually arranged tables and chairs suggest a languid sociability. The interior, with the trees clearly visible, is full of interesting places to sit and things to look at. It is all done out in the best possible taste. At the same time, the higher-resolution images show the roughness of the concrete surfaces, with the traces of the wooden formwork clearly visible, a technique still unfamiliar in a domestic setting. Around the

141   The Aesthetics of Poverty

Vilanova Artigas,
Casa Elza Berquó,
São Paulo, 1967,
interior.

roof, great concrete panels hang down in a scarcely credible manner, like concrete curtains. Overall, the house has the precariousness of a tent – it is little more than a concrete canopy held up by sticks, and at ground level the interior and exterior spaces blur, rhetorically and in actuality, into each other.

A much larger instance of the same allegorical structure can be found at Artigas's building for FAU-USP of 1961–9. This is a very large, reinforced concrete, horizontal pavilion, rising to about four storeys; the surfaces are again exceptionally rough. It has a massive, light-filled atrium covered with glass, and it is open to the elements at ground level. It is held up by columns of improbable lightness, which suggest the idea that materiality cannot be transcended. They taper in the middle, creating an apparent structural weakness. Not only that but the upper storeys of the building are rhetorically exaggerated in mass. Windowless, they cantilever out all around the building, as if more than half of this already massive structure rests on these comically insufficient stalks. It looks as if it has a duty to fall down. But it suggests, as Adrian Forty has written, a 'strategy' for building in Latin America, combining a simple technology

Vilanova Artigas,
Casa Elza Berquó,
São Paulo, 1967.

143 The Aesthetics of Poverty

Vilanova Artigas,
FAU-USP, São Paulo,
1961–9.

Vilanova Artigas,
FAU-USP, São Paulo,
detail, 1961–9.

(concrete) with unskilled labour, the latter a resource that Brazil is supposed to have in abundance.[26]

In reality, FAU-USP is as technically sophisticated as any building of
the time, with huge spans describing equally huge voids. It is also notoriously expensive to maintain. But it articulates on a large scale the *aesthetics*
of poverty; an allegory of underdevelopment informed by Marxist political beliefs, it *looks* poor even if in reality it is not. Unlike Niemeyer's
Modernism, its intent is desublimatory. It does not, in other words, seek
to lift one out of the everyday world, to achieve a sense of the Surrealist
merveilleux or have any other transcendent experience. Quite the reverse:
it seeks to bring one down to earth, to remind one of the limits of everyday existence, and in so doing suggest more realistic ways of living.

Other projects by Artigas worth citing include the Taques Bittencourt
house (1959) in São Paulo for its formwork imprints and stone wall; the
dressing rooms for the São Paulo football club (1961) for an astonishingly rough concrete finish; the Santa Paula yacht club in São Paulo the
same year, for a great concrete roof teetering on inverted triangular
columns (a sketch for the later FAU-USP); the Zezinho Magalhães public
housing project at Guarulhos, close to São Paulo's international airport
(1967); and the Jaú bus station (1973). In all these projects, structure and
materials are explicit, and very little is concealed. It is obvious how each
building is built and with what. The materials are rough and readily
available, and the techniques pre-modern or vernacular as much as they
are modern. And there are, as is so striking at FAU-USP, highly rhetorical
formal contrasts: fat concrete roofs balanced on feeble-looking columns
or vernacular stonework set against reinforced concrete. The same formal
sensibility can be found in several other architects of the Paulista school:
Joaquim Guedes, Fábio Penteado, Ruy Ohtake and Paulo Mendes da
Rocha. The work of the Curitiba-born João Filgueiras Lima (Lelé) is
important in terms of its continuation of the Modern Movement as an
ideological project rather than a stylistic one. His administrative centre
for Salvador (1974–5) makes use of prefabricated elements on a massive
scale through which the landscape penetrates.

For some of his followers, however, the radical potential of Artigas's
work was curtailed by the nature of his patronage (see chapter Five). I
have already shown how Artigas's affiliation to the PCdoB 's line on proletarian revolution allowed him to concentrate on high-class housing for
select clients. The emphasis on the re-education of the wealthy now seems
perverse, a deferral at best, while the precise nature of this 're-education'
remains obscure. Nowhere is it made clear how living in surroundings
of *béton brut* and tree trunks may inform a revolutionary attitude.
Whatever revolutionary sentiments these buildings were supposed to

produce are ameliorated by soft furnishings and luxuriant vegetation. In any case, in Brazil as everywhere, revealing the frankness of the building process is no guarantor of sympathy with those who laboured in the building. As a revolutionary tool, Artigas's work remains obscure.

What can be said about it with certainty, however, is that it supplies a critique of the developmentalist aesthetic of the Carioca school. Paulista buildings *age*. Artigas's works look good regardless of their condition, because they seem to have been built as ruins in the first place. That of Reidy, by contrast, or Niemeyer needs constant attention to maintain an illusion of newness. The actually ruinous condition of parts of the FAU-USP building (its leaky ceiling, for example, dripping with stalactites) seems part of the aesthetic programme rather than a negation of it. The appalling physical state of Reidy's Pedregulho by contrast seems only to indicate its failure.

Bo Bardi and 'Poor Architecture'

Such ideas were pushed to their limit in the work of Lina Bo Bardi, an Italian-born naturalized Brazilian, who had trained and worked in Italy in the office of Gio Ponti, and amongst other things documented the ruined condition of Italy's cities after the war. Her own office had been destroyed in an air raid in 1943. In Brazil she built little, but what she did build was outstanding. She was also the founder and first editor of the design magazine *Habitat* (1949–53), highly regarded outside Brazil, as well as the creator of the Museum of Popular Art of Bahia.[27] Through her drawings, writing and her cultural activity, she made a more complete case than anyone else for an aesthetic of poverty. The two best-known projects both occupy crucial sites in São Paulo, and make an appeal to a collective social life, making public space as much a part of the building as concrete or glass.

Bo Bardi's Museu de Arte de São Paulo (MASP) of 1957–68 sits opposite the Parque Trianon, midway along Avenida Paulista, then the financial heart of the city. With the exception of the park, it is an area that conspicuously lacks public space. One is either inside a building or part of the traffic of the avenue, symptomatic of an exclusionary system that, consciously or not, divides the worlds of work and non-work, wealth and poverty. The one big exception to this is the MASP. It occupies four floors on some of the most densely built up and expensive real estate in Brazil. But it manages to occupy space without taking publicly accessible space away from the city. The means of doing this is a remarkable, probably unprecedented structure. The building is split horizontally in the middle, with the two lower floors – a temporary exhibition hall and

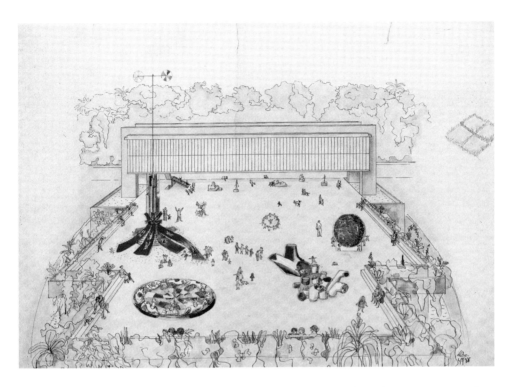

Lina Bo Bardi, MASP, São Paulo, sketch, 1968.

a restaurant – effectively below ground. These floors support a platform, which forms a covered public square. Above that are two immense pre-stressed concrete beams each 70 metres in length, from which hang two further floors containing the main offices and the galleries of the main collection.

The public plaza is, unusually for Brazil, permanently open to the street. The huge span of the beams means it is unobstructed, although it is mostly shaded by the upper floors of the museum, no bad thing given the summer climate in the city. The plaza extends to the rear of the building, providing views of the city to the north. In a particularly hard urban environment, with few areas of public space, the MASP is, and has always been, well used throughout the day. Aldo Van Eyck wrote after its construction that it was 'an amazing feat for the building is indeed both there and not there, giving back to the city as much space as it took from it. An impossible site if ever there was one – all the more so because it was destined to remain open – not built on.'[28]

Bo Bardi's sketches of MASP before its completion show the sublimation of this public space. In one sketch done on 4 May 1965 in a *faux-naïf* style, the plaza is depicted from the north, and is shown surrounded by

Lina Bo Bardi, MASP, São Paulo, under construction, 1968.

Three further views of Lina Bo Bardi's MASP, São Paulo.

vegetation; the strip of planting around its edges appears continuous with the Parque Trianon on the south side of the street. Meanwhile, the great Brutalist gallery recedes, to be replaced by what is in effect a children's playground. Where you expect to find sculptures are in fact slides and carousels. Bo Bardi's original treatment of the exhibition spaces continued the theme of public access to culture. She wrote:

> The new museums should open their doors and let pure air and new light in . . . it is in this new social sense that the MASP was conceived and directed specifically at uninformed, unintellectual, unprepared masses.[29]

The original concept for the exhibition spaces had the painting collection displayed on glass stands in the centre of the space; the usual arrangement of walls and partitions and the accompanying linear progression through museum space was abolished. At the same time, the uninterrupted curtain walls of the east and west fronts of the museum suggested the interpenetration of inside and outside spaces, as if the collection and its surroundings were no longer to be considered separate from each other, or the one valued any higher than the other. The effect was reminiscent of the famous image of André Malraux, de Gaulle's minister of culture, contemplating a vast, de-hierarchized array of photographs of sculpture for his book *Le Musée imaginaire*, a book Bo Bardi undoubtedly knew.[30] Bo Bardi herself wrote of her antipathy to

Lina Bo Bardi,
MASP, São Paulo,
interior with original
arrangement of
pictures, 1968.

traditional arrangements for viewing art: in the new setting 'pictures
and public are liberated and free'; viewing pictures becomes a matter of
choosing a dance partner; one approaches the work of art in the same
way one chooses a dancing partner, as a meeting of equals rather than
one in which one party has the upper hand.[31]

The MASP project materializes a number of crucial ideas in Bo Bardi's
thought. As an Italian immigrant, she had a formative experience between
1958 and 1963 living in Salvador in the north-eastern state of Bahia, one of
the poorest of Brazil's cities and one with the highest Afro-Brazilian population. Partly as a result of that experience, she came to regard Brazil as
essentially a childlike nation, undeveloped and naïve by First World standards, but strong in this essential character.[32] Crucial terms in Bo Bardi's

thought were 'happy', 'pretty', 'simple' and 'poor'. Her language now seems patronizing and neo-colonial. But equally, in using words like these she empathized with a version of Brazil normally kept from view by the authorities, except in carefully controlled circumstances. Her Bahia museum of popular art was thought subversive by the military, which occupied and closed it in 1964, and forced her to resign as director; she spent much of the subsequent decade away from both Brazil and architecture. At the same time her identification with the poor seemed to have something of the same exoticizing character seen in (for example) the 1959 movie *Black Orpheus* by Marcel Camus, a version of the Orpheus myth set in a Rio *favela*. Like Camus, Bo Bardi seemed to wish to keep Brazil in a state of attractive underdevelopment, perhaps because she herself had ways of escaping it. Her houses, such as the house built for herself and her husband Pietro in the luxuriant suburb of Morumbi that now houses her archive – are sophisticated exercises in a rustic modern style, calculatedly rough weekend houses for a client base that had enough wealth and sophistication to enjoy a bit of austerity.

These reservations apart, MASP remains if nothing else an astonishing form, and its programme of public space is one of the most successful in the history of modern architecture. Like the Place Beaubourg in Paris or the Rockefeller Center in New York, this is a modern space that appears to be both well used and well liked. Even more extraordinary is Bo Bardi's last major building, the Serviço Social do Comércio (SESC)-Pompéia (1977–86), a publicly funded arts and leisure co-operative in a post-industrial no-man's land. To describe the SESC as a leisure centre suggests something prosaic and functional, when it is neither. It is enormous, first of all – 16,500 square metres – the size of a large office building. It is by conventional standards perhaps the ugliest building in this book, deeply inelegant, awkward and brutally finished, with no apparent relation to its surroundings. This was all apparently intentional: Bo Bardi declared that she wanted the SESC to be 'even uglier than the MASP'.[33] But an extraordinary range of activities are possible in the centre, from theatre and art exhibitions to ceramics and metalwork classes to film, to swimming to aerobics. There are two swimming pools, a gym and a very cheap (and good) restaurant.

Lina Bo Bardi, SESC-Pompéia: site as factory before construction.

But the most remarkable features are formal. The SESC occupies the site of a former brick factory, and reuses a number of low, functional brick structures from it. Then there are two towers housing the sports facilities. One deliberately recalls the demolished factory chimney, and has a crude construction in thick bands of concrete visible from afar – if anything, it looks cruder than the simple industrial structure to which it alludes. Bo Bardi wrote that its detailed design was left to the builders who themselves developed the look of the final structure, defined by ply-wood formwork sliding up the tower to provide room for 56 piled rings, each 1 metre in height. The cotton waste on the external face was used as a sealing element during the concreting phase and moulded the final lace effect of the surface.[34]

The other tower, containing swimming pools and other sports facilities, is a big cuboid of the same height as the water tower, and is characterized by strange irregularly shaped holes covered with metal grilles. These were made to provide natural ventilation, replacing the need for air conditioning, a technology that generally horrified the architect. Bo Bardi described the holes as 'prehistoric', turning the users of the building into temporary cave-dwellers.[35] The sympathetic Catalan critic Eduardo Subirats has referred to the building's aesthetic of play, turning a space or work into a space of leisure. The original site was a site of hard manual labour, transformed into a space of creativity and relaxation. Subirats relates this explicitly to notions of poverty (see Rocha, cited at the outset) and to Johann Huizinga's notions of creativity and play from *Homo Ludens*, still fashionable on the libertarian left.[36] Subirats and others therefore describe the SESC as a poetic transformation first and foremost, rather than one driven – as it would have been in the US – by a rational imperative, however superficial. Subirats defines the SESC as such:

> It's a model of poetic intervention in a real situation . . . it defines a specific sense of civilizing architecture through the dignification of human life, through the active participation in collective processes of artistic communication, of the collective management of know-ledge, of the collective creation of a collective identity.[37]

All Bo Bardi's work was justified in terms of 'poor architecture', which she related to her experience of living in the north-east:

> I was looking for simple architecture, one that could immediately communicate that which in the past was known as 'monumental'. . . I made the most of my 5 years in the northeast of Brazil, a lesson

Lina Bo Bardi,
SESC-Pompéia,
São Paulo, 1977.
Concrete walkways
linking the towers.

of popular experience, not as folkloric romanticism but as an
experiment in simplification. By means of a popular experiment
I arrived at what might be called Poor Architecture.[38]

Poor architecture, like those things, was the product of a privileged,
but sympathetic, imagination: it is not simply touristic in that it does
more than merely appropriate poor forms for rich use, as it were; it seeks
some kind of engagement with, or identification with, poverty. Bo Bardi's
perspective sketches of MASP, for example, do not for the most part represent the typical visitors to a museum complex, the wealthy and the
privileged; instead, she represents children, a section of society that she
rhetorically blurs with the poor; children and the poor are for Bo Bardi
in effect the same thing, simple, undeveloped, but natural people from

Lina Bo Bardi,
sesc-Pompéia, São
Paulo, detail, 1977.
'Prehistoric' holes.

whom civilization can and should learn. According to Roberto Conduru, poor architecture is materially poor 'yet rich in fantasy and inventions. It is a premise for a free and modern future that, together with the achievements of the most scientific practice, will retain at the beginning of a new civilization the values of a history full of hardships and poetry.'[39] An architecture, in other words, that is mostly poor in a poetic sense, that holds poverty to be the locus of authentic culture. As society progresses, and becomes materially richer and more sophisticated, it has a moral obligation to remind itself of its origins. Something of this can be seen in the sesc-Pompéia, a building that symbolically exists outside modern time. In its harsh, but unmistakably modern, surroundings, its history is hard to disentangle. The new bits of the building in some ways look older than the refurbished old bits; like a castle or keep, the main tower might be medieval. Its strange window openings at first sight look as if they may be evidence of decay, and as the architect makes clear, they are technically a means of denying the rich world.[40] The sesc-Pompéia takes the logic of Artigas's work as far as it may conceivably go in a monumental building. This is some achievement, and as virtually all critics are agreed, it supplies a set of remarkable, unique spatial experiences. But at the same time, it could not supply a model for mass housing as its author really wanted: it was far too individual and irrational for that.

After Brutalism

From outside of Brazil, it is tempting to regard the indigenous form of Brutalism as something of a dead end. Unlike in England, for the most part it did not become an official style, except for university buildings. It enjoyed occasional patronage from individual states, but not from the federal government. There is very little in Brasília that could be regarded as Brutalist, hardly a surprise given the calculated opulence of most of the capital's official architecture; its rhetoric of poverty was too uneasy, too critical to make much sense for any but a few buildings, and least of all public housing. England may have had its own divisions of wealth in the 1950s and '60s, but they were nothing like as extreme as Brazil's, and the topic of poverty nothing like as charged. Perhaps the biggest problem with Brazil's Brutalism was its fundamentally negative

156

relation with its surroundings. As Wisnik has written, Brutalism in Brazil was a radically introverted architecture, creating often luxurious interior worlds, but at the expense of positive engagement with the world outside. This was an understandable response to the urban condition of São Paulo, but it made for an architecture that could stand only in critical relation to its surroundings.[41] Its indifference to the exterior world is perhaps a metonym for the tendency's ideological xenophobia: this was an ideologically, as well as physically, inward-looking architecture. This inwardness contrasts directly with the presentation of Brutalism in Europe, where (contrary to much popular opinion) buildings often make a direct address to their surroundings, and may have decorative or highly modulated exteriors.

There are, however, at least three ways in which the project of Brutalism, and its accompanying aesthetic of poverty, were continued into the 1970s and beyond. First are the vault-house experiments of the Arquitetura Nova group. Discussed in more detail in the following chapter, this group took up and extended the political language of their teacher, Artigas, developing a set of architectural principles and methods that, they argued, could be applied on a large scale and in a popular context. They attempted to move Brutalism beyond the provision of bespoke buildings for sophisticated clients. Second was the work of the

architect João Filgueiras Lima (Lelé), whose work carried on the project of Brutalism as a political project in large-scale public commissions, including a series of well-known and well-liked special hospitals. The Hospital Sarah Kubitschek (1980) on the Avenida w3 in Brasília is a good example, a building organized around unstinted spaces for the patients' benefit, exemplified in a set of generous balconies. Third is the success of Paulo Mendes da Rocha, recipient of the Pritzker Prize in 2006. Mendes da Rocha's more recent work is discussed in chapter Eight. But what is clear as early as 1970, and his extraordinary pavilion (built with Ruy Ohtake) for the Osaka Expo in Japan, is that Paulista Brutalism could be reconfigured as a formal spectacle, stripped of any political meaning it once had. That pavilion, a great concrete roof resting on the ground on a few

Paulo Mendes da
Rocha, Expo '70
Pavilion, Osaka.

incongruously tiny points, reiterates precisely the same design language as that deployed by their teacher, Artigas, in his FAU-USP building. But where Artigas meant his building as a metaphor for Brazil's under-development, Mendes da Rocha and Ohtake meant only to show off their skill with reinforced concrete. It was an amazing building formally, but no longer communicated an aesthetic of poverty.

João Filgueiras Lima
(Lelé), Hospital Sarah
Kubitschek, Brasília,
1980.

Hospital Sarah
Kubitschek, detail.

chapter five

The Politics of Liberation

For architects like Artigas, the invocation of poverty was a means to a revolutionary end. Their politics were straightforwardly Marxist, and they did not much depart from the line set by the PCB, ideologically one of the least compromising communist parties in the world. This approach well describes the architecture of the Paulista Brutalists. By the end the 1960s, however, the Paulista approach was arguably beginning to look tired. In a process that parallels the shift from 'old' to 'new' left thinking in Europe and the US, architects and artists on the left in Brazil began to experiment with forms and activities more suggestive of social and sexual liberation rather than revolution per se. The key architectural figure in this process was the *favela*, that is, the informal and usually illegal settlement found on the periphery of all Brazil's big cities, and (in 2008) housing approximately 20 per cent of Brazil's urban population. From being a representation of the problem, an embarrassment that must be swept away, the *favela* came to embody a set of positive values: self-help, freedom from state interference, liberation from convention.

The shift in thinking was international. In 1964 Bernard Rudofsky, an Austrian-born architect who had worked in São Paulo in the 1930s, curated a popular exhibition *Architecture without Architects* at the Museum of Modern Art in New York, suggesting that informal settlements might have their own worthwhile aesthetic.[1] The following year, John Turner, a British architect, began publishing what would turn out to be a long series of articles advocating the aesthetics and lifestyles of the Peruvian *barriada*, a settlement with which he was familiar. But the shift had a particularly powerful representation in Brazil, where the repressive political context of the *anos de chumbo* – the banning of all opposition political parties, the orchestrated attack on the left, the imprisonment and exile of significant cultural figures – meant that the orchestrated expression of dissent was difficult. But an identification with the informal city, aligned to an understanding of New Left politics (such as the writings of Herbert Marcuse, popular in Brazil), could have

Rio *favela* above Tijuca, 2004.

a powerful effect in changing attitudes. This chapter describes in effect a revolution in the head, rather than on the barricades.

There is a huge amount of fantasy in the re-evaluation of informality, and the *favela* in particular, a fantasy based around a peculiar form of cultural tourism, a literal 'slumming it'. But the *favela* has a cultural power that helps to sustain the fantasy, for it is the *favela* that produces most of Brazil's most arresting popular culture. This chapter explores the fantasy of liberation through architecture in the work of a number of contrasting figures: artists such as Hélio Oiticica, who was fascinated by architecture, and whose work (such as the iconic *Tropicália*) powerfully responds to it; Lygia Pape, trained as a philosopher and then an architect; and the Arquitetura Nova group from São Paulo, whose political trajectory led them away from formal architecture towards the informal city. An important bridging figure between 'old' and 'new' left thinking was Lina Bo Bardi, whose invocation of the poverty of the north-east was always connected to concepts of social liberation. She made these concerns clear herself repeatedly through her work and her actions. Late in her career, in 1988, she opened her Espaço Glauber museum in Salvador de Bahia dressed in bags of coconut fibre, invoking both the poverty of the region and the liberatory potential of performance art.[2]

The centrality of images of poverty to 1960s architectural discourse is well illustrated by Oscar Niemeyer. Reflecting on the experience of the construction of Brasília, what he remembers with most affection is not the Modernist city that he helped design, but a semi-legal squatter camp, the Cidade Livre or 'Free City'. This lay some 10 kilometres from the centre of Brasília, straddling the main southern highway, the BR040, the road that eventually forks and leads either to Rio de Janeiro or São Paulo. It was established in 1956, at the same moment as construction began, and at its peak officially housed 11,600 people, although unofficially probably many more. It comprised mostly roughly built wooden shacks, sprawling out from a main street. Haphazard in appearance, it was nevertheless a legal settlement, founded by the capital's development company NOVACAP as a temporary camp to service construction, with legal concessions for banks and businesses. It was for many years the centre of commercial activity in the capital.[3]

Cidade Livre had, as almost all visitors reported, something of the atmosphere of the cinematic Wild West, a breathtaking contrast with the self-conscious modernity of the emerging capital. It was nevertheless often represented in romantic terms. Niemeyer referred to the period he spent living in Brasília at the beginning of its construction as a period of great hardship, but also a quasi-utopia in which physical adversity appeared to liberate the city temporarily from the normal boundaries of

Cidade Livre, Brasília, unknown photographer.

social class. The taking part in the experience of the construction of the city was an 'adventure', not least because of the isolation of the construction site. The site was four days' drive from Rio de Janeiro along perilous dirt roads, and one left unsure if one would arrive in safety, not knowing, given the difficulty of return, when, or even if, one would see one's family again.[4] But in spite of the harsh conditions, the work was an experience of which Niemeyer had 'like everyone, a fond memory. It wasn't just a professional opportunity, but something of greater importance, more of a collective movement'. He continued: there was something about the nature of the collective hardship that produced a 'fighting spirit . . . that levelled everyone, a natural affinity that made class differences . . . almost impossible to establish'.[5] The Cidade Livre was an essential part of this experience of social levelling; more than that, perhaps, it was its symbol:

> we would go out to the Cidade Livre, attracted by its 'wild-west' atmosphere. We normally went, by choice, to Olga's Bar, where a clientele of exotic appearance amused themselves, dancing animatedly in a state of euphoria produced by alcohol, with boots dirty with mud, in the middle of the hubbub of those sitting around. There occurred the most bizarre scenes, and unexpected brawls.[6]

For Niemeyer, in fact, it was precisely the nights of *cachaça*-fuelled entertainment in the Cidade Livre that materialized the dream of a classless utopia, where each man, regardless of his social origins, could feel he had a place in the city.[7] This dream was momentarily realized during the construction – or at least in Niemeyer's memory of it – in a way that never came to pass in the formal housing projects.

Niemeyer was by no means the only one to promote the myth of the Cidade Livre. Juscelino Kubitschek's unofficial visits to the place, usually to eat at a restaurant named after him (*Restaurante JK*), were legendary.[8] For Niemeyer and Kubitschek, and countless other privileged visitors, the Cidade Livre, whatever its privations, represented a form of social liberation that actually seemed to work, exceeding the liberation envisaged in the official architecture of the city. Niemeyer's position is compromised here for obvious reasons: what he says about the informal city is always circumscribed, and in any case, his experience of it, however profound, had little ostensible impact on his architecture. But others made the informal city, and its liberatory myth, central to their work. This becomes increasingly visible after the military coup of 1964. With Brasília, and the official Modernist project, increasingly identified (however accidentally) with the military, radical practices in architecture were increasingly informal, low key and temporary.

Theories of Liberation

Such architectural practices were all powerfully informed by a politics of liberation: from poverty, from the limits of bourgeois social and sexual behaviour, from psychological repression, from social class. Precisely what we mean here by liberation needs further explanation. A good starting point is the work of Herbert Marcuse, the Frankfurt School philosopher whose psychoanalytically informed critiques of Marx became the totemic texts of the New Left in the later 1960s;[9] Marcuse arguably supplied the theoretical basis for the worldwide events of 1968. Oiticica's interest in Marcuse is well documented. In published letters to his fellow artist Lygia Clark during the 1960s, he describes the impact on his thought of reading Marcuse's *Eros and Civilization: A Philosophical Inquiry into Freud*, first published in 1956.[10] Oiticica's interest in Marcuse occurred at the moment (1968–9) when the philosopher's theories were well known in the developed world, but had only just arrived in Brazil. Marcuse and other philosophers of the Frankfurt School were only published in Brazil from 1968 onwards, and their critiques of Marxism from within the Marxist tradition were a minority interest.[11] It is not clear exactly what Oiticica was reading, and in which language, but in his letters of 1968 to Lygia Clark (then based in Paris, and a close witness of the May 1968 'events') he glossed important parts of Marcuse's theories and encouraged her to read them too. On 15 October he writes of *Eros and Civilization* that he now 'rejects any prejudice deriving from the established order'; further, he now sees himself as profoundly 'marginal', 'marginal to marginality'. Such a position gives him 'surprising freedom of action'.[12]

In *Eros* Marcuse provides a critique of Freud's earlier essay *Civilization and its Discontents*, arguing for a new kind of society based around the free play of the libido rather than its repression. For Freud, repression was a necessary part of civilization because of the general condition of scarcity. Marcuse by contrast argued that repression was no longer necessary in advanced societies, given the relative abundance of food and material things. An erotically liberated society would be organized around pleasure rather than work. Gilberto Freyre had (as we saw in chapter Two) advanced the idea that Brazil was already in certain crucial senses erotically liberated; it is no surprise to find that Marcuse's ideas had an attraction there.[13] Both Freyre and Marcuse showed in different ways how a distinctively Brazilian variant of leftist politics might be developed, one that celebrated the erotic, in marked contrast to the somewhat puritanical leftist imagination in Europe and Russia.

In Brazil itself, Paulo Freire supplied another variation on the theme of liberation. This sociologist, trained at the University of Recife, completed a remarkable PhD thesis in 1959 on literacy in the north-east of Brazil. He began immediately thereafter on campaigning work to improve the educational level of the rural poor, work that saw him achieve both a public profile and unwelcome attention from the authorities. On the arrival in power of the military in 1964, Freire was arrested and jailed for allegedly subversive activities. He re-emerged shortly thereafter to become one of Brazil's major intellectuals of the 1970s and beyond, as well as a member of the international jury of UNESCO, the United Nations cultural heritage committee that (as described in chapter Three) gave protection to Brasília.[14] Freire's first book was *Educação Como Prática da Liberdade* (1967, 'Education as the Practice of Liberty'), in which he argued that for liberation to have any meaning at all it needed to be rooted in educational practice. Liberation was, he argued, a state of mind that could be taught.

He developed the argument at greater length in the bestselling *Pedagogy of the Oppressed*. Here, education is described as traditionally a tool of oppression, so effective that those whom it oppresses acquire the habits of thought and the values of the oppressors. The oppressed internalize the 'image of the oppressor'; they 'fear freedom' and therefore never achieve it; they participate, in other words, in their own oppression. Freire's liberatory solution was a process of *conscientização* ('consciousness-raising') to reveal the location and nature of oppression. Then followed praxis, in other words liberation imagined as a process involving both action and reflection.[15] The emphasis on liberation as praxis resonates with the artistic practices described in this chapter; likewise Freire's emphasis throughout on the importance of individual subjectivity. Here in other words is a set of ideas in which liberation is imagined as an individualistic process, a challenge to the left's monolithic ways of organizing society.

Freire's work on liberation through education closely relates to Augusto Boal's theatre work, best known though his *Teatro do Oprimido* ('Theatre of the Oppressed'), a collection of essays written in exile between 1962 and 1973.[16] In many ways it is a theatrical equivalent of Freire's work. Just as Freire sought to interrogate and break down the power relations between teacher and student, Boal sought to rethink the relationship between actor and audience in the theatre, replacing it with a situation in which all parties are fully engaged, both in effect 'writing' and 'performing'; like Freire, liberation is achieved through a process of reflective practice, 'praxis' in his terminology, a process that never achieves an end, but is an end in itself.

The Favela as Liberation

Such theories of liberation are made materially manifest first through the figure of the *favela*. The *favela* (sometimes just *morro*, or hill) is a shanty of a kind that formally resembles other informal, peripheral settlements in Latin American cities, such as the Peruvian *barriada*. It has been an important geographical feature of the Brazilian city since the late nineteenth century, but has grown rapidly only since 1945.[17] It is a phenomenon that varies a good deal in size, sophistication and permanence, making a clear definition difficult, if not simply 'futile'.[18] The *favela* has also long been surrounded by negative myths: the 2002 movie *Cidade de Deus* (*City of God*) presented a fictionalized account of violence equal to that found in any war zone.[19] In these contemporary reports, the *favela* is not merely poor, but also a place of quite exceptional and excessive violence.

In spite of the negativity surrounding the *favela*, its status as the locus of social liberation has a long history. Both Le Corbusier and the leader of the Futurists, F. T. Marinetti, made well-documented visits to Rio *favelas* in the 1920s.[20] Marinetti had been photographed in a *favela* in 1926 with four black *favelados* and two policemen.[21] In each case, the European visitor feared the *favela*, but was at the same time drawn to it, hoping (as Styliane Philippou has put it) that their work would be 'liberated through contact with it'.[22] Marcel Camus' well-known *Black Orpheus* of 1959 reiterates the exoticization of the *favela* in film.[23]

The first large-scale attempt to explore the potential of the *favela* in architectural theory, however, was probably John Turner's polemical writings of the 1960s. Turner's anarchist advocacy of Latin American squatter housing first appeared in the London-based *Architectural Design* in 1963, and, much encouraged by its editor, Monica Pidgeon, he continued to contribute throughout the rest of the 1960s and '70s.[24] His particular expertise lay in the Peruvian *barriada*, but he travelled widely during the 1960s and his work became well known in Brazil. The squatter settlement, he wrote in 1968, had no less than an existential value. It was the product of 'three freedoms':

> the freedom of community self-selection; the freedom to budget one's own resources; and the freedom to shape one's own environment ... squatters have a homogeneity of purpose but maintain the heterogeneity of social characteristics vital for cultural stimulation and growth.[25]

This is not a Marcusian freedom – it is far too pragmatic for that. But it is a concept of freedom founded on distaste for authority that is both visceral and poetic. The squatter settlement in his work is always contrasted with the architectural products of authority, always Modernist. The photography and commentary on these buildings are not of a measured analysis, but of a feeling that is as poetic as anything in Oiticica. In that sense, the freedom articulated here is as much a matter of aesthetics as anything else.[26] Other important critical readings of the *favela* include *Quarto de Despejo* (published as *Beyond All Pity* in English), a bestselling diary of despair by a *favela* resident, and an anthropological study, Janice Perlman's *The Myth of Marginality*.[27] The latter elaborates Turner's suggestion that the *favela* is an embryonic suburb, an essentially respectable place whose values are conservative.[28] But where Turner emphasizes self-reliance and suspicion of authority, Perlman finds support for the state, tradition and order.

Architecture and Para-Architecture

Given their profoundly critical relation with state power, these theories of liberation tend to be most clearly manifest in para-architectural projects. These are works derived from, or made in critical response to, architecture, but cannot be located within the professional practice of

Hélio Oiticica, the
artist visiting
Mangueira *favela*.

architecture. Hélio Oiticica (1937–1980) is the main figure here, an artist
whose work persistently referenced architecture and was itself built on
an architectural scale, but stood in critical relation to it; his extensive
published writings also make clear his long-standing interest in both the
favela and broader theories of liberation. In a diary entry from 7 June
1969, he explains to his friend Lygia Clark about the appeal of these
things and, in his worldview, their connectedness. Here he describes his
first visit to Mangueira, a *favela* 6 kilometres from Centro on Rio's poor
north side, a part of the city that is mostly flat, lacks access to the beach

and has little of the picturesque character of the south side. His friends tell him not to go, expressing the ubiquitous middle-class fear of the *favela*. But Oiticica decides to ignore them:

> I thought: I won't say anything, and just go, and I loved it; suddenly, here, everything that was a sin turned into a virtue; all the folk tales they told me were put aside, because in place of the dope-head and decadent they would find an intelligent and creative person.[29]

Here, Oiticica makes clear that the *favela* represents something distinct from the working-class quarters of European cities, which might tolerate Bohemia. In Rio, the *favela* is known by the people who live there, but not otherwise. It does not represent a possible lifestyle option for a young artist.[30] But having gone, Oiticica found an unexpected appeal: 'everything that was a sin' in the bourgeois world he had temporarily abandoned, here 'was a virtue'. For Carlos Basualdo, Oiticica managed to experience the *favela* fully because he managed to extricate 'himself from the limitations of his social class'.[31] It might be more accurate to say that the *favela* was the means of escape. Oiticica's view of it, well informed by experience, has much in common with the writings of de Quincey or Huxley on drug experiences: the *favela*, like opium or mescaline, is a vehicle for social liberation.

Oiticica's cultural tourism was nevertheless adventurous and extensive: his association with Mangueira began in 1964 and he had got to know it well, joining its samba *bloco* and producing an extensive body of work in response to it.[32] The early works include the *parangolés*, large, cape-like objects halfway between architecture and items of clothing. The cover of Oiticica's Whitechapel exhibition catalogue from 1969 provides a good illustration of one: a friend of the artist's, Jerônimo, from the Mangueira *favela*, wears *Parangolé* number 5. A tall, athletic man, Jerônimo stares out from the photograph at the viewer with an expression of some intensity. This is not a joke – he wears the cape with some seriousness. There are numerous film records of the *parangolés* in use, so to speak, their wearers throwing them around with abandon. They are more then clothes; this is portable architecture made to frame an idea of bodily and social liberation; the wearer of the *parangolé* could, temporarily at least, do anything.

Oiticica's crucial work in this context is, however, the iconic installation *Tropicália*, installed for the first time at the Museum of Modern Art (MAM) in Rio de Janeiro in April 1967 as part of a group exhibition *Nova Objetividade Brasileira* (New Brazilian Objectivity), accompanied by a week of performance events. An amalgam of two existing installations

known as *PN2* and *PN3* – the letters *PN* stood for 'Penetrable' – it was a
large environment that could be entered physically by the spectator. Its
heterogeneous materials included painted wooden panels, a door, glass,
sand, plastic accessories, fabric, Duratex (a textured plaster), a television
set, potted plants and two live macaws.[33] It was noisy: the birds
squawked unpredictably, the television blared. It was, as the artist put it,
a 'sort of tropical scene'.[34] Occupying roughly 20 square metres of floor,
it was organized in two zones: a kind of beach zone, with rocks and
pebbles arranged in a path, along which the visitor walked, and a building
zone comprising two roughly improvised pavilions resembling canvas

windbreaks, simple wooden frames, stretched with blue, orange and floral prints. Visitors were encouraged to remove their shoes and pad around the sandy floor, poke their heads in the two pavilions, sit on the floor if they liked, watch TV or square up to the macaws. Calculatedly informal, temporary and poor, it had a desultorily festive air, like the aftermath of a party.

Its relationship to *favela* architecture was clear enough. It was not a representation of, or a reconstruction of, a *favela*, but it appropriated some of its typical materials and informal qualities. In the reconstruction of the work at the Whitechapel Art Gallery in London in 1969, the equivalence was underlined. In the Whitechapel exhibition catalogue, the MAM installation is illustrated on one side of a double spread, with the other side fully occupied by a photograph by Desdémone Bardin of the *favela* of Mangueira. As an image, it shows the *favela* in a good light. The hill is precipitous, as all Rio hills are. Down these hills normally cascade water, refuse and sewage, staining the rocks. The low resolution of this image obscures this, however, and Mangueira blurs into unlikely respectability. The buildings are not shacks for the most part, but what would elsewhere be called cottages, with tiled roofs, wooden shutters, whitewashed plasterwork, water tanks, outbuildings. While the houses occupy every usable bit of the hill, they make an attractive picturesque composition.

Tropicália was a striking contrast with its surroundings in the first showing at Affonso Reidy's Museum of Modern Art, one of the classic structures of Carioca Modernism. The museum is a low, horizontal concrete structure with a dramatic parabolic roof, supported by slender columns. It anticipated the sweeping vistas opened up by the creation of the Aterro do Flamengo, a generous network of highways and parks along by the harbour.[35] And it made clear reference to airport architecture, the obvious reference point being the Roberto brothers' Santos Dumont airport, little more than ten minutes' walk from the gallery. The contrast

171   The Politics of Liberation

Hélio Oiticica,
Tropicália as
reproduced in
the Whitechapel
catalogue, 1969:
double page-spread
with image of
Mangueira.

between these two structures is very great: one is a great optimistic structure, looking forward to a spacious, modern, decongested city; the other is a *faux* slum, a representation of everything the gallery's architecture sought to abolish. Yet both are in different ways visions of social liberation, the gallery in the form of an official solution imposed from above, the installation by Oiticica representative of liberation from below.

On the same curious site was staged a work by Oiticica's contemporary and friend Lygia Pape (1929–2004), a trained architect whose work explored the fringes of architecture, often with an explicitly political dimension. Pape's *Divisor* (1969) is well known as an image if less as a material object. *Divisor* is architectural in the same sense as Oiticica's *parangolés*, that is, a temporary way of activating space made of flexible materials. But where the *parangolé* accommodates just one person, *Divisor* is a vast sheet 20 by 20 metres, with openings cut in it for a hundred people. Various images of it exist, including one outside Reidy's Museum of Modern Art in Rio, where – like *Tropicália* – it makes a poignant contrast with the architecture. Also like *Tropicália*, *Divisor* staged a confrontation between the official city and the *favela*, for the people Pape chose to activate the work were children from the *favela* and the work had already been staged there. There are echoes of *Divisor* in

172

Pape's work in the grounds of the Museu do Açude – *New House* – is a
small box of a house, filled with light but at the same time almost completely overgrown, consumed by the tropical forest. Like Oiticica's work,
it works with architecture but conceives of it as something light and
temporary, and built from ordinary materials – whatever comes to hand.
It is not a professional activity, but something empowering; in this it can
be related to Freire's work in which education is imagined as a liberatory
rather than repressive activity.

Oiticica and Pape showed how theories of social liberation might
challenge the formal practice of architecture. Their work has close connections with the practice of other artists including Lygia Clark, whose
installation environments (often architectural in scale) staged a psychic
liberation based on Kleinian psychoanalytical theory – architecture
become therapy as it were.[36] Later artists, including Artur Barrio, Grupo
3Nós3 and, much more recently, Ducha, have explored notions of liberation through large scale and sometimes dramatic urban installations,
and it is here that the legacy of artists like Oiticica is carried on. Even
Ernesto Neto's well-known and popular sculptural installations draw on
this tradition; their use of distinctively Brazilian materials (especially
food and spices) makes explicit reference to informal architecture, now

recuperated as picturesque. What is striking about all this work is the way it creates a different, anti-official view of architecture using temporary and low-key materials, readily available techniques and local knowledge; its concept of liberation is based on the activation of local knowledges rather than professional ones.

Arquitetura Nova

Oiticica, Clark, Pape and their followers were not, however, architects, and however much they took from architecture and informed a critique of its development, they operated in a different, and in many ways freer, world: they did not have clients to satisfy, regulations with which to comply or teams of builders with whom to negotiate. In São Paulo, Arquitetura Nova took the prevailing ideas of liberation as a starting point and looked to apply them in the tougher and more compromised environment of architecture, and popular housing in particular. Even they struggled with the limits of professional architectural practice, however, and, as we shall see, their activities dissolved variously into painting, theatre or terrorism. They built little, and their existence (like their contemporaries Archigram in the UK and Superstudio in Italy) was based less on architecture than a cultivated notoriety. In this – their existence as a kind of radical think tank rather than a viable architectural practice – they functioned not unlike the artists already described. But they were tougher and grimmer, realistic rather than idealistic; there was little of the hippyish idealism found in Oiticica. Their liberation meant freedom from alienated work, wage slavery and social class.

Arquitetura Nova was a group of three – Sérgio Ferro, Flávio Império and Rodrigo Lefèvre – all pupils of Vilanova Artigas at FAU-USP in the early 1960s. They adopted Artigas's idea of an aesthetics of poverty (see chapter Four), but took it as far as it might reasonably go in architecture before it became something else. As they found with the last of their built projects together, the Casa Juarez Brandão Lopes (1968), the deployment of unlikely forms and materials did not of itself satisfy their radical political aims. To be radical involved direct actions against specific targets – and it is no surprise to find that the explorations of two members of the group, Ferro and Lefèvre, led them away from the practice of architecture and towards art (painting and theatre, often politically charged), as well as more direct forms of confrontation with the military regime.

Ferro was the group's theorist. His writings show a more or less complete disregard for professional niceties, starting with the 1967 manifesto 'Arquitetura Nova' itself, first published in the journal *Teoria e Prática*.[37]

Flávio Império and
Rodrigo Lefèvre,
Casa Juarez Brandão
Lopes, São Paolo,
1968.

In this angry and uncompromising piece, architecture as a professional practice is repeatedly and savagely criticized. It exists within a capitalist system with an unparalleled 'anthropophragic' capacity to neutralize the most radical work; it is 'tame', 'corrupt', a 'pantomime', a business of disguising the truth. Ferro later developed and expanded his ideas in his best-known text, *O Canteiro e o Desenho* ('The Building Site and the Design'), first published in exile in 1979, the major elaboration of the Arquitetura Nova project.[38] The title refers back to a dispute between Vilanova Artigas and his followers at FAU-USP over the relationship between architectural practice and social change. As we saw in chapter Four, Artigas maintained a lifelong commitment to the profession of architecture, which is to say, a belief in the ability of a professional elite to deliver revolutionary solutions. His houses, for example the Casa Elza Berquó, were imagined as part of a broader avant-garde project, in which architecture (it was never made clear how) would help deliver social change through design. Artigas's position is inseparable from Niemeyer's here: both have everything invested in the design process. By contrast, Ferro and his group laid the emphasis on the process of building. Broadly, it was through identification with building, not design, that a radical architecture could be achieved. As long as it was subservient to design, it would be by its nature a process that was not only inefficient and alienating, but violent and exploitative, almost everything about it being contrived to alienate the builder further from his work.[39] In a manner analogous to the theorizing of conceptual artists of the late 1960s, Ferro argued that a truly radical architecture should ally itself with *process* rather than product; architecture as it stood was little more than a function of capital and to focus on design, that is, a finished, consumable product, would only entrench its commodity status further.[40]

For Arquitetura Nova, Brasília represented for them everything that had to be overturned: it was (so they thought) a place that elevated design at the expense of building, with the result that its realization involved profoundly exploitative processes. At the National Congress, Ferro described the building in terms of endemic cruelty. The twin bowls were beautiful forms, but to construct then out of reinforced concrete required an immense amount of manual labour. Worse, the work was physically dangerous. As contemporary images of the construction show, the bowls are formed from a vast but dense network of steel rods, which had to be tied together before the concrete could be added. This work with the rods turned out to be brutal, trapping hands and limbs as the concrete was poured, causing, he said, terrible injuries.[41]

Precisely how Arquitetura Nova planned to realize their critique is less clear. In some ways their writings point to a revival of pre-modern, artisanal ways of working – there are hints of a South American arts and crafts revival here. In the Brazilian context of the 1960s, this was a radical suggestion, given the social chasm between the two sides: an architect's education in Brazil, like everywhere else, was about forming an elite as much as technical knowledge, an elite who systematically removed themselves from the building process. Yet recent Brazilian history contained examples of persons for whom design and building were the same: in early twentieth-century São Paulo, Italian immigrant builders specialized in certain aspects of the construction of residential buildings, like the *escadeiro* who would design and build a stair in a gap left for him in a new house – a complex process involving design and improvisation with materials and labour.[42]

Arquitetura Nova's buildings are surprisingly restrained given the incendiary rhetoric. The built legacy consists of a series of individual

villas, built on relatively small budgets mostly for friends, all in São Paulo. In chronological order, the most important include Império's Casa Simon Fausto (1961), Ferro's Casa Boris Fausto (also 1961), Ferro's Casa Bernardo Issler (1962), Império's and Lefèvre's Casa Hamburger (1965), Lefèvre's and Império's Casa Juarez Brandão Lopes (1968), Lefèvre's Casa Dino Zamataro (1971) and Lefèvre's and Nestor Goulart's Casa Pery Campos (1972). By the early 1970s it was all over. The most interesting of these houses are those that employ a simple vault to define the house, a device used for both pragmatic, and rhetorical reasons. The group built in a 'poor' way as a way both of reducing costs (their clients were mostly their friends) and of finding models of building that would be appropriate for Brazil's poor. Hence their development of houses in the form of a curved vault, uncannily reminiscent of the Nissen Hut.[43] All three were involved in houses of this design. The choice of vault was

Sérgio Ferro, Casa Bernardo Issler, Cotia, 1962.

significant symbolically. As Arantes has described, the vault was 'an expression of the most primitive kind of human habitat: a covering that produces a womb-like, cavernous space. A reinvented cave'.[44]

The vaults of Arquitetura Nova recalled the simplest forms of dwelling, and were meant to look as such. Ferro elaborated further: this was a technology that was simple, cheap and easily mass-produced.[45] Their vaults were distinctly different from those employed by Niemeyer in his Memorial da América Latina in São Paulo. The vaults there, Ferro complained, were all decorative, covering up a pre-existing structure.[46] They were wasteful, unlike those Ferro advocated, which represented a cheap way of building a shelter. Recalling the most primitive forms of housing, these used the minimum materials and were simple to build. In practice, the vault appeared in houses like Lefèvre's Casa Dino Zamataro. In the perspective drawings of it, and the photographs of it realized, it appears as a single curved volume, rising to two storeys in height. The vault itself is steel-reinforced concrete (expensive materials in Brazil, but here used sparingly). Externally, it is an exceptionally simple form, a half-cylinder, glazed at both ends. A brick box forms the entrance and extends into the interior, forming a platform at mezzanine level. The simplicity of the exterior form largely continues inside: this is a big, informal, open-plan space that absorbs a wide range of possible activities, both work and leisure. In early perspectives, an artist's studio

178

Sérgio Ferro, Casa
Bernardo Issler,
Cotia, 1962, interior.

Sérgio Ferro, Casa Bernardo Issler, Cotia, 1962, interior.

is depicted on the mezzanine, while hammocks hang informally in the main space. The liberatory programme of the construction continues inside, it could be said, providing a stage in which new forms of social behaviour might take place. The free-flowing quality of the space, the lack of division between workspace, eating space and bedroom, was an explicit challenge to middle-class Brazilian houses, whose complex internal divisions represented rigid social hierarchies. The vault houses abolish these internal divisions, and suggest that the social divisions they represent might also disappear.

Rodrigo Lefèvre and
Nestor Goulart, Casa
Pery Campos, São
Paulo, 1972.

Lefèvre and the others in the group refined the vault for use in further houses for individual clients, and sketched out plans for its use in *casas populares*, although because the group ceased to exist as an effective architectural practice, these remained at the level of proposals.[47] In retrospect, these vault houses suffer from the same problems as Artigas's villas, in that they approach the condition of the *casa popular* without ever really acceding to it. What we are presented with is the *look* of poverty -- the use of rustic or quasi-rustic materials and processes to make, in the end, fabulous weekend houses for privileged clients. But the quality of engagement with process is qualitatively different here compared with Artigas's houses: the design seems less fixed; the materials and building processes are of a decidedly lower grade; the houses, both before and after completion, have an improvised quality about them that Artigas's did not. Ferro wrote of the importance of jazz as a metaphor for their practice: jazz was unlike other western music, he stated, in that it was a music of the players, 'everything in it was subordinated to the individuality of the players'. Moreover, it was a music that privileged improvisation, which is to say, it emphasized process and was informed by contingencies.[48] So it is with the vault houses, at least in theory.

Rodrigo Lefèvre,
Casa Dino
Zamataro, São
Paulo, 1971.

Casa Dino
Zamataro,
interior.

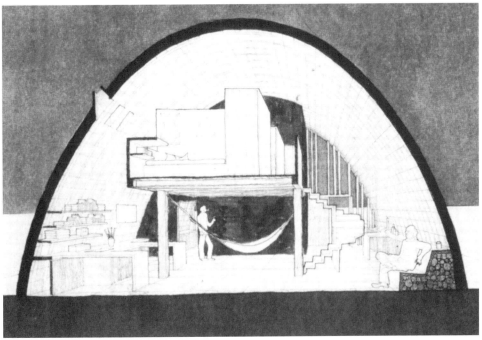

In 1964 Ferro was called as a witness in the trial of the Faculty of Architecture and Urbanism (FAU-USP). Although under suspicion by the Brazilian authorities, he continued to work, and to publish articles directly and indirectly critical of the military regime. He continued as a member of the Communist Party until 1967, when he left for Ação Libertadora Nacional (ALN), a group advocating armed resistance against the government. In 1968 both Ferro and Lefèvre staged bomb attacks and bank robberies in São Paulo. Imprisoned in 1970, Ferro was sacked by FAU-USP the same year for having 'abandoned his responsibilities'. On his release in 1971, he made his way to France, where he took up a teaching position at the University of Grenoble. At the time of writing, Ferro was the only surviving member of the group, and maintaining an uncompromising view of architecture and politics, little altered from the 1960s. Lefèvre also spent a year in prison during 1970–71 as a result of his terrorist actions with Ferro. Império meanwhile abandoned architecture in 1968, and turned to theatre and painting, resigning from his teaching position at FAU-USP in 1977 after being denied space for experimental theatre by the authorities. The impact of external political events on the work of the group was considerable, and led away from architecture altogether. The group's experiments remain important, however. Like the artistic experiments of the circle around Oiticica in Rio, they point up the contradictions in the official rhetoric of modernization and progress, and they argue convincingly that any meaningful process of liberation will necessarily be driven from below, rather than imposed from above. The objects they produced, finally, show how an aesthetic of play might be made central to building. Niemeyer and his circle wished to generate a sense of dumbstruck awe in the beholder – a position in which the beholder is (albeit temporarily) powerless. By contrast, the artists and architects described in this chapter wanted to empower the beholder.

These ideas have not persisted long in the architectural imagination. They have, however, proved durable in other cultural areas. Oiticica's international reputation as an artist has grown markedly since his death in 1980, with particular interest being generated by the para-architectural works. In London alone it was possible to see a reconstruction of the iconic *Tropicália* in both 2006 and 2007. The Whitechapel Art Gallery, the venue for the first London showing of the piece in 1969, had shown three architectural-scale installations by the artist as recently as 2002.[49] All these exhibitions drew attention to the liberatory potential of the *favela*, albeit in a somewhat deracinated form. The task was achieved most thoroughly, however, in the book *Cidade de Deus* by Paulo Lins and its immensely popular cinematic version by Fernando Meirelles in

2002. Both book and film deal with a dense, claustrophobic situation, a grim state housing project of 1966 that had degenerated into a quasi-*favela*.[50] The literary critic Roberto Schwarz wrote of the 'closure of the horizon' in the book, with all human existence reduced to what could be contained within the *favela*.[51] Yet, as Meirelles's immensely popular film made clear, in this terrifying place, liberation (albeit of a temporary and morally dubious kind) is crucial: anything can, and does, happen. The violence invariably has an erotic, sometimes sadistic, dimension. One major set piece, the celebration of the departure of one of the *favela*'s hoods, is both a bloody massacre and a marvellous party: the massacre interrupts the party, but in many senses the pleasure and the violence are inseparable, the more extreme the violence, the greater the accompanying pleasure.[52] This, arguably, is the perverse legacy of the 1960s experiments in liberation.

chapter six

The Politics of Spectacle

The low-key and often subversive activities described in chapter Five exist in the context of ferocious urban development, which Modernists often sought to oppose. As Lúcio Costa wrote as early as 1951, in the context of so much commercial development in Brazil, any architecture was a 'miracle'.[1] For much of the twentieth century, Brazil's rates of urban growth were among the world's highest. This was manifest most visibly in the astonishing growth of São Paulo, which increased from a town of 70,000 (1890) to a megalopolis of 18 million a century later.[2] More significant in some respects has been the rate of urbanization of the country as a whole: in 1930 there were 20 million Brazilians, only 32 per cent of whom lived in cities; in 2007 there were 185 million Brazilians, of whom 82 per cent lived in cities. During the course of less than a century, a small, mostly rural country became a large, almost entirely urban one. The Brazil of the *fazenda* has gone, and the nostalgia for it expressed by such unlikely figures as Costa and Freyre was in some ways an expression of mourning for its passing. The new Brazil is dense, urban and heavily industrialized. During the period covered by this book the rates of urban growth in the twentieth century in Brazil compare with or exceed those of the Industrial Revolution in Europe, while the cities they produced were on an unprecedented scale, in excess of anything – with the possible exception of New York – in the developed world.[3] Such development was by no means confined to informal settlements on the urban periphery, but included, and profoundly redefined, the formal city. With the sole exception of Brasília, Brazil's cities became cities of high-rise towers.[4]

In terms of individual buildings, there was also a notable, but underreported, tendency to giganticism during the years of the economic miracle. Huge infrastructural works were matched by huge architecture, such as the Petróbras headquarters in central Rio de Janeiro (1969–73, team led by Roberto Gandolfi), for the state-owned oil company; this has both an extraordinary form (a squat Miesian tower punctuated by huge voids) and extraordinary scale. With a floor area of 115,000 square

Roberto Gandolfi,
Petróbras head-
quarters, Rio de
Janeiro, 1969–73.

metres, it approaches the World Trade Center in New York (1970–2001) in scale; it used concrete sufficient to build 30 ten-storey buildings; its lifts could take 500 passengers in one go; its electricity transformers supplied 15MW, enough to power a city of 120,000.[5] However, it occupies a site adjacent to Lapa, a fragment of Rio's delicate nineteenth-century landscape, making its size all the more striking. Adjacent to Rio's equally vast metropolitan cathedral (completed in 1968), the Petróbras building appears as a harbinger of a future when all buildings will be equally monstrous.[6]

Brazil's urbanistic megalomania, however, is best represented by São Paulo. It was its epicentre, and it remains its most extraordinary product. Its high-rise landscape is as epic as anything in Hong Kong or New York, and it remains after these two cities the world's largest concentration of tall buildings, with about 4,000 high-rises.[7] It is a landscape of such density that the rich have apocryphally taken to helicopters to avoid congestion and crime, only rarely now descending to street level.[8] Such development in São Paulo's case did not, whatever its appearance to the contrary, appear from nowhere, but has a politics as profound as that underpinning the building of Modernist cities. It is not mere accumulation, but the result of a variety of processes, some conscious, some not, that legitimized such ferocious development regardless of its environmental or social consequences. It has also been a process largely ignored by mainstream architectural discourse, both inside and outside Brazil. Inside the country, there was a remarkable tendency by architects to repress it, or to declare (in Ruth Verde Zein's words) that 'after Brasília nothing happened.'[9] Little could be further from the truth, as Zein argues: in the late 1960s and early 1970s Brazilian architects were busy providing the material frame for the economic boom of the period, and in so doing transformed the urban landscape more completely than at any other time in Brazil's history. That they could not somehow admit that this is what they were doing has to do with their complicity with both an authoritarian political regime they generally despised and a real estate boom they could not sanction.

The situation produced a city that can only be described as *spectacular*. Spectacle is an over-used word, yet its various connotations to do with both the worlds of entertainment and the accumulation of capital are exactly appropriate here. This is one of the few instances when Guy Debord's definition of spectacle – 'capital to such a degree of accumulation that it becomes an image' – really is correct.[10] In the case of São Paulo, it works well because this is a city that is so nakedly the result of the accumulation of capital above any other process. When you stand on the observation deck of the Edifício Itália, once the city's tallest building, you see wave on wave of high-rises as far as the horizon. Interrupted only by the mountains of São Paulo state 50 kilometres to the northwest, it is one of the great sights of the modern world.

Very few of the buildings taken individually have much architectural merit. Almost all have been put up to maximize the commercial potential of the site, built to – or slightly exceeding – the absolute limit of local regulations on height and density. Yet despite the complexity of the forces involved, and the number of different individuals and sources of finance, the view condenses into a coherent image. It is by European

São Paulo, view from Paraiso looking east, 2004.

standards a remarkably undifferentiated landscape. The churches and parks (what few there are) do not stand out, or establish themselves in any kind of urban hierarchy. There is, as the Brazilian architectural historian Luz Recamán has commented, no sense here of the European civil society life that developed in Europe and the United States.[11] It is an ant heap. That ant heap is nonetheless extraordinarily impressive, not to mention economically effective, and this effectiveness explains why the ant heap (and not, say, the formal planning of 1920s Rio or 1950s Brasília) has become the model for all major urban development in Brazil. I use the image of São Paulo here, but it is in reality the São Paulo

189 The Politics of Spectacle

São Paulo, Avenida
Paulista, eastwards
from MASP.

model, which one sees replicated everywhere in urban Brazil. Brasília's
Pilot Plan may discursively represent Brazil's architecture of the 1950s
abroad, but whatever its prestige, it is in many ways the antithesis of the
modern Brazilian city. This is a vital distinction. Both Brasília and the
spectacular city can be said to be equally modern. They employ many of
the same architectural forms (high-rises, slab bocks, urban motorways),
but in radically different formats, and to radically different ends.

We must therefore not be too prescriptive about the distinction
between spectacular and planned cities. The distinction is nevertheless
worth making because the spectacular city remains urban Brazil's most
striking aspect, yet remains only weakly present in architectural discourse. This chapter explores the spectacular city in a number of ways.
First it considers further the notion of spectacle in relation to São Paulo,
bringing into play a wide range of literary and artistic accounts of the
city, not all of them positive. Then I look at notions of spectacle in relation to architecture, especially in relation to what Brazilian architects say
about it. I discuss a number of historic São Paulo buildings in relation
to the concept of spectacle. Finally, I look at the way a certain number of
contemporary architects in Brazil have taken on board the notion of
spectacle directly, chief among them being Ruy Ohtake.

City as Spectacle

São Paulo is the signal case of the spectacular city. Although founded in the fifteenth century as a trading post by Portuguese Jesuits, the modern city was the creation of immigrant businessmen such as Francisco Matazarro, an Italian from Calabria who, in the first decades of the twentieth century, established an industrial empire based around the production of flour. It became the greatest industrial complex in South America. In the second half of the century, the main industry was car manufacturing. As the city grew, local politicians became more ambitious, and helped develop the architecture and infrastructure to represent and encourage that growth. The spectacular landscape of highways and high-rises that so characterizes the city is in many respects a political product, the result of a desire on the part of local mayors to provide appropriate visual images for the industry that increasingly defined the city. The crucial political figures here include Francisco Prestes Maia and José Vicente Faria Lima, who controlled the city from 1961 to 1969 respectively, a period in which the city's spectacular appearance was properly consolidated. A significant product of this time was the Elevado Costa e Silva, a violently disruptive elevated motorway that sliced through the historic centre. Known locally as the

São Paulo, Elevado Costa e Silva, or *minhocão*, 1971.

minhocão ('Big Worm', a terrifying mythical creature of the Amazon), it was inaugurated in 1971.[12] Throughout the 1950s and '60s politicians at a local and national level helped produce a climate in which the development of the city of this kind was justified in the name of progress. As Korawick and Bonduki have reported, during the 1950s and '60s the 'self-congratulation and flag-waving' of the city's ruling class 'soon spread contagiously to the mass media and took the middle classes by storm'.

> Slogans such as 'São Paulo must not stop', 'São Paulo is the fastest growing city in the world' and 'Latin America's biggest industrial center' were heard on all sides, justifying any initiative purporting to be progressive. Progress meant demolition of anything that was old.[13]

The period has been described as 'an uncontrollable will to modernize, that is build, grow, progress'; there was 'money for everything'.[14] It is a process that in many ways still continues: the development of the Avenida Berrini since the 1990s is a good example.[15]

Although São Paulo's growth during the twentieth century was meteoric, its culture of development was in many respects fixed by the middle of the 1930s. During this decade its spectacularity made it an object of special fascination for foreign visitors. The fascination had nothing to do with individual buildings or history, but rather the impression of collective activity, superficially chaotic, but ultimately directed to the single goal of the accumulation of capital. The impressions of São Paulo closely resemble those of industrial Manchester a century previously, particularly those of Friedrich Engels.[16] Both cities represent a prototype of future urban development, which both thrills and terrifies; both cities are in some way sublime, representations of the unrepresentable; both are, in the Debordian sense, spectacular.[17]

The French anthropologist Claude Lévi-Strauss provides a good example from his first visit in 1935, when he arrived to take up an assistant professorship at the newly formed University of São Paulo. His response was one of simultaneous wonder and horror. Nevertheless, the extraordinariness of the city is not only to do with the desire for the exotic on the part of the tourist, but also an understanding by the city's own residents that they live in a place that defies comprehension. Lévi-Strauss makes two essential points, first being the speed of development. He wrote:

> The town is developing so fast that it is impossible to obtain a map of it; a new edition would be required every week. It has

been said that if you take a taxi to an appointment several weeks
in advance, you are in danger of arriving before the builders have
finished.[18]

Lévi-Strauss's second point concerns the quality of the development. At
various points in the description, he relates how the city has an almost
ruined appearance, that it appears to have been destroyed before it has
yet been finished. There is something about the careless nature of the

construction and the demands of the tropical climate that prevents newness. He remarks on the rapid degeneration of the decorative façades of buildings with the humidity and pollution: they are 'reminiscent of the scrolls and crusts of leprosy'.[19] Everything is built 'so as to be renewable . . . that is, badly'. New districts are 'hardly integral elements of the urban scene'. They are 'like stands in a fairground, or the pavilions of some international exhibition, built to last only a few months'.[20]

Lévi-Strauss's classic account of the city is reiterated in the form of photographs taken at the same time. A series of thirty or so city views have been published showing the city in a frenzied state of construction. Particularly striking are those images that show the points of the borders or edges of the city, points at which high modernity collides with either nature or rural life. An image of the construction of the Avenida Paulista in the 1930s, now a forest of high-rises the equal of midtown Manhattan, shows the formal city – at this point a row of elegant villas in the English style – emerging from a chaos of little ravines where, as the author puts it, 'nature still has the upper hand'.[21]

Lévi-Strauss's view of the city is affirmed over the subsequent decades by other visitors, foreign and Brazilian alike. All were shocked by the violence of the city's development. A few years after Lévi-Strauss's visit,

Claude Lévi-Strauss, photo of São Paulo, 1936.

Stefan Zweig wrote of the city's unequalled dynamism and ambition, but also the violence of the process. 'One has the sensation of not being in a city, but on some huge building site', he wrote; it was 'not a city built for enjoyment; nor is it built for ostentation. It has few promenades and no *corsos*, few views, few places of amusement; and in the streets one sees almost exclusively men, hurrying, busy men.'[22] The founder of the Bauhaus, Walter Gropius, visiting ten years later in 1954, described skyscrapers springing up overnight 'like mushrooms' in an utterly disorganized regime of development, unlike anything he had seen in his life. He was both appalled and impressed.[23] Max Bill decried the 'jungle growth' of São Paulo;[24] Siegfed Giedon, writing in 1956, deplored the city for the same reasons, describing it as a 'cancer'; it had to be restrained.[25]

In all of these accounts the reader is presented with a city that defies belief, a place that exceeds comprehension: too big, too fast, too chaotic to be represented. These were the defining tropes until the end of the 1950s. After that point, and especially with an unstable economy after the inauguration of Brasília, combined with deep political uncertainty leading to the military coup of 1962, perceptions of São Paulo took on a different tone. The trope of unrepresentability persisted. This was still a city that defied belief in its extraordinary scale, in its relentlessness, but with that had come a sense of melancholy. In some ways this was an extension of the ruinous quality that Lévi-Strauss found in 1935. But where he identified ruins as by-products of the city's modernization, in later years the ruin came to define it. In later reports, the city came to seem hollowed out, falling down, defined by its degradation and lack of civic sense. It still grew, but lethargically; it had become a ghastly accumulation of poor-quality concrete serving no apparent purpose. This was no longer an efficient machine, attuned to the purpose of making money. It existed for its own strange purpose, now long forgotten. Simone de Beauvoir, writing in 1962 after a grumpy visit to Brazil with Jean-Paul Sartre, detected an epic melancholy in the city, manifest in its many construction sites: 'they haven't finished building: everywhere there are unfinished buildings. We noticed however that the masons worked at a slow pace, and on certain construction sites, not at all: the enormous inflation has brought with it a recession; many businesses have been abandoned'.[26]

Bernd Witte, a German literary critic, noted something similar twenty years later. 'I saw São Paulo for the first time from my hotel window,' he wrote,

> and I have to say that it seemed like a city of the dead. Seen from the height of a thirty-storey building, the city presents itself to the

viewer like an underworld, like a realm of shadows, on which the skyscrapers, in their uniformity, appear like tombstones. And when people pass through the city, they see what is unfinished is already falling down.[27]

Nelson Brissac Peixoto provides a gloss on Witte's remarks: 'These constructions', he says, referring to the city's skyscrapers, 'lack the traces of history, the memory of a successful life, such as exists in European cities. Of course one can't call ruins those inexpressive conglomerations of skyscrapers. A ruin implies a memory of something successful, whose traces even the most competent researcher will be hard-pressed to find.'[28] Another account from a foreign observer, this time Eduardo Subirats, describes an immense confusion in the city's landscape, a mixture of construction and destruction, which previously might have been called 'sublime':

> Viaducts, factories, skyscrapers, the febrile movement of masses of people and machines grant to this area a heavy futurist dimension. A chaotic and aggressive polyphony of strident volumetric forces. The keen poverty of façades and faces, the dirt and pollution of the streets, the unavoidable presence of ruins and industrial waste together with the aggressive energy of the mass together create a powerful expressive tension. There is something crackling and nervous in the air. Destruction and production confuse their signs. Meanwhile among them exist signs of unexpected tenderness. In the urban texture of the industrial region, there are residential fragments of pre-industrial settlements which grew up with the coffee plantations and the sugar plantations, with their family houses and little backyards, a delicate reference to tropical vegetation at the door. A typical Paulista landscape.[29]

More recent accounts, especially those developed from an economic or anthropological perspective, have emphasized the emerging chaos in the city; it has become not only a ruin that may – just – be appreciated in aesthetic terms, but is also actually out of control, a situation that again many writers have compared with that of British industrial cities in the middle of the nineteenth century, prior to their reform. According to Korawick, the city is 'plummeting' towards conditions of Third World cities.[30] It is, in the words of another commentator, William Goldsmith, the 'City of Misery' populated by 'survivors in Dickens' Manchester';[31] for the anthropologist Teresa Caldeira, the city is obsessed with crime: the 'talk of crime' is contagious, breeding ubiquitous fear.[32]

These exotic views of the city find visual form in the work of a number of contemporary artists, among them Candida Höfer, Thomas Struth and (in Brazil) Rubens Mano, Rogério Canella, Luisa Lambri and Paulo Climachauska.[33] The best-known artistic representations include Anselm Kiefer's *Lilith* (1987–9), one of the outstanding works in the São Paulo Bienal of 1989, now in the collection of Tate Modern, London. A gigantic picture, 3.3 × 5.6 metres, it provides an immersive environment in which the viewer loses him or herself. It depicts the view from the Edifício Itália in the centre of São Paulo, a view composed exclusively of Modernist towers, a dense array that excludes everything else; there is barely space to breathe. The city is drawn roughly in acrylic and emulsion paint. Over this rough sketch is scattered, haphazardly, a series of crude materials, all of which have about them the unmistakeable sense of decay – ashes, chalk, human hair,. The city is undeniably spectacular in these images, but the spectacle is profoundly negative: the city is a horror, a view underwritten by the title itself, *Lilith*, an evil deity in Hebrew myth who rains destruction from above. The allusions to aerial bombardment in *Lilith* are clear enough, and consistent with Kiefer's obsession with German history. São Paulo,

Anselm Kiefer, *The Grass Will Grow Over Your Cities*, 1999. A book work by Kiefer making use of São Paulo's imagery, in this case the approach to Congonhas airport.

of course, never suffered the fate of Dresden in the Second World War, but in alluding to those events, Kiefer suggests that a similar, spectacular, destruction may take place by other means.

The spectacle of São Paulo has less to do with the agency of architects than the movement of capital, and developers building to the limit – or slightly exceeding – local building regulations. As the anthropologist Teresa Caldeira has described, it is two regulations in particular dating

Oscar Niemeyer, São
Paulo Bienal
pavilion, interior, 1951.

from 1957 that most define the look of the city. These are the *coeficiente
de aproveitamento* (municipal law 5261), which declares that the 'total
built area cannot exceed 4 (residential) or 6 (office) times the area of the
total lot', in other words, a restriction on the height of buildings. The
second regulation declares that the *cota minima de terreno* per apartment should correspond to at least 35 square metres of the terrain area,
in other words, a restriction on the minimum size of apartments to
avoid crowding. In a city with few other planning controls, and a free
market in land, the implications are obvious: a forest of high-rises of
more or less the same height and design, built as close together as permissible, aimed at maximizing what the law would allow.[34] Given this
control on density, from this moment on, wrote Caldeira, the high-rise
had de facto legal status as housing for the affluent. Here were, to put it
another way, regulations enshrining low density, and therefore high cost,
in city-centre housing. The spectacular landscape of São Paulo is therefore also for the most part a wealthy landscape. The poor, as we have seen
elsewhere in this book, occupy informal parts of the city, far from the city
centre, and built at much higher densities than the spectacular city itself.

Most of the architects described in this book remained implacably
opposed to the spectacular city: Costa, Niemeyer, even Artigas, despite
spending his entire working life in São Paulo. Artigas took a particularly dim view of the developing financial centre of the city along the
previously residential Avenida Paulista. This showcase of commercial
development could rival Fifth Avenue in New York in scale by the end of

the 1960s. But in an interview in 1984, Artigas decried it as bastardized Modernism: Brazil had been robbed, having had some of the most famous architects in the world (thinking, presumably, of Niemeyer), it had imported a watered-down, commercial variant of Modernism for Paulista, a representation of a 'desperate reality'.[35] What emerges from this litany of complaints is a profound, perhaps irreconcilable divide in the architectural profession between an elite who disparage the modern world as it is, and refuse (at least in public) to participate in it – and a professional mass who by contrast engage with the world, and in effect build it.

Centro to Paulista

Nevertheless (as Zein hints with relation to Brasília), the architectural profession in Brazil was more engaged with the production of spectacle than might first appear. There is a long history of buildings in São Paulo and elsewhere that have contributed to the sense of spectacle, rather than stand in opposition to it. Most of these are tall buildings, meant to give form to the city by providing it with landmarks, icons and viewpoints from which the city's spectacle could be apprehended. A good, early starting point is the Prédio Martinelli, in the Avenida São João in Centro, for eighteen years São Paulo's tallest building. It was planned in 1922 by Comendatore Martinelli, an Italian developer from Lucca, who aimed to build the tallest building in South America. Construction began in 1924, and was completed in 1929. The original plan was for a ten-storey block; the building as realized reached 27 storeys and 105 metres, with a built area of 40,000 square metres. The architects were José Campos do Amaral and Raul Silveira Simões, and at the time of its completion it was the largest concrete-framed building in the world.[36] Functionally, it was an unusual building for the time, combining a variety of commercial and other functions including offices, a hotel, cinema and shops. It quickly became an icon of the city during a period of widespread verticalization, displacing the elegant cast-iron bridge of the Viaduto do Chá (Tea Viaduct) over the bed of the Anhangabáu River as the city's most recognizable symbol. Its illuminated advertising was famous, giving it the status of a southern hemisphere Times Square. The view from its roof terrace also became important, a place from which the burgeoning metropolis could be viewed, and be understood as a single entity.

The Martinelli was widely celebrated. It was photographed extensively, and came to represent the city metonymically in those images. It was also celebrated in poetry by Mário de Andrade, one of the principal Modernists in the literary scene in Brazil. Like the Woolworth Building in New York, built a decade earlier, this is not a Modernist building from the outside. Its 27 storeys are highly decorative, hiding the concrete frame. The façade is stone, with a heavy cornice: this is an inflated, extruded Renaissance *palazzo*. It is not Modernist, but it nevertheless communicates what could be achieved by the modern world. The height alone could only be made usable by means of the elevator.

One of the most arresting images of the Martinelli shows it on 11 May 1933 when it was circled by the immense *Graf Zeppelin* airship, itself a symbol of technological sophistication. Circling slowly around the Martinelli at the level of the seventeenth floor, the two immense objects are in surreal dialogue with each other: there is no question in the mind of the photographers in each case that this monstrous ballet represents the future. Yet the very spectacularity of these images marks them out as modern, but not Modernist. The absence of buildings such as the Martinelli from Modernist histories of architecture is striking – yet the achievement of the building was, by any standards, huge.

Whatever the achievement of the Martinelli as spectacle, its commercial history was uncertain. Owing to the collapse of the developer, it was sold to the Italian government in 1934, and during the Second World War, for reasons of national security, it was appropriated by the government of Brazil. It fell into decline from the 1950s onwards, crudely

José Campos do Amaral and Raul Silveira Simões, Prédio Martinelli, São Paulo, 1924–9.

José Campos do Amaral and Raul Silveira Simões, Prédio Martinelli, São Paulo, 1924–9, detail.

converted into cheap flats, and it was restored only in the 1990s.[37] By this time the surrounding area – once the financial heart of Brazil – had itself fallen into decay, having long been superseded by the Avenida Paulista. In other words, Martinelli's status as urban spectacle was as short lived as the airship with which in image it was often associated. Two much more durable cases can be found less than a mile or so from the Martinelli. Adjoining each other, they are Oscar Niemeyer's Edifício Copan (1955) and Franz Heep's Edifício Itália (1965). The Copan is a sublime building, one of the architectural sights of Brazil, yet little has been written about it.[38] Built between 1951 and 1954, it consists of a 32-storey block containing parking for 500 cars, nightclubs, restaurants, art galleries, shopping and no less than 1,700 apartments. It is a modernistic world in miniature, the Unité d'Habitation relocated to the tropics, twisted, and blown up. Located at the apex of the Avenida Ipiranga and the Rua da Consolação in the city's old financial district, adjacent to the leafy Praça República, it has two distinct sides. The front, as it were, is an enormous serpentine façade, comprising horizontal *brises-soleil* in concrete that transform the building into a 32-storey sculpture.[39] Affonso Reidy's Pedregulho in Rio is a clear reference point (see chapter Two). But Reidy's appropriation of the curve had some residual justification in terms of function: it was legible as a means of getting the best out of a difficult, hilly site, allowing access to light and space for each apartment in the block. The Copan, by contrast, is pure sculpture, an image made simply to connote modernity regardless of function.

The Copan's functions, unsurprisingly, are compromised by the spectacle. The shopping centre is cramped and gloomy, a labyrinth of badly lit tunnels snaking up and down through the ground floor, disgorging its few customers at the service entrance. The views from the apartments are hampered by the hefty *brises-soleil*. The cultural facilities seem to have failed: at any rate, the author failed to find much evidence of them in 2006. The complex as a whole is shabby and uninviting, in parts distinctly foreboding. But as spectacle it has few parallels in a city that is not short of such things. This quality has given it a curious afterlife as a subject in art and advertising. The crucial formal feature of the Copan, its sculptural *brises-soleil*, is reiterated in two further buildings by Niemeyer from the same period, the Copan's near neighbour, the Edifício Montreal (1950–51), on the Avenida Ipiranga, and the Edifício Niemeyer in Belo Horizonte (1954).[40]

The Copan was completed in 1955, at which point it was by far the most substantial building in the area. Since 1965 it has been joined by Franz Heep's Edifício Itália, and the two exist in a formal dialogue with each other. They are both essentially Modernist, but both extend or

Franz Heep, Edifício Itália, São Paulo, 1965.

exaggerate Modernist forms to become spectacular. Their forms no longer connote function – their forms just connote form. Heep (1902–1987) was an Austrian of an impeccably Modernist pedigree, having worked with Le Corbusier in Paris in the 1930s. Emigrating to Brazil in 1947, he became a naturalized citizen in 1952. The Edifício Itália is his best-known, and largest, work in Brazil. It was the result of an architectural competition for a new headquarters building held in 1953 by the organization representative of São Paulo's huge Italian business community, the Círculo Italiano. Other entrants in the competition included Gregori Warchavchik, the Russian émigré long based in São Paulo, and the Italian architect Gio Ponti.

At 168 metres, Heep's winning entry was double the height of the still iconic Prédio Martinelli. Its site, at the corner of the Avenidas São Luis and Ipiranga, then had much prestige, a kind of southern hemisphere Fifth Avenue. The building, triangular in plan, bisected the site dramatically, defining the corner of the two avenues. It was vast in scale, as well as tall: a total constructed area of 52,000 square metres. The *brises-soleil* were borrowed from a Le Corbusier plan for a skyscraper in Algeria from the 1930s. The complex was crowned by a famous, if mediocre, restaurant, the Terraço Itália. The view from the Terraço Itália is the one depicted by Anselm Kiefer, looking south along the Avenida São Luis, towards the Avenida Paulista. It is Paulista that captures most visitors' attention, for this high ridge – the highest point geographically in the central city – marks the greatest and densest concentration of high buildings in the city, and it remains, despite relative decline, the place of work for close on a million Paulistas.

Paulista is a vital element of the spectacular city, and whatever its origins, it can no longer be read as the straightforward expression of either the military period or the simple accumulation of capital. Travelling from east to west, the following buildings stand out: the Citicorp Center by Croce, Aflalo and Gasperini, completed in 1986, for Fernando Serapião, the last important intervention along Paulista before its usurpation by the lower density, less urban architecture along the Marginal Pinheiros;[41] the so-called Gazeta building, officially the Fundação Cásper Líbero, a 44-storey tower with a giant radio mast (1950); the Rino Levi-designed FIESP headquarters (1979); the vast 25-storey multifunctional Conjunto Nacional by Studio David Libeskind (1958); the 'L'Arche' building (1994), now occupied by HSBC. Each of these buildings calls attention to itself through spectacular form, from the Gazeta's leaning wall at ground level, to the FIESP's dramatic triangle form slicing out at ground level towards L'Arche's vast but clumsy pastiche of the Grand Arche de la Défense in Paris. Paulista is full of self-consciously spectacular buildings, whose

Studio David Libeskind, Conjunto Nacional, São Paulo, 1958. Ohtake's Renaissance Hotel is visible in the background.

appearance represents a politics of accumulation. Each seeks to outdo the other; forms become ever more baroque within the confines of the demands of the high-rise tower; surfaces become ever more decorative.

After Paulista

As local critics including Ruth Verde Zein, Fernando Serapião and Luiz Recamán have pointed out, Paulista is now in relative decline, and in pure financial terms no longer represents the core of the city's economy.[42] From Centro, to Paulista, the economic centre has now moved decisively towards the Marginal Pinheiros, a strip of relatively low-density development along the margins of the River Pinheiros, to the south of both the previous centres. This development is closely modelled on refurbished waterfronts in old northern hemisphere cities: Battery Park City in New York and Canary Wharf in London are essential reference points. The developments in all these cases are – to invoke a term invented by the sociologist Manuel Castells – meant to represent the 'space of flows', that is, an international space in which capital can move freely, and be seen to move freely.[43] The architecture of the space of flows is therefore functional on one level – it is office space of a certain kind that facilitates such transactions, but it also represents such transactions. It is vital that it looks modern, and that it looks placeless. The individual structures must have enough individuality in their envelopes to differentiate themselves from each other (too much similarity would suggest a planned economy in which capital implicitly cannot move freely), but such differentiation is mostly symbolic. The density at which these developments are built is relatively low by comparison with the old city; too much density would inhibit vehicular traffic, but also, more importantly, provide an unwelcome image of congestion. The result is the eerie, evacuated, quasi-Downtown familiar from any medium-sized North American city. As Zein describes, this new centre of São Paulo is barely urban at all:

> Like a large part of the great avenues of sp, Av. Berrini doesn't link anything to anything else. In fact, it's not an avenue: it's the cover for one of the innumerable canalized streams of the city. Overlaying the disconnected mesh of narrow streets, and parallel to the avenue along the banks of the river Pinheiros, seen from above, it is today a grand scene of battle: countless lots left vacant or with old houses awaiting demolition contrasted with buildings of varying heights and forms, in a space of transition from the peaceful neighbourhood of twenty years ago, to the tertiary subcentre of today. A good number of these new buildings are not on the Av. Berrini itself, but on the little cross-streets congested with parked cars. Temporary gaps between the buildings still permit you to see them from various angles, should the distracted visitor feel like leaving the square framing of his car window. It's not an easy task: the narrow pavements, the lack of continuity of access levels, and the excessive demarcation between private and public space make a stroll scarcely more than that between the parked car and the entrance to the elevators, and almost never the pleasure of the urban.[44]

This place may be dysfunctional for the pedestrian tourist, but it makes absolute sense from a helicopter. The main buildings are Postmodern boxes that would look at home in Atlanta or Houston: the Centro Empresarial Nações Unidas by Botti Rubin Arquitetos (1989–99), three enormous towers in reflective glass, each describing a different variation on a triangular plan; the central tower, at 158 metres, is the second tallest building in the city. As Serapião notes, the group relates formally to the World Trade Center, adjacent (1992–5, Aflalo and Gasperini architects).[45]

Botti Rubin Arquitetos, Centro Empresarial Nações Unidas, São Paulo, 1989–99.

In its emphasis on surface, it also relates to a smaller, explicitly Postmodern building by Königsberger Vannuchi architects, the Terra Brasilis. Enormously controversial when completed in 1990, this is one of the few genuinely Postmodern structures in the city. It makes ironic reference to the architecture of Niemeyer, the Paulista school, the historicist architecture of Centro and 1930s Moderne. The reference points are largely local, but the effect international.

Ohtake in São Paulo

The work of Ruy Ohtake, little known outside Brazil, defines better than anyone else the present-day politics of spectacle in São Paulo. Ohtake (born 1937) is a generation younger than Niemeyer. He was taught by

Königsberger
Vannuchi Arquitetos,
Terra Brasilis, São
Paulo, 1986–1990.

Artigas at FAU-USP in the mid-1960s, and his early work is recognizably Modernist: there are a series of well-detailed apartment and highly functional blocks in São Paulo, for example.[46] His publicly expressed views on politics and Brazilian society indicate – at least on the surface – support for a similar range of views to those of his teachers. In 1964, following the military coup, he was prevented from taking up a teaching post at Mackenzie Presbyterian University's School of Architecture in São Paulo by the School's board because of his association with the politically suspect FAU-USP. If he was not a member of the Communist Party as were Artigas and Niemeyer, he nevertheless appears to share their suspicion of the consumer society, of property speculation, of the accumulation of capital in general. Publicly, he seems to regret that so many of his compatriots are so poor. There is a well-publicized scheme of 2005 to brighten up 278 houses in Heliópolis, São Paulo's largest *favela*, with a few licks of paint.[47] Like Niemeyer, Ohtake felt that the world would be a better place if it were oriented more around art and less around making money – a sentiment represented in built form perhaps in the Ohtake Cultural (1995–2004), a striking pink and gold mixed-use tower in the Pinheiros district, named after the architect's mother, a successful abstract painter.

In all his public pronouncements, Ohtake is a romantic of the left, who publicly disdains the symbols of consumer culture. He claims to have no car, computer, mobile phone or even wristwatch.[48] For his advocates, his architecture represents a retort to the spectacular society: for the critic Roberto Segre, it is 'a learned and socially responsible alternative to the proliferation of anonymous shopping malls and strict duplicates of Disneyland and other First World theme parks. It is not by mere chance that, due to his ethical and aesthetic standing, Ohtake has never been commissioned with this type of job.'[49]

Yet during the past decade, no other architect in Brazil has provided such an effective image *of* the spectacular city. Ohtake's projects – with the exception of Heliópolis – are for a series of more or less blue-chip clients: private villas, shopping centres, luxury hotels, private cultural centres. And the form of these luxury projects updates the meaning of architectural spectacle. Most of the spectacle of São Paulo becomes rather tawdry at the level of individual buildings. The sense of spectacle is produced by accumulation; the astonishing skyline of Paulista, for example. Ohtake is an exception, however. His individual works have the capacity to surprise or astonish in the same terms as the best recent work by Libeskind or Hadid.

The towers for the Renaissance Hotel, at the far western end of the Paulista district, and the Ohtake Cultural arts centre are good starting points. Neither is particularly high, nor are they structurally remarkable; both are concrete-framed, clad in coloured glass panels. But the use of colour is extraordinary. Both make use of rich, vibrant colours – pinks, purples, bronzes – that are quite unlike anything seen before in local building. The cladding itself and the use of horizontal bands of contrasting colour make these exceptionally graphic buildings. They have no depth; they appear two- rather than three-dimensional, almost exactly like oversized cigarette packets, an effect exaggerated by the

Ruy Ohtake, Ohtake
Cultural, São Paulo,
1995–2004.

overwhelmingly grey colour of the surrounding city. The same tricks
are in evidence in the Edifício Berrini 500 and the Edifício Santa
Catarina, the latter, at the time of writing, under construction on the
Avenida Paulista and a sign perhaps of that area's revival. All these buildings make use of strong colour applied in large, flat areas. At the same
time, they also deploy some unlikely forms. The Berrini 500 and Ohtake
Cultural both have floors offset in a rippling pattern, a sculptural trope
seen in a number of buildings. Ohtake Cultural, meanwhile, has bizarre
projections that serve only to advertise its own presence: a great jutting
half-cornice (in pink) and two giant purple pilasters at ground level in
the shape of starfruit.[50]

More striking still is the Hotel Unique, rated by the *New York Times*'
architecture critic Paul Goldberger as one of the new Seven Wonders of
the World in 2004.[51] Unlike any other building in existence, this is a giant

Ruy Ohtake,
Renaissance Hotel,
São Paulo, 1998.

slice of watermelon propped up at each end by the thinnest of columns. Its port-holed bedrooms are the melon's seeds. The vast lobby and grounds are patrolled by Armani-clad guards. On the occasion the author visited in 2005, they seemed to outnumber the guests. The hotel's owners, perhaps under instruction from the architect, control the distribution of the hotel's image, of its spectacle. It is forbidden to take pictures unless one is a guest: the guards spend much of their time controlling this aspect of the hotel's life. The major everyday security issue here seemed to be the security of the hotel *as image*.[52]

The Spectacular City

The tendency to spectacle is, however, best seen not in the work of individual architects, but, as in São Paulo in the 1960s and '70s, in the

Ruy Ohtake, Edifício Berrini 500, São Paulo, 2008, detail.

Ruy Ohtake, Hotel Unique, 1999–2002.

creation of vast cityscapes by developers. São Paulo's growth has lately slowed, but many parts of Brazil, typically those that missed out on earlier development booms, have become spectacular. Recife, for example, the capital of the north-eastern state of Pernambuco, has developed in a decade a remarkable strip of beach hotels in the southern suburb of Boa Viagem, which locals claim – with justification – to be as impressive as Copacabana. Águas Claras on the north-western outskirts of Brasília, an instant high-rise city, planned by Paulo Zimbres, is now rapidly

supplanting the Pilot Plan in scale (discussed in more detail in chapter Three). Most extraordinary of all is the neighbourhood of Barra de Tijuca, a 10-kilometre strip of high-rises and shopping malls 20 kilometres to the south of Rio de Janeiro, which is now the place where the city's wealthy live and play. Barra, organized around the great six-lane Avenida das Américas, was designed by Lúcio Costa in a project of 1968 that reiterated some of the principles of Brasília. Traffic and pedestrians were well separated; urban spaces and housing types were defined by a strict formal hierarchy; and access to transport (both public and private) provided a rationale for the overall form of the city. The development as realized under the agency SUDEBAR was something else – a wild, undisciplined sprawl little different in character from any other highway development in any Brazilian city.[53] This common assessment, however, devalues the epic scale and colour of the development that has occurred. Among its more remarkable sights is New York City Center, a huge indoor mall replete with a half-scale replica of the Statue of Liberty, now a local landmark. These spectacular new cities exist largely outside architectural

Boa Viagem, Recife, 2006.

EM BREVE UM NOVO PARQUE PARA A CIDADE

Barra da Tijuca,
Rio de Janeiro,
looking north
towards Copacabana.

discourse, and are normally discussed as representations of Brazil's problems – its inequalities of wealth distribution, for example – rather than attempts to solve them. But in scale, ambition and proliferation, in their own way they are as impressive as anything produced by the Modern Movement.

chapter seven

The Politics of Public Space

The development of an architecture of spectacle (described in chapter Six) coincided with, and in all probability contributed to, an erosion of Brazil's realm. Brazil's historic architecture includes some of the same luxurious public spaces as one might find in Portugal, Spain or Italy. For the best Modernist architecture built on this tradition in the twentieth century, think of the well-appointed public space around the MES building in Rio. But in the second half of the twentieth century, and particularly from the 1970s, Brazil's public spaces increasingly became associated with fear and violence. São Paulo's great civic space, the Praça da Sé, which frames the cathedral, became the centre of the city's homeless population, and was increasingly perceived as dangerous.[1] Crime, violence and the fear of these things produced an inclination to live and work in secure environments. Gated compounds, *condominios fechados*, have proliferated, eroding the very concept of public space. Traditional, unsecured neighbourhoods in the big cities have decayed. Civic spaces have come to be associated with crime and disorder, and, sometimes, officially sanctioned violence. It is a pattern repeated throughout the Americas, but Brazil's experience, as usual, is peculiarly exaggerated. The problem is well represented by the pattern of urbanization of Brazil's largest cities. Avenida Paulista, for example, has, with the exception of the well-used space underneath MASP, virtually no useable public space; the Parque Trianon opposite is perceived by many as too dangerous to be frequented on a regular basis.

This chapter discusses the politics of public space in the Brazilian city since the 1970s through a series of iconic urbanistic projects. First is Roberto Burle Marx's remodelling of Copacabana beach; then Oscar Niemeyer's Memorial da América Latina, a monumental reinvention of the ancient form of the agora; Paulo Mendes da Rocha's involvement in the remodelling of the Parque da Luz in São Paulo in the late 1990s; and finally, the mother of all gated communities, Alphaville. In each of these projects is an attempt to engage with the problematic of the public realm, underwritten by a belief in the agency of public space to change

Roberto Burle Marx, Avenida Atlântica, Rio de Janiero at Leme, renewed 1971.

(and, specifically, improve) public behaviour. It is also motivated by a belief – similar to that found in the Anglophone world – that large-scale pieces of urban infrastructure, such as São Paulo's *minhocão*, could be profoundly inimical to the cultivation of the public realm and that a more sensitive approach might be required.

The projects I discuss in this chapter were built during the forty years after 1970. In international architectural practice during this period, there was a revival of interest in the public realm. Often a vehicle for a critique of mainstream Modernism, the advocacy of the public realm held it to be a complex socio-cultural phenomenon that could not be produced by rational means. Art, in other words, needed to be reinserted into the urban process. A crucial statement of this idea can be found in Aldo Van Eyck's preface to Joseph Rykwert's seminal book, *The Idea of a Town*. Here the Dutch architect describes the renewal of interest in urbanism as a problem of aesthetics more than function; he describes town planning as fundamentally irrational, art rather than engineering; it should act as a reminder to architects that a city 'also had to enshrine the hopes and fears of its citizens'; it should be symbolic.[2] Statements of this kind suddenly abounded in the mid-1970s, especially in the Anglophone world, and they can be traced back to the work of Lewis Mumford, as well as related to such diverse contemporary figures as the sociologist Richard Sennett, the architect Leon Krier, the new urbanist planner Andrés Duany and the polemicist prince, Charles, Prince of Wales.[3] All these figures in different ways found fault with Modernism through its indifference to the art of urbanism.

To some extent, Brazil's Modernist urbanism has been subject to the same critique. James Holston's book on Brasília, *The Modernist City* (discussed in chapter Three), is infused with nostalgia for the Portuguese colonial public realm. Holston longs for cities of street corners and squares, cities whose traditional public spaces gently mediate between private and public lives – or at least do so in the imagination. Brasília by contrast has no street corners and consequently 'lacks the bustle of street life'.[4]

But as both Sérgio Buarque de Holanda and Gilberto Freyre described, Brazilian notions of civic life are notably different from those of Europe.[5] Brazil never developed the civic life of the European city-state like sixteenth-century Siena, in which the church, government, commerce and the individual were all seen to hold each other to account.[6] Such institutional conditions were, and generally are, alien in Brazil, in which, barring the church, one or other power tends to hold sway, with all the problems that entails. The result, in architectural terms, is a relative absence of attempts to frame civic life – and where such attempts exist, a general indifference to them, and a relative willingness to see them decline. Great public spaces undoubtedly exist, but are infrequent by comparison with Europe.

In part this has to do with the pattern of colonization in Brazil. Brazil's early settlements are characterized by informality above all. As Norma Evenson has described, early Portuguese settlements were imagined simply as frontier or trading posts, rather than the material form of a superior colonizing civilization. The contrast with Spanish colonial practice could not be more marked, in which every new city in Spanish

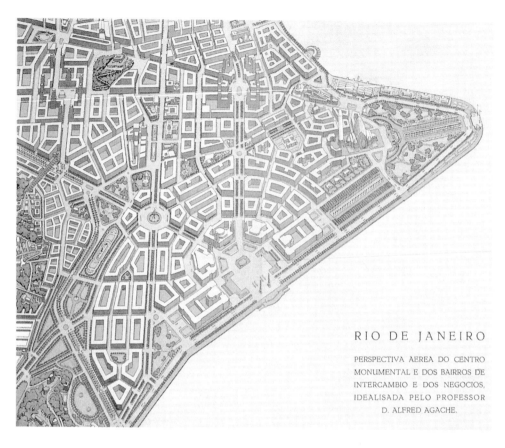

RIO DE JANEIRO

PERSPECTIVA AEREA DO CENTRO
MONUMENTAL E DOS BAIRROS DE
INTERCAMBIO E DOS NEGOCIOS,
IDEALISADA PELO PROFESSOR
D. ALFRED AGACHE.

Alfred Agache, plan
for Rio de Janeiro,
1930s.

America was laid out with military precision, institutions clearly marked
and given a place in the urban hierarchy, and a clear place for civic life
defined.[7] Portuguese colonial urbanism was by contrast informal and
provisional.

It occasionally, however, flirted with authority, and when it did so,
it set few limits. Jean-Baptiste Debret's plan of 1839 for Rio is one early
instance of this, a precursor of Baron Haussmann's mid-nineteenth-
century plan for Paris. Debret's ideas were played out in certain aspects
of late nineteenth-century Rio, especially the laying out of the neo-
classical Avenida Rio Branco. In 1930 another Frenchman, Alfred Agache,
proposed a much more comprehensive re-planning of the capital on
neo-classical lines. The centrepiece was a gigantic new square facing
out to sea at Flamengo. It was 87,500 square metres in area, and defined
a new government quarter, comprising new buildings for both houses
of parliament, exhibition halls for the fine arts, commerce and industry,

Alfred Agache, plan
for Rio de Janeiro,
1930s.

as well as a great ceremonial hall, all built in the 'ponderous stripped
classicism' later favoured in 'Nazi Germany' and 'Fascist Italy'. Evenson
wrote of a plaza serving as the site of 'military parades, civic demonstrations [and] a ceremonial place of welcome where officials could
receive visitors disembarking from their ships by means of launches
which would carry them to a waterfront stair of honour flanked by
ceremonial columns'.[8] The life imagined in this great square was official
and authoritarian, concerned primarily with the display of power. It
was a 'megalomaniacally scaled vision of an imaginary superstate'
where 'antlike formations of troops would echo in their geometric
formations the rigid massing of the buildings while at night search-
lights would illuminate and unify the assemblage'.[9] A *Zeppelinfeld* in
the tropics, in other words. Needless to say, Le Corbusier admired the
Agache plan for Rio, and his own plans for the city have much in common
with it. Both plans are attached to the idea of civic space as an expression of power. Everything is gigantic, and social life is replaced by
mass demonstrations. The distractions of bourgeois civic life are kept
to the minimum.[10]

Burle Marx on the Beach

Both the informal and authoritarian approaches to urbanism are much
in evidence in Brazil. The development of Brazilian cities remains by
(continental) European standards fundamentally disorganized. At the
same time, all its big cities have been touched by expressions of authority: Rio has the Avenida Rio Branco, Belo Horizonte has its gridiron,

Roberto Burle Marx,
Avenida Atlântica,
Rio de Janiero at
Ipanema, renewed
1971, photographed
in 2006.

São Paulo its Avenida Paulista. Then there is Brasília, a city whose central areas one struggles to read as anything but expressions of authority. On its monumental axis, there is no better large-scale expression of Le Corbusier's imagination of an ideal modern social life. The case studies of this chapter are those spaces that have been conceived of in some critical relation to these default modes of informality and authoritarianism.

The first case is the remodelling of the Avenida Atlântica (1969–72) by the landscape architect Roberto Burle Marx, a close friend and collaborator of Oscar Niemeyer. It is without question the best-known public space in Brazil, and the defining feature of Copacabana. It was (and remains) apart from the beach, an 'unbroken wall of high-rises'.[11] By the early 1970s the former resort town was a metonym for Rio in general, supplanting the original city in the local, as well as the tourist imagination. Failure to live there, wrote Evenson, was 'regarded as a major eccentricity requiring apologetic explanation'.[12]

Burle Marx's scheme was part of the largest infrastructural project since the creation, between 1892 and 1904, of the tunnels providing access to Rio, and the laying out of the original Avenida Atlântica. The remodelling involved the building of a six-lane highway along the beachfront, in an attempt to alleviate the chronic traffic congestion in

Detail of mosaics on Av. Atlântica. Probably the largest mosaic in the world.

the neighbourhood. Building the highway without adversely affecting the beach involved (as described by one critic) 'moving the Atlantic ocean about 60m to the south'.[13] The National Hydraulic laboratory of Lisbon dealt with the engineering problems.[14] Burle Marx had already designed the huge land reclamation scheme of the Aterro do Flamengo in 1962.[15] His design was straightforward: the original pavement along the Avenida was defined by a wave pattern in black and white Portuguese mosaic tiles, an iconic design first seen in Manaus during the late nineteenth-century rubber boom. Burle Marx retained all 3 km of this, but had it shifted to its new position. The remainder of the project

223 The Politics of Public Space

was the amelioration of the impact of the highway. He added a further two pedestrian boulevards parallel to this one, a surface area of a further 45,000 square metres in total, which he decorated with mosaic tiles arranged in his own neo-Cubist designs: overall, it was probably the largest mosaic design in the world.[16] The patterns were varied, and designed to be visible from all levels. Their effect is most striking from a height, but they are also well visible at street level, and (even) from a car (a means of alleviating the 'monotony' of the drive, thought one critic, although this avenue scarcely needs more distractions).[17] As well as the tiles, there were Italian almond trees, arranged in clusters of four or five with benches beneath.[18]

The Avenida Atlântica is a fantastic piece of urban architecture, in scale, in popularity and in critical status: Burle Marx, like his contemporary Niemeyer, seems to have largely evaded criticism. For such a large piece of architecture that involved such a dramatic alteration to the seafront, one hardly notices that it is in fact a piece of architecture, rather than a natural extension to the beach. As Leenhardt suggests, in the project 'the city became landscape; landscape became architecture'.[19] And at first sight, it bears comparison with the world's most popular public spaces. In its cafés, its kiosks, its beach bars, its groves of trees, bodies are in different ways put on display, observed and consumed. Tourists mingle with locals, street hawkers sell baseball caps and coconuts, joggers and cyclists speed up and down, bodybuilders lift weights, sunbathers work on their tans, street children pickpocket tourists, and prostitutes tout for business at the doors of the high-rise hotels. Hardly anyone wears anything apart from bathing costumes and flip-flops. It may be heterogeneous, but it appears also for the most part civilized, a manifestation of the Freyre myth of a multicultural Brazil, a country cheerfully tolerant of difference.

Brazil's inequalities are, however, manifest here as strongly as anywhere else. The very generosity of the space sustains criminal activity as well as promenading. And it is obvious too how much the erotics of the promenade is always imbued with power. As I have argued elsewhere, the promenade is never a free space, but is about the enactment of social rituals that are acquired, and in which power is always, one way or another, enacted.[20] Perhaps this is why, after a gap of fifteen years, and when Brazilian modern architecture was as unfashionable as it could be, the *Architectural Review* took a sudden interest in Burle Marx's work at Copacabana.[21] At the time the AR was writing, in 1985, Postmodernism as an architectural style was at its height, and in Europe and the United States schemes proliferated for public realm works, in which the city was reimagined as a space of leisure and consumption:

Léon Krier's work in Luxembourg and Richard Rogers's in London are good examples, both concerned with remaking the city as a fundamentally theatrical space. In both cases, social reform is abandoned in favour of theatre.[22]

The Memorial da América Latina

The remodelled Avenida Atlântica could be interpreted therefore as a proto-Postmodern space. A revival of the bourgeois public realm, it is a space for promenading and display underpinned by an understanding of architecture as decoration rather than social engineering. Dating from a little over a decade later, it is another attempt to imagine the public realm in the Brazilian city beyond the usual poles of informality and authoritarianism. This is the Memorial da América Latina (Latin American Memorial) by Oscar Niemeyer. An extraordinary public space in north-western São Paulo, it is widely considered a failure, but is no less interesting or important for that.[23]

    The Memorial was commissioned in 1987 by Orestes Quércia, then governor of the state of São Paulo, and completed in a remarkable 519 days at a cost of approximately US$48 million. Inaugurated by Quércia at 10 a.m. on Friday, 18 March 1989, its completion coincided with a worsening economic crisis in Brazil, and the start of a presidential electoral campaign in which the governor was to play an important role.

Oscar Niemeyer,
Memorial da América
Latina, 1987–9.

One measure of the crisis was the incumbent president José Sarney's popularity, or lack of it: a poll conducted on the same day as the Memorial's inauguration found that an unprecedented 62 per cent of Brazilians regarded Sarney's premiership to be 'bad' or 'very bad'.[24] Quércia, as leader of Brazil's richest and most powerful state, and de facto kingmaker, wasted no time at the Memorial's inauguration in declaring support for his favoured candidate. But this was in many respects not the time for such grandiose gestures, and the Memorial was controversial from the start.

The Memorial lies at Barra Funda, a piece of post-industrial inner city, about 8 kilometres to the north-west of Praça da Sé. The area is cut through with urban motorways, rail lines and the canalized River Tietê, and punctuated with huge office towers. The Memorial occupies an area of some 150,000 square metres on a roughly horizontal, east–west axis adjacent to the metro station. It consists of two related spaces, split by the six-lane Avenida Auro Soares de Moura Andrade. The two pieces of land are linked by a curving concrete footbridge, designed, like everything else here, by Niemeyer. The two parcels of land that define the space are roughly the same size, but irregular, and slightly offset. They do not corres- pond, at any rate, to any traditional form of a public space. The Memorial's surfaces are exceptionally hard. There are a few, largely symbolic, palms, but otherwise the concrete and glass are unremitting. There is no shelter and no sense of enclosure. The towers and motorways of the surrounding

Oscar Niemeyer, Memorial da América Latina, São Paulo, 1987–9.

Oscar Niemeyer, Memorial da América Latina, auditorium interior.

city intrude visually and aurally. The Memorial *is*, however, enclosed, by a 2-metre-high steel security fence, which allows entrance and exit to be controlled to a small passage near the Barra Funda metro station. The presence of the security fence and the harsh character of the concrete give the Memorial the feeling of a military compound. The Praça dos Tres Poderes in Brasília was criticized on the same grounds, but is positively picturesque by comparison, its formality alleviated by some luxurious planting and the extensive use of marble and other tactile materials.

The Memorial, like the Praça dos Tres Poderes, is a space that inverts traditional figure–ground relationships. It does not therefore enclose space, but leaves it open. The individual buildings are conceived as sculptures, and the Memorial space a form of sculpture park. It is, to invoke Colin Rowe and Fred Koetter on the Modernist city, 'the sparse, anticipatory city of isolated objects and continuous voids, the alleged city of freedom and "universal" society'.[25] Nevertheless, about half of the space is built up, with six major architectural elements, all of which deploy the same basic materials, white-painted concrete and black solar glass. The forms are quasi-*gestalts*, instantly recognizable: here is a curve, there is a double vault, there a cylinder, there a pyramid, each form clearly identifiable, and clearly separated from the others. On the northern side there is a 'Salão de Atos' ('Hall of Events' – a kind of secular

cathedral), a library and a restaurant; and on the southern side a 'Pavilhão da Creatividade' (Pavilion of Creativity), an exhibition of handicrafts from all over the continent, an auditorium and an administrative block. In the middle of the northern part stands the Memorial's metonymic sculptural image, an abstracted 7-metre-high concrete hand in whose palm is inscribed a map of the Americas in red, like a wound. Blood drips from this down the wrist, as if to say that the history of the continent is marked everywhere by violence. Niemeyer provided an uncompromising text to accompany the sculpture: 'sweat, blood and poverty have marked the history of this oppressed Latin America. Now we must unite it, defend it, and make it independent and content.' Under pressure from Quércia, he changed this to 'this is a hand that reminds us of past days of strife, poverty and abandonment'.[26] One final building makes up the Memorial, although not strictly within its boundaries. The site of a future 'Latin American Parliament' (Parlatino) occupies a large, cylindrical, glass-clad building at the hinge between the two parts of the site, but just outside its boundary.

What ideas motivated the construction of the Memorial? For one local critic the Memorial might be conceived of first as a 'post-*abertura*' project along with the Sambódromo in Rio de Janeiro, in other words a spectacular public project designed to provide the country with a new image after the military government.[27] The idea apparently came from Quércia; the sociologist Darcy Ribeiro provided the main theme. Ribeiro's work had long explored the nature of Latin America, and he had long argued for a political organization to match the continent's scale and population. His work of the 1960s and '70s argued in favour of a continental conception of Latin America, despite some obvious difficulties. Its geographic unity seemed clear enough in terms of a continental outline, but within the continents of Central and South America, communications were extremely poor. In Ribeiro's *América Latina: A Pátria Grande*, he wrote of the geography that 'we live as if we were an archipelago of islands linked by the sea and the air, and that, more frequently return abroad, to the great world economic centres, than inside'.[28]

It is also, however, a civic square, with specific effects intended. Both the library and the Salão de Atos were meant to 'create a sense of ritual gravity and religious solemnity'; the Salão de Atos was meant to be 'the most solemn space in SP as well as the most popular'.[29] The architectural forms, although Modernist, were supposed to echo the typical form of a Plaza de Armas of a Spanish American city – a space in other words in which the elements of civil society would come together in one architectural scheme. Here one would find typically the major church or cathedral, the town hall or other representative of government, and a space for markets or other informal commercial events. São Paulo, Darcy Ribeiro declared in an interview on the Memorial's inauguration, 'needs a square like this'.[30]

However, the critical response to the project was profoundly negative, partly a result of the timing. As the *Folha de São Paulo* noted, the inauguration took place in a period of deepening economic uncertainty.[31] On the day before the Memorial's inauguration, a student protest against cuts in the level of grant funding led to a violent battle with the military police, briefly closing the Avenida Paulista.[32] Against this background, the Memorial seemed an unnecessary extravagance, a luxurious gesture the city and the state could at that moment ill afford. There was suspicion too of the political motives behind the project, and possible corruption.[33] The inauguration was itself something of a failure. Its organizers expected 350,000 to turn up on the day, and were somewhat embarrassed to welcome just 1,000. Even so, the Memorial struggled to cope: the March sun and the lack of shade in the Praça Cívica threatened to dehydrate the guests, and emergency supplies of water were twice required.[34]

The most direct criticisms came from Brazilian architects, marking something of a sea-change in attitudes to Niemeyer, a figure who had lived in a world largely free of criticism since Max Bill in 1954.[35] Ruth Verde Zein complained that Niemeyer's best work was done in conjunction with an urbanist, namely Lúcio Costa. Of the Memorial, she wrote, 'Niemeyer is, unhappily, alone'.[36] The result was a series of buildings and spaces that did not conform to any conventionally understood norms. The Pavilion of Creativity was so 'fluid' a category of building as to be effectively meaningless, 'and nobody has the least vague idea to what end is served by the Salão de Atos'.[37] Edson Mahfuz identified a number of functional mistakes. There was no shade, because the architect forbade it; the sun shone directly into the library, threatening the collection of books; the detailing was poor; the peripheral location prejudiced from the start the likelihood of it being able to perform any meaningful civic functions. The right place for that would of course be the Praça da Sé, the literal centre of the city and traditional locus of political protest.[38] His main impression was desolation. Eduardo Comas wrote simply that the project was 'rancid', 'an unequivocal sign that the dream ended; it has the flavour of a hangover, the Ash Wednesday of a modernity that has now passed'.[39] Comas's bleak assessment is hard to disagree with now: the complex is little visited, and seemingly little cared for, an incipient ruin.

Mendes da Rocha's Public Space Projects

Contemporary with the Memorial da América Latina is a comparable public space, MUBE (Museu da Escultura Brasileira / Brazilian Museum of Sculpture), by the Pritzker Prize-winning Paulistano architect Paulo Mendes da Rocha (born 1928). Since the mid-1980s Mendes da Rocha's work has made the public realm central to his work. MUBE was built between 1986 and 1995, and as can be seen readily from photographs, is not really a building at all, but a square on a street corner. Located in Jardim Paulista, an upmarket São Paulo neighbourhood, its site was the venue of a proposed shopping centre, fiercely opposed by a local residents' association (the Sociedade de Amigos dos Jardins Europa e Paulistano e Sociedade de Amigos dos Museus). In its place they proposed a museum, although the brief asked for a building that did not

Paulo Mendes da
Rocha, MUBE, São
Paulo, 1986–95.

impose itself on the site. This was possible because the museum was envisaged not as the home for a collection, but a space for the *study* of public sculpture focused on 'documentation, courses, exhibitions' and so on.[40] No more than 30 per cent of the land area was to be built on – it was therefore conceived of less as a building devoted to the exhibition of an archive of work and more as a modern take on the garden.[41]

As built, it is indeed at first sight barely a building at all, more a park on a street corner. The museum is essentially subterranean, set beneath a concrete beam, no less than 60 metres in length and supported only at each end; the beam sets the limits of the site and shades both the entrance to the two exhibition spaces and the diverse activities that now regularly fill the plaza, providing rental income for the museum. An antiques fair regularly occupies the space, and it is also apparently a popular setting for weddings, and launches for new models of car. The rich variety of the museum's uses, plus the now decayed surface of the concrete structure, describe a more humane experience than that suggested by photographs at the time of its opening. What seemed an unforgiving, austere and depopulated structure in image is now a mostly successful

Paulo Mendes da Rocha, Praça do Patriarca, São Paulo, 1999–2002.

public space. Nevertheless, its success needs to be qualified: this is a public space that provides some relief from the frenetic market economy, but it is not value-free. Very much like the reformed public spaces of Oriol Bohigas's Barcelona, realized at the same time, MUBE communicates an essentially bourgeois conception of the public realm based around a small number of conventional and highly regulated leisure activities.[42] This is not a space of free expression, but of politeness. Its relative success compared to the Memorial da América Latina has to do in large part with its acceptance of its role. It is far less ambitious in concept than the Memorial, it occupies an already privileged space; within its limited parameters, it seems to work.[43]

Mendes da Rocha's other public projects represent similarly conservative, but successful, tactics in addressing the problem of the approach to the public realm. The Praça do Patriarca (1992) is a remodelling of a public square in the old commercial centre of São Paulo. Close to the iconic Viaduto do Chá, it is superficially no more than the refurbishment of the entrance to the Anhangabaú metro station, but it does it with minimalist grandeur. A huge white steel canopy, suspended from a concrete beam, now shades the restored paving tiles of the square, the latter the same formal device as found at MUBE. It is on the one hand an extremely simple solution to the problem, comprising just two simple forms. It is huge in scale, however, and has – as a number of critics noted – a serious effect on the views of the surrounding square, including a rare seventeenth-century church.[44] Its simplicity connotes functionality in the Modernist tradition. In reality, this is a piece of minimalist sculpture, whose real function is simply to mark place. The remodelling of the Pinacoteca do Estado (1997), alongside the grand Victorian promenading space of the Parque da Luz, is a brilliant conversion of a nineteenth-century school of engineering into a modern art museum. Mendes da Rocha simply stripped out everything from the old building – up to and including the plastering of the walls, inside and out, revealing a rich red brick. The building now resembles a Roman ruin. He then glazed the interior courts, and added oxidized steel gangways at first-floor level for access. It is again a marked contrast to the building's surroundings, the fag-end of São Paulo's old centre, in 2008 still a mess of urban motorways, vacant lots and prostitution on an industrial scale. In these projects, Mendes da Rocha is working in an essentially conservative tradition in which the small-scale intervention is privileged over the grand plan, and in which European bourgeois traditions of public space are reasserted.

Urban Acupuncture

During the 1980s and '90s there were a number of widely publicized urban projects in Curitiba, the capital of the state of Paraná in southern Brazil. Here, in this city of two million, an architect, Jaime Lerner, was, most unusually, elected mayor three times between 1971 and 1992 (Lerner went on to be elected twice to become governor of the state of Paraná). Lerner's initiatives in the city received much attention from architects outside Brazil, perhaps because on the one hand they conformed to First World notions of what good city governance might be in the 1980s and '90s, and on the other, his projects for Curitiba went further than was normally possible in Europe and North America.[45] Lerner had romantic notions of city life, but was also a pragmatist of the first order. As an urbanist, he abandoned the Modernist belief in total planning, a reversal of everything that Costa and Niemeyer stood for at Brasília. By contrast, he was a believer in cities as processes, in which forms could be influenced by small actions, but not controlled. He was also an aesthete. His urbanism was strongly informed by the look and texture of the nineteenth-century European city; his plans for Curitiba invoked the civic spirit of nineteenth-century urban reformers in Europe and the United States, and sublimated their preferred urban forms: parks, pedestrian boulevards, public squares, covered arcades, museums. Curitiba was, in other words, another experiment in the bourgeois public realm.

His position is well described by the book *Acupuntura Urbana* ('Urban Acupuncture').[46] Written for a mass audience, this is a series of tiny vignettes describing ideal urban spaces. His preferred solution to urban problems – 'acupuncture' – is a telling metaphor, suggesting a preference for small-scale, local intervention, therapy rather than surgery. There is a great emphasis on spaces of culture: in the introduction the Guggenheim Museum in Bilbao and the Pompidou Centre in Paris are cited as exemplars of good practice. And the urban space of the Ramblas in Barcelona – the subject of a chapter – is identified as an ideal public space. The Ramblas is good, he writes, because of its essentially theatrical nature, turning all those who walk through it into either spectators or performers; it is always busy, always full of life. 'Acupuncture' may not always involve architecture per se: in another section of the book, Lerner recalls as mayor being presented with a request from the representatives of a neighbourhood who wanted improvement work to cease as a matter of urgency in order to protect a local spring. About New York, he writes how Korean immigrants have revitalized the city's urban life by opening stores around the clock. In terms of Lerner's work in Curitiba, significant

Paulo Mendes da Rocha, Pinacoteca do Estado, São Paulo, 1993–7.

Pinacoteca do Estado, interior.

projects include public spaces such as the refurbishment of the city's botanical gardens and the creation of the pedestrian-oriented realm of the Rua das Flores, imagined as a southern Brazilian Ramblas. His best-known public project is not, however, a space per se, but a piece of transport infrastructure; this is the city's rapid bus network, introduced from the 1970s and making use of federal money earmarked for a metro system. Lerner's administration found that they could build a far more extensive bus network running on segregated lanes than an equivalent heavy or light rail metro. It invested in articulated Volvo buses (capable of carrying 600 passengers) and a network of metro-style bus stops, controlling access to the system and providing ticket machines. The system was much admired outside Brazil, not so much for its efficiency, but for its aesthetics. This is a system that provides, if nothing else, a compelling image of what a dense, pedestrian-oriented city might look like. Lerner's work may be criticized on the other hand for its very emphasis on the look of the public realm; his projects are dominated by the idea of the city as theatre, in which the real beneficiaries are the better off. Some projects – such as one that exchanged bags of refuse for bus tickets – seemed to be aimed at the superficial beautification of the public realm rather than the social problems that might have caused its degradation in the first place. Reading *Acupuntura Urbana*, it is hard to escape the impression that its imagination of the city is a fundamentally touristic one: the city is a space of leisure and pleasure above all, not work.[47] Perhaps this is why Curitiba's experiments have not been much replicated outside the city.

Lerner's perspective is nevertheless important because it maps onto a recent Euro-American attitude towards the city. In this view, public space and civic life are represented principally as image. It becomes very important to supply architectural images of ordered city life, without necessarily paying attention to the institutions that underpin such order. The urban promenade becomes a civic duty. Something of this can be seen in a number of large-scale urban regeneration projects around Brazil in the 1990s. *Rio-Cidade*, run from 1993 to 2004 under three administrations, was an ambitious programme of urban housekeeping in the city of Rio de Janeiro. Focused on upgrading basic street infrastructure, it replaced drains, upgraded street lighting and replaced telecommunications networks, burying cables underground. Its scope was broad, and the disruption it caused considerable – but its aesthetics were pragmatic and conservative. This was, like Oriol Bohigas's Barcelona, a city concerned primarily with tidying things up rather than doing anything radically new. Many of the results – such as the tastefully refurbished Paço Imperial, an eighteenth-century square near the old port, incorporating a contemporary arts

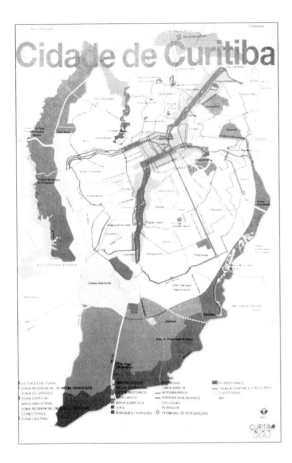

Curitiba plan.

centre – recall Bohigas's city, and they have achieved something of the same popularity with tourists and locals alike.

At the opposite end of the social scale, the same pragmatic aesthetics can be found in a variety of schemes from the 1980s to the present to revitalize *favelas*. As discussed in chapter Five, official policy towards the *favela* has lurched from acceptance to refusal and back again, but since the 1980s most policy has concentrated on accepting them as fact, and gradually bringing them into the official built realm. A crucial political project in Rio has been *Favela-Bairro*, begun in 1995 with a grant of $180 million from the Inter-American Development Bank. The project focused on the pragmatic upgrading of *favela* infrastructure combined with educational programmes. At the level of architecture, the shift in attitude towards the *favela* has been reflected in the increasing discussion of *favela*-based schemes in professional journals such as *Projeto Design*. Recent projects in Brazil's large cities have moved beyond questions of basic infrastructure or housing to the aesthetics of the public realm. In January 2000 *Projeto Design* described a scheme for four Rio *favelas* (Fubá-Campinho, Vidigal, Salgueiro, Fernão Cardim) by the architect Jorge Mário Jáuregui, in which, through the introduction of new public areas, it would 'plant a seed or urbanity in the heart of each community'.[48] In Fuba-Campinho, Jáuregui proposed a giant urban space, containing many kinds of cultural and sporting facilities. In a statement worthy of Oriol Bohigas, he made clear his belief in the capacity of well-designed public space to inculcate good behaviour:

> urbanizing *favelas* implies above all thinking about architecture and urbanism in its function as a social service, capable of facilitating

access to citizenship . . . the improvement in the quality of everyday spaces produces a positive influence on the self-worth of the citizen.[49]

In 2006 *L'Architecture d'aujourd'hui* carried a feature about a similar scheme, this time actually built, for the remodelling of the market at Rocinha, Rio's biggest and best-known *favela*.[50] This was on the one hand a piece of simple infrastructure, a 150-metre-long covered street, whose roof was composed of a series of steel masts holding a tensile roof; located between a busy bus stop and an evangelical church with 50,000 daily visitors, and intended for 24-hour use, it was made of tough materials. But the rhetoric about it extended far beyond function. This was a piece of public space, designed for the 'diffusion of information', the 'preservation of popular culture', 'modes of alternative consumption' outside the formal market, 'an urban landmark'. The rhetoric about this space was remarkably similar to that found in that about both Barcelona's reconstruction in the 1980s and the so-called new-urbanism. In all these examples, the civilizing influence of public space is upheld.

Alphaville

But drive a few kilometres south of Rio de Janeiro, and it is hard to escape the impression that these worthy, but small-scale bits of urban house-keeping are more or less futile: the city's real future lies elsewhere. The city's growth is polarized between the continued sprouting of *favelas* (of which only a few will ever be properly urbanized) and the development

Alphaville, 2005.

of gargantuan gated communities in the Barra da Tijuca. Both Lúcio Costa and Oscar Niemeyer had a hand in the original development of this coastal strip in the 1970s, but the place now represents traditional urbanism turned on its head. From a distance it might be another Copacabana, a long strip of high-rises set along a curving beach. But get closer, and the impression is quite different: the density is low; the buildings are isolated elements set within their own high-security compounds; neighbourhoods have been replaced by air-conditioned malls.

The apogee of this tendency in Brazil is undoubtedly Alphaville, begun in 1974 by the architect Yojiro Takaoka and the engineer Renato de Albuquerque.[51] Alphaville lies about 30 kilometres to the west of São Paulo, adjoining the River Tietê and the established city of Baueri. It has been a remarkably successful phenomenon, with offshoots now to be found outside Fortaleza and Curitiba, and even in Portugal. The São Paulo Alphaville is, by land area, one of the biggest gated communities in the world. As the anthropologist Teresa Caldeira has described, Alphaville has benefited from the decline of São Paulo's inner suburbs, such as Moóca. A self-contained town behind a 6-metre steel wall, 90 minutes by bus from the inner city, it promises security above all. It has its own police force, miles of huge new houses in a variety of historical styles from New England to Art Deco to Second Empire French and a city centre, the size of Los Angeles' revitalized downtown, with a cluster of 30-storey towers. The whole city is laid out on a grid as formal as Brasília's, and in some places feels subjectively bigger than Brasília, which is, for all its grandeur, a low-rise, horizontal city. Everything is under CCTV surveillance. The commercial centre is a grid of little two-storey buildings in a variety of historical styles, a local take on American new urbanism; its bustle, street cafés and shady plazas represent urban life as leisure, in a way that is directly comparable with Celebration in Florida or Poundbury in England. Alphaville, like those places, has all the infrastructure to create the illusion of a healthy civic life: schools, healthcare centres, streets, squares and parks, all organized within walking distance of each other. The commercial centre is impressive, bustling and not at all contrived, and registering high levels of satisfaction, according to one study.[52] But the illusion of civic life is created at some cost: Alphaville's residential population of 15,000 is serviced by a much larger army of cheap labour, imported from the surrounding towns. Neither is the urbane ambience of the city a guarantor of psychological health: in 2005, Alphaville had, according to its directory of local services, no less than 96 psychologists or psychotherapists – on the evidence of the *Páginas Amarelas*, roughly 3,000 times the number of analysts per head of population in Alphaville than in São Paulo in total. And in the late 1980s in a bizarrely Freudian episode, all the things Alphaville sought to repress returned with a vengeance, from within. Its youth took to stealing cars, drugs, rape, even murder. For the *Folha de São Paulo*, Alphaville was nothing less than a real-life *Twin Peaks*.[53]

Underwriting all the projects I have described in this chapter is the same fantasy of civic life that can be found in public space works in Europe and North America. Architects have much invested in this idea, and it is as strongly present in Niemeyer's strange Memorial da América Latina as it is in Alphaville, or the reurbanization projects in Rio's *favelas*. In each case, however formally different, there is an unquestioned belief in the value of public space, in the creation of spaces for public assembly. As in Europe and North America, however, Brazil's new public spaces have a slightly puzzling quality about them, built for civic traditions that no longer really exist – or perhaps never did. And the relative inequality of all these societies, especially Brazil's, means that the publics for whom these spaces are intended may regard them with hostility. The spaces need physical protection in order to survive. The Memorial da América Latina is a military compound in all but name, separated from the public that it ostensibly serves by a 3-metre steel fence. Alphaville's developers are obsessed with public order, their strongest selling point. *Favela-Bairro* has been well meaning, but its spaces have a fleeting quality about them, tiny, fragile civil interventions that look unlikely to survive long in what are often brutal conditions. In Brazil as elsewhere, the public space agenda is a matter largely of aesthetics and surfaces: the real future is represented for the time being by the proliferating privatized spaces of the gated community and the mall. That said, the sophistication of Alphaville, or the newer parts of Barra da Tijuca, shows that such spaces need not sublimate their paranoia. They do not look like prisons, these places; they at least create the illusion of public life as effectively as more genuinely public schemes.

chapter eight

Brazil's Legacies

In June 2003 a peculiar structure was erected in the genteel surroundings of Kensington Gardens, London. Made of steel, glass and concrete, but more of a sculpture than a building, it had an airy loggia with inclined walls, a catenary roof and a dramatic red zigzagging ramp. It looked like the set for a 1950s sci-fi movie. The loggia was open to the elements, while one of the two end walls contains a great oval window, framing views of the park. The whole structure sat on a cylindrical podium containing some calculatedly retro-futuristic furniture and an exhibition of architectural photographs. This was Oscar Niemeyer's pavilion for the Serpentine Gallery of contemporary art, one of an annual series, which had previously displayed designs by Zaha Hadid, Daniel Libeskind and Toyo Ito. Superficially it resembled Niemeyer's earlier work: the ramp seemed to be a quotation of the Museu de Arte Contemporânea (MAC) of 1997 at Niterói, while the catenary form of the roof (as well as the size and proportions of the building overall) recall the so-called Igrejinha (1959), one of the first buildings erected at Brasília and one of the few landmarks in the residential south wing of the city. A temporary building, the pavilion was nevertheless larger and more substantial than that iconic church. This effect had been achieved without the architect ever having visited the site. At the age of 95, and long suffering from a fear of flying, he worked out the designs with Julia Peyton-Jones, the gallery director, in Rio de Janeiro, who then had them built in London. Despite the design process, the building was widely regarded as a success.

Niemeyer had not built in Britain before, but had lately become the object of veneration by a new generation of architects outside. Niemeyer was awarded the Gold Medal of the Royal Institute of British Architects in 1999, having already received the Pritzker Prize in 1988.[1] His Niterói gallery was widely praised outside Brazil (despite some rather obvious flaws in the construction). At the opening of the Serpentine Pavilion, Norman Foster declared his enthusiasm for Niemeyer's work, while admitting (in common with many of his contemporaries) that until this moment he had known it only from photographs. The Serpentine

Pavilion was widely discussed in the professional press throughout Europe and North America. Perhaps more significantly, the project was an object of fascination for the mainstream press throughout the summer of 2003.[2] Accounts of it were unusually reverential in tone, remarkable in that they dealt with a normally reviled architectural tendency, Modernism. Niemeyer's best-known works at Brasília had not been favourably represented in any part of the Anglophone press for the best part of forty years, while the city was generally supposed to represent the nadir of Modernist planning, and was assumed to lie in ruins if it still existed at all, a dreadful warning against of hubris of architects (see chapter Three for more on the status of Brasília).[3]

In the intervening period, something happened to Niemeyer's reputation and that of Brazilian Modernism in general. This chapter discusses what, and asks: who wants what from Brazilian Modernism? The broad narrative set out here describes a shift in the perception of Brazilian Modernism from a social project aimed at reforming Brazilian society to a formal one, in which architecture is mostly a diversion, popularly consumed, but of negligible social importance. It is a shift characterized by an increasingly exoticized perspective, oddly so in view of Brazil's greatly increased accessibility. The chapter deals with these questions through three architectural case studies. First is the rise of Paulo Mendes da Rocha, whose neo-Brutalist work is now almost as highly regarded as Niemeyer's outside Brazil. Second is a series of case studies of recent Niemeyer buildings and their critical reception, particularly the MAC at Niterói. Third is the revisiting of Brasília, and its reclamation as an object of enquiry, particularly artistic enquiry.

The Rise of Paulo Mendes da Rocha

Few architects describe the changing status of Brazilian Modernism as well as Paulo Mendes da Rocha, who received the Pritzker Prize for architecture in 2006. His has always been architecture for the sake of architecture, 'concrete poetry' as Ruth Verde Zein put it.[4] Mendes da Rocha's work is increasingly visible in São Paulo (his public space project has already been discussed in chapter Seven). The Forma building (1993), an upmarket furniture store, is a vast, but highly disciplined exercise in architectural minimalism. It has a two-storey glazed façade revealing the activity within, on a site where a standardized retail shed might have been expected. The FIESP cultural centre (1998), on the city's Avenida Paulista, is a restrained remodelling of a tower of 1979 by Rino Levi to provide a coherent entrance and art gallery on the basement and ground floors. The materials are revealed; the whole thing has an air of cool restraint, in marked contrast to the visual chaos of the surroundings, not to mention the baroque character of most of the architectural surfaces. The Galeria Leme (2004), a small contemporary art space close by in Butantã, an area of light industry on the south side of the River Pinheiros, is a simple top-lit structure done entirely in concrete. From the outside it is initially hard to distinguish from the simple, but functional industrial sheds of the surroundings. Inside it is a cool, airy, space with a somewhat ecclesias-tical atmosphere.

That atmosphere is developed in a more explicit way in the chapel of Nuestra Senhora da Conceição on the outskirts of the north-eastern city of Recife. The project, for a chapel on the site of the artist Francisco Brennand's factory-estate, is a conversion of an eighteenth-century house, long fallen into ruin, into a restrained chapel for family use. A small project by the standards of the others discussed here, its methods are in the same tradition; in its approach to an older building it strongly resembles the much larger Pinacoteca. In both cases the original remains, but in a dras-tically stripped-down form, while the contemporaneity of the insertions is emphasized.[5]

Why might these buildings have begun to assume a special impor-tance now? The answers come partly from internal Brazilian discourses about Modernism, in which, for the architectural elite, Mendes da Rocha's work represents a way of continuing the Modernist project, but without its ideological baggage. If Mendes da Rocha shared the uncom-promising politics of his teachers, he kept it well hidden: he has rarely published and his interviews say little about politics. In place of ideology came something seemingly imported from the United States – the notion of site-specificity. This concept was originally associated with Mini-malist sculpture, a form of large-scale, inexpressive and geometrical work that emerged from New York art studios in the mid-1960s. Some of Minimalism's chief exponents went on to meditate on the effect these strangely inexpressive objects would have on their surroundings, espe-cially when those surroundings were public.[6] In particular, Richard Serra's work from the mid-1970s onwards became almost exclusively about this dialogue between a landscape – usually an urban one – and a Minimalist object, and each project would begin from a detailed obser-vation of the site and its use or inhabitation. The results were strikingly uniform. Nonetheless, Serra and his advocates claimed that the work was site-specific, dependent on a set of unique spatial relationships, and that to remove a work would be to destroy it. Crucially, Serra claimed that the work stood in *critical* relation with the site; in other words, it did not seek to adorn it (as conventional public sculpture would have done) but underline its true nature.[7]

This concept of site-specificity seems to have informed so much of the literature around Mendes da Rocha, to the point where he is no longer really an architect in a recognizably Brazilian tradition, but a kind of southern hemisphere Serra. Hugo Segawa has described his relative lack of alignment with local architecture: he has preserved 'in his own way' an affinity with Brazilian Modernism, but he is out of step with 'postmodernism, orthodox rationalists and pragmatic functionalists' and 'international trends' in general.[8] Sophia Telles, describing the MUBE, brings in to play a set of ideas more commonly associated with public sculpture. The architect's idea from beginning, she claims, was to understand the site in its entirety. It was not about putting an object on a site, and thereby constructing a figure–ground relation, nor was it about 'dissolving' the museum, by putting it underground. Instead, the construction and the site were coterminous, inseparable and inter-dependent. The function of the great concrete beam was to make the site, nothing more.[9] Josep Maria Montaner refers to the work directly in the context of Minimalism, providing a gloss on the artistic movement and implying that a cultural puritanism is at work in both cases: he identifies a reaction to 'excess', to 'decoration, symbolism and eclecticism', as well as the 'elitism' of recent architectural theory.[10] Otilia Arantes refers directly to work of Richard Serra in her account of Mendes da Rocha. Mendes da Rocha, like Serra, she argues, is concerned with 'revealing and redefining a place', and both often add a discordant note; they do not simply wish to embellish the sites they work with.[11] Bastos's conclusion is vital in establishing Mendes da Rocha's place in Brazilian Modernism. Referring in particular to one of her sources, Montaner, she describes Mendes da Rocha as an architect involved with the reordering of space, but, vitally, one who sees the role of modern architecture to work with what already exists. No more 'does modern architecture occupy the virgin lands of Brazil, instead it is an architecture that returns to the essential with the objective of regeneration'.[12]

This is a Brazilian expression of the differentiation between Modernist and Minimalist sculpture: the forms in each case may be similar, but the understanding of the surroundings quite different. The result is an architecture freed from the widely felt doubts about Modernism. As Guillerme Wisnik has written, Mendes da Rocha is an architect who appears to be 'immune' from the criticism of Brazilian Modernism, having somehow sidestepped it. His 'structural formalism' may be similar to that of the Modernists, but it 'ceases to be didactic since it no longer conveys a morality of construction'.[13]

These critics' views of Mendes da Rocha are underlined by the views of the jury for the Pritzker Prize, awarded to the architect in 2006. The views of such juries are necessarily bland – but what is clear in this instance is the way in which Modernism here has been evacuated of its social ambitions, to be rendered as formal experiment. It is an architecture of 'universal' appeal. Carlos Jimenez cited Mendes da Rocha's 'exceptional economy', producing an architecture that 'transcends the limits of construction to dazzle with poetic rigor and imagination'. Balkrishna Doshi, of the Pritzker jury, cited his 'generous architecture' created in circumstances of scarcity and constraint, his 'largeness of vision'.[14]

As I have argued throughout this book, for many in Brazil, Modernism became a somewhat toxic tendency, representative of discredited ideas or having the wrong associations. Mendes da Rocha represents a detoxified Modernism with immense appeal outside Brazil. It is no longer the default mode for large public projects, but has assumed a special niche, building art galleries, private chapels and design-orientated retail outlets, in which it serves a small, interested public, for whom architecture is mainly a matter of aesthetics. It has become an architecture of art galleries, not housing estates.

Niemeyer and Exotic Brazil

Mendes da Rocha represents one way that Brazilian Modernism might successfully inhabit the present. Another is similarly evacuated of ideology, but plays up the exoticism of the work's origins. This is arguably what led the revival of interest in Oscar Niemeyer's work outside Brazil during the 1990s.

Brazil has always been constructed as exotic by the European, and Niemeyer's architecture, whatever the architect's humanism, has always played to the exoticizing view of the tourist. In writings and interviews, Niemeyer has simultaneously insisted on his humanistic rational desire to house and serve the population of Brazil in a better and more egalitarian way, and on his work's essential strangeness. Not that he would put it quite like that – but the desire to make strange objects that unsettle is hard to separate from the exoticizing perspective of the tourist. His remarks about Brasília are well known: the priority in creating the major public buildings was not function in the first instance, but to create a sense of 'shock' or 'surprise', equivalent to that experienced by the tourist at the first sight of Chartres Cathedral or the Doge's Palace in Venice.[15] He wrote later that he wished the lasting impression of Brasília to be of its singular formal qualities: the visitor might not like or appreciate what he has seen, but he would leave certain that he had not seen anything like it before.[16] It is sensibility that is profoundly anti-rational, closely related, in fact, to a taste for Surrealism.[17]

Foreign appreciation of Brazilian architecture has always been tempered by a suspicion of this local tendency to the exotic. Max Bill's revulsion at Niemeyer was discussed in the Introduction.[18] Bill's reaction to what seemed to him a revival of the Baroque is understandable, given the puritanical tendencies in European Modernism. Here was 'utter anarchy in building, jungle growth in the worst sense'.[19] But Bill's disgust at the exotic in Brazil's architecture had little effect on its development. Niemeyer's work since the 1950s has become if anything more baroque, ever less related to function, ever more sculptural and surreal. We have looked at some of these projects already, the Memorial da América Latina for example (1989). Consider also a series of foreign projects built during Niemeyer's exile from Brazil: his campus for the University of Constantine in Tunisia (1969), his Maison de la Culture in Le Havre

(1978) and his headquarters building for the French Communist Party (1980), all calculated to give the impression of having arrived from another planet. Two of Niemeyer's more recent projects since his return to Brazil have even exaggerated this tendency to science fiction: the great flying saucer of the MAC in Niterói (1997) and more recently the Museu Oscar Niemeyer in the southern city of Curitiba (2002), a giant glass eye on a stick.

Of these more recent projects, Niemeyer had a particular regard for the MAC, considering it one of his top three buildings (the others were the National Congress and the cathedral in Brasília).[20] It was very widely discussed outside Brazil, and was an important factor in securing the architect the RIBA Gold Medal in 1999, as well as the Serpentine Pavilion in 2003; it has become as iconic as the architect's earlier work, celebrated in image, for example, in his autobiography, *The Curves of Time*, in which it appears as a sketch on nearly every page. It is located on a rocky outcrop of the coastline, with spectacular views across the bay to Rio, from where it can be seen on clear days. Formally it is an upturned bowl, 40 metres in diameter, not dissimilar in profile from the upper house of the National Congress. It has two levels of exhibition spaces, built on top of a central trunk 8 metres wide. The whole complex sits in a concrete plaza. An artificial pool reflects the museum by day; it is spectacularly floodlit by night. There is dark glazing in a band at the top level, framing panoramic views of Rio from the circulation space of the interior. Linking ground- and first-floor levels is a serpentine ramp, in pink, a baroque variation on a favourite circulation device of Niemeyer. It is unmistakably a flying saucer of 1950s vintage that has come to land, improbably, in Niterói. The architect himself plays on this in an officially sanctioned documentary made by a Belgian production company shortly after the MAC's inauguration.[21] The film's opening sequence depicts an animated saucer circling over Rio, to land in a great cloud of smoke in Niterói; a

Oscar Niemeyer,
Museu de Arte
Contemporânea,
Niterói, 1997.

Oscar Niemeyer,
Museu de Arte
Contemporânea,
Niterói, 1997: view
towards Rio de
Janeiro.

ramp unfurls, and the building reveals itself as the MAC. The architect, with slicked-back hair, dressed in a high-buttoning Chinese-style jacket and smoking a cheroot, descends the ramp, a messenger from another planet. The message is clear: this architecture comes from space.

The MAC, however, is by no means a sophisticated building. Built of concrete, it has a hand-made quality the closer you get to it. The quality of the surfaces is poor – so poor, as the critic Hattie Harman noted in a review shortly after its opening, that the whole building had to be painted white to give the surfaces some consistency; the work on the ramp, meanwhile, was even worse and had to be covered up with poly-carbonate boards. An administrative wrangle meant that the ramp was never properly functional, never being – as was supposed – a ceremonial route directly into the gallery, but instead curtailed at the first floor. The lack of ticket sales facilities on the top floor meant that visitors needed to enter at first-floor level, pass a temporary desk and make their way up inside via a stair meant originally for staff.[22] The staff areas, as Harman went on to note, are grimly claustrophobic, conspicuously lacking the high ceilings, windows and spectacular views of the rest of the building. But even as an art gallery, it has some obvious failings. The architecture dominates any installation, demanding (as the director has said) that artists work with the building rather than try to fight it. And there is a structural flaw too: leave a window open for ventilation, and an internal tornado is allegedly created around the central core, whipping around the building with such speed that it will pick up any object that is not securely fastened. 'O acelerador de partículas' ('The particle accelerator') is the building's unfortunate nickname.[23]

Niemeyer, as usual, seemed largely indifferent to such earthbound matters. What mattered to him was the creation of an icon, an original shape; he is the heroic form-giver, brought in to give shape to a site. As Harman wrote, the chief purpose of the building is not to be an art gallery, but to supply an iconic image. In this, Niemeyer's work is oddly Postmodern, preoccupied with the creation of icons that may or may not be related to their supposed functions.

Niemeyer's work at Niteroí has been exceptionally successful in this respect, providing an iconic image for a city that previously lacked one. Niemeyer has now been involved in a much larger scheme in the area, incorporating the MAC. The Caminho Niemeyer, begun by the city in 2001, is 72,000 square metres of public space on the city's waterfront, incorporating Catholic and Protestant cathedrals, a theatre, a museum

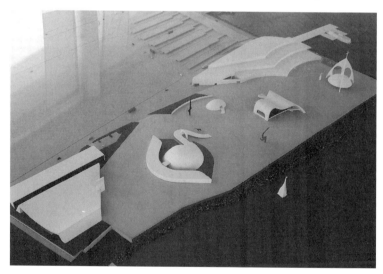

Oscar Niemeyer, Camino Niemeyer, Niteroí, model, 2005.

and other cultural facilities, with the MAC as one pole of development. All the respective parts of the project deployed Niemeyer's usual repertoire of curves and ramps, all done in concrete. At the time of writing, some of the buildings had been started, but the project was a long way from completion. While the forms of the project may have been unfamiliar to those outside Brazil, perhaps even archaic, the project was in other respects remarkably close to regeneration projects in the developed world: a waterfront site, an emphasis on culture, architecture as a vehicle for producing icons, a relative disregard for function. In all this, public life is imagined as a series of polite diversions in pleasant surroundings – it is the European bourgeois ideal.

As well as his buildings, Niemeyer himself has also become an object of fascination, much apparent in the critical treatment of the 2003 Serpentine Pavilion. Reviews by critics in the *Guardian* and *Observer* newspapers refrained from judgement on the pavilion as a piece of architecture per se in favour of awestruck commentary on the fact of Niemeyer's (re)-emergence, and, for that matter, his continued existence at the age of 96. He was, it was made clear, a representative of a virtually extinct species, 'the last of the great, decisive, form-giving modern architects of the 20th century', a man who had personally known every great Modernist architect, and most great artists of his lifetime.[24] The critics' awe therefore derived not only from the fact that he was still alive, but also that he still worked in the exact same mode as before. His pavilion showed no deviation whatever from the formal vocabulary established at Brasília. Not only that, but Niemeyer himself still spoke an ancient dialect of

Oscar Niemeyer, Camino Niemeyer under construction, Niterói, 2005.

architectural Modernism, a thrillingly unreconstructed mixture of existential philosophy and machismo. The project was 'different, free and audacious . . . a palace, a cathedral, the figure of a woman appearing'.[25] Niemeyer's unmodernized views on women were for one critic somewhat unappealing.[26] For most, however, they were evidence of his authenticity, their old-fashioned, corny sexism providing a delicious frisson.[27] Such uncomplicated use of the female body, such as in the pavilion's interior mural, was permissible only because it no longer represented any kind of threat. Modernism here was no longer a realistic way of building but a kind of retro kitsch.[28]

Exotic Brasília

The re-emergence of Niemeyer as popular kitsch is the case of a single architect, but something similar can be seen on the latter-day representation of Brasília, a city, which, as I explained in chapter Three, has now re-emerged from a long period of effective disappearance. But its reappearance is in the guise of a place that is no longer a model of good practice, but a surreal entertainment. The real city, as I have already described, continues as a more or less successful medium-sized metropolis, a 'city like any other', as Niemeyer claimed in 1983; its representation has profoundly changed, however.[29]

The latter-day Brasília is both exotic and dystopian. The city is presented as unique, exotic, remote and singular; its aesthetic characteristics are generally praised, but it appears as a fundamentally bad place. There is an important difference, however, from the early reports of the city. In the years around inauguration, reports of Brasília were fraught with anxiety about the city's value as a *model* for contemporary architecture and urbanism. Its success or failure was a matter not just of local, but global concern, for here, on the largest imaginable scale, was an experiment in Modernist urbanism.[30] Max Bill's derogatory remarks about Brazil, made in 1954, are indicative: his displeasure at the perceived arbitrary and baroque character of contemporary buildings is much more than a matter of personal taste, but a perceived traducing of the principles of Modernist architecture itself. The offence he takes is not personal, but on behalf of the movement: here Modernism itself appears under threat from within. The early criticism of Brasília infuses judgements about local taste with anxieties about the future of the Modern Movement. For European critics writing in the early 1960s, Brasília was an object in which they had much invested. They owned it, in effect, as an experiment, and their criticism of it was informed by a keen sense that it represented a European as much as a local future.

Oscar Niemeyer,
Procuradoría Geral
da República, Brasília,
1995–2002.

That sense of ownership prevalent in the early criticism is absent in the more recent critiques. The city is still bizarre, dysfunctional and dystopian, but it no longer exists as an object of anxiety, but pleasure. Its eccentricities, and even its failings, can, to put it another way, be experienced as sublime. In this scenario, the city's negative character is frequently exaggerated for literary effect, and its eccentricities played up; here, with the writer in the position of uncommitted visitor, Brasília can be the stuff of adventure.

So the British critic Jonathan Glancey referred to Brasília as a 'science fiction city', its Congress buildings the 'headquarters of a Martian leadership'.[31] Hannah Baldock in *Icon* describes a city made for a 'race of hyper-intelligent Volkswagens' rather than people, a city designed to speed up Darwinian processes of natural selection by murdering its residents in traffic accidents, and a city in which day-to-day survival for visitors is a test of wits.[32] Carlos Moreira Teixeira wrote in 2005 for the French journal *L'Architecture d'aujourd'hui* that the city was simultaneously ghastly and beautiful, a kind of anti-city, a species of 'desert' or 'wasteland' in which architecture was a futile business in the face of the enormity of the *cerrado* landscape.[33] 'Let more filth come forth!', he declaimed: let, in other words, the city become even worse. The report was accompanied by large-scale photographs by Emmanuel Pinard, which showed a vast, barren landscape, all dust, cracked earth and discarded plastic bags, in which are located the semi-ruins of the modern city. It is an apocalyptic vision no less, but one that provides both the writer and the photographer with the pleasure of the sublime. In accounts like these, the city's faults become a source of temporary amusement or distraction; they become in effect a necessary part of the visit, a motivation for it; it would be a disappointment, one senses, if the city *failed* to live up to its dystopian reputation.

L'Architecture d'aujourd'hui had, in fact, already re-imagined the city as sublime dystopia as early as 1997. Its authors were the architectural journalist Yannis Tsiomis and a well-known French novelist, Jean Rolin, but a vital part of the exercise involved returning the Swiss photographer René Burri to the city after a gap of 37 years. Burri's images of the inauguration in 1960 were canonical. Rolin's brilliant travelogue is organized around a series of nine vignettes of the city, from the hotel and shopping areas in the centre, to the experience of life in the residential wings (both south and north), to the phenomenon of the 'invasion', to life in a satellite town, Ceilândia. It is highly poetic – Rolin is drawn to the perverse, the extreme and the contradictory throughout. He demands the city be exotic, and when it is not, he is disappointed. The Conjunto Nacional shopping centre, for example, lets him down because it reminds him too much of Bagnolet, a western suburb of Paris.[34] The Conic, an adjoining mall, is better for his purposes, because it contains both a lively evangelical church (which has taken over the local cinema) and also, by poetic contrast, a striptease joint.

Rolin's account of the residential areas of the Pilot Plan plays up the differences between two corresponding areas, the 308 South and the 306 North, with similar situations in relation the centre. At 308 South, 'not a button' is missing; the architecture (some by Niemeyer) and landscaping (by Roberto Burle Marx) is superb; the polished marble of the entrances to the super-blocks gleams with such intensity one hesitates to step on it. By contrast, 306 North is, according to Rolin, 'definitely the ugliest place I laid eyes on', all cracked paving and abandoned supermarket trolleys, populated by youths apparently transplanted from South Central LA. Rolin and Burri pause to reflect on the city's predilection for 'mysticism' – a giant pyramid apparently covers the city in the fifth dimension while its residents are the reincarnation of ancient Egyptians – before they move on to visit the satellite towns, which do not disappoint. Ceilândia is big, confusing and centre-less, with an impressively high murder rate, ten times that of the Pilot Plan. They move on further away from civilization to a 'gigantic, open dump' where

> swarms of tip-up trucks and bulldozers are constantly at work, along with hundreds of poor people – many of them children, busy picking over garbage . . . There are thousands of more or less dung-eating birds too: Eagles (caracaras), vultures (urubus) and white egrets, which last named, on weekends, are the delight of the rich Lake-side residents, who apparently think they feed on nothing but fresh fish.[35]

This passage, the last of a series of vignettes, strikes me for two reasons. First is the fact that Rolin ends his account on the margins rather than the centre. The lasting impression of the city – the one the author wishes to leave as true – is therefore not the monumental centre, but the informal and mostly illegal city excluded by it. The second thing that strikes me is the image of the white egret, a beautiful bird held in much affection by *Brasilienses* whose bright plumage belies its revolting diet. A metaphor for the city as a whole, it asserts that whatever beauty exists has its roots in filth. What Rolin does here is to reiterate the dystopian narrative about Brasília, but this time for entertainment value. No longer does the critic have any commitment to the city, or feel it offers a useful model. Brasília exists instead as the pretext for adventure tourism. One visits much in the same way one would go white-water rafting or bungee jumping. And this is increasingly how the city has been marketed to internal tourists, a continuum of spectacular possibilities, all, in the true sense, extra-ordinary.[36]

Brazilian Modernism and Art

The re-emergence of Brazilian Modernism in recent years has often happened in the context of art. Niemeyer's best-known recent projects have

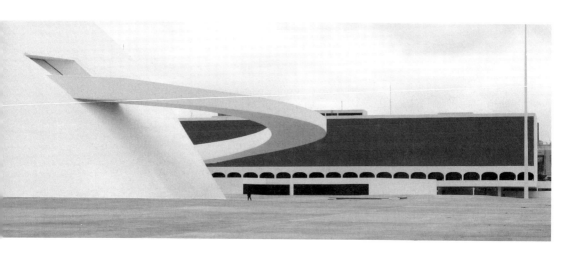

been either art galleries themselves or have been commissioned by art galleries, and have been both used and conceived as works of art – that is, they are unapologetically useless. There have been no housing projects or hospitals, few government buildings. Niemeyer has in most senses been absorbed by the art world, as has Mendes da Rocha, whose restrained Minimalism both makes reference to and reiterates the sculptural tendency of American Minimalism of the 1960s. Like Niemeyer, it is significant that his best-known recent projects have been essentially urban sculptures. The Praça do Patriarca, for example, is not a metro station per se – a problem that might have interested an early Modernist – but the exterior decoration for a pre-existing station. Niemeyer and Mendes da Rocha therefore no longer seek to remake the world as they once did, but to adorn a pre-existing world. It is a significant recasting of the Modernist project as art.

It is no accident therefore that Brazilian Modernist architecture should itself become an object of fascination for contemporary artists, as it has done for advertisers (see chapter Six). I have already shown how this might be done in the painting of Anselm Kiefer, in which in the paintings *Barren Landscape* and *Lilith* the city of São Paulo and some of its main buildings have been represented as an urban chaos. The slicker surfaces of Brasília and Niemeyer's Modernism have increasingly become an artistic subject too, although in a different way. Where Kiefer uses São Paulo as a stand-in for a rather pessimistic modernity, photographic artists such as the German Candida Höfer have explored the specificity of the architecture. Höfer's series of large-scale c-type prints from 2005 depict several major public buildings in Brasília. Her images – all interiors – represent the city as something ineffable and anachronistic,

Oscar Niemeyer,
Biblioteca Nacional
complex, Brasília,
2006.

surprisingly pristine, but unquestionably of another time. The spectacular stair of the Itamaraty palace is depicted in a way that manages to be
both empty and pregnant, an elaborate piece of interior design waiting
to be filled by some undefined – but vast – ritual event. Höfer's images
of Brasília are continuous with her pictures of Portuguese Baroque
buildings, both genres of building presented as equally out of time and
spectacular.

Other artists have sought to make a more obvious visual transformation of the source material. The São Paulo-based artist Jair Lanes, who
exhibited photographs of Brasília in Paris in 2005, depicted the city's
architecture in a series of large-scale, out-of-focus but colour-saturated
photographs, in which all detail was evacuated, save the gestalt of the
essential form.[37] The architecture was reduced to its elements, but also
something hazy, like a memory, removed from real time and place as if the
architecture itself was no longer really of contemporary importance, but
a kind of mirage. The transformation of the architecture into something dreamlike was emphasized by showing the pictures opposite the
straightforward monochrome reportage of the city by Alberto Ferreira.
At Leeds, the following year, several artists from Brazil made different,
but comparable work based on Brazil's Modernist architecture. The
vast photographs by Rubens Mano and Rogério Canella of the Bienal
pavilion in São Paulo show the iconic interior of the building between
installations; the scale of the picture conveys something of its grandeur,
an effect clearly desired by the architect. At the same time, the high resolution of the images shows up the building's history, how it has become
worn and institutional, distancing it from its original utopian condition.
At the same exhibition, Paulo Climachauska did a big wall drawing of

the same building, reducing it to a line drawing, whose line comprised a series of tiny numbers; the numerical series was hard to read from a distance, giving the line a halting, fragmented quality analogous to the pavilion's construction. In common with all Niemeyer's large-scale work, the futurity of the design contrasts with the crudeness of the construction methods. At the pavilion, as elsewhere, the utopian first impression does not long survive. Climachauska's image makes this plain.[38] Perhaps the best-known Brazilian artist to be exhibited outside Brazil in recent years is Hélio Oiticica, whose work has been the subject of major exhibitions at the Whitechapel, Tate and Barbican galleries in London since 2000. Oiticica's attitude to architectural Modernism was ambiguous. On the one hand, his interest in the *favela* (see chapter Four) suggested a profoundly critical attitude to the formal city; on the other, many of his sculptural and relief works extend Modernist architectural formal experimentation.

Perhaps it is this attitude of Oiticica's that now best defines the legacy of Brazilian architectural Modernism. Its social project is a ruin, so to speak, and it no longer exists as a template for all development. But a great deal of fun can be had playing in the ruins. One of Oiticica's most impressive, but lesser known, works exemplifies this condition beautifully. *Magic Square No. 5 – de Luxe*, installed in the Museu do Açude in the Atlantic rainforest above Rio is a great, architectural-scale sculpture, installed in the middle of the forest. A set of brightly coloured, almost fluorescent planes in Perspex and painted concrete, it is a staggering contrast to the surrounding forest, an object that might as well have landed from Miami Beach, if not another planet. At the same time, it does not seem to represent a model of doing things, any other kind of future. It is architecture reduced, as it were, to folly building. And like the follies built by eighteenth-century English aristocrats, this one accedes to the condition of the Picturesque, falling into a mouldering ruin, a state of which its maker would have approved. Like all ruins, this one speaks of an essentially conservative worldview. Like *Magic Square*, a neighbouring installation by Lygia Pape, a contemporary of Oiticica and a trained architect, is architectural in scale and similarly appropriates the language of Modernism. But it is built as a ruin to start with, and the surrounding jungle has grown up through it, destroying it from within. Seemingly an allegory of the futility of human endeavour, it is a melancholy sight.

By way of a conclusion, it is worth noting the views of a Brazilian critic, Fernando Luiz Lara, on the re-emergence of Brazilian architecture in international architectural discourse. Writing in the major journal *Projeto Design* in 2001, he notes that by one measure, the Avery Index, there were almost as many international citations of Brazilian work during the 1990s as there were during the previous ninety years.[39] The revival is real, and it is also characterized by a marked shift of interest away from the traditional axes of Rio–São Paulo or Rio–Brasília. It marks not only a revival of interest by critics outside Brazil, but also an internal revival in the country's architectural heritage – Brazilians, he says, are 'voracious' consumers of international journals. But, he continues, Brazil retains a peculiar, and ultimately peripheral, character: the country is always cited in terms of the 'exotic, erotic, or chaotic'; the country is always a curiosity rather than something more serious.[40] The re-emergence of Brazilian Modernism we have seen in this chapter fits this description. If this is the case, it is an architecture that is – however well patronized – fundamentally marginal. There are a few exceptions to this, notably the continuing work of João Filgueiras Lima (Lelé): his Lago Norte hospital in Brasília for the Sarah Kubitschek foundation (2001) deploys the swooping forms of Brazil's high Modernist period, but in the service of a profoundly humanistic project, namely the treatment of patients with neurophysiological disorders. The centre is beautifully sited, luxuriously equipped and provides world-class facilities for diagnosis and long-term physiotherapeutic treatment. But Lelé apart, Brazil's Modernism has arguably become another style, from which the humanistic, and socially progressive, project has been removed. It remains to be seen whether the Brazil of the early twenty-first century finds an equivalent architecture to match its progressive ambitions.[41]

References

Introduction

1   L. Costa, 'Relatorio do Plano Piloto de Brasília', *Revista Arquitetura e Engenharia*, 44 (1957), pp. 9–12.
2   A. Conan Doyle, *The Lost World* [1912] (London, 1979).
3   F. Lara, 'Arquitectura Brasileira Volta as Páginas das Publicações Internacionais na Decada do 90', *Projeto Design*, 251 (January 2001), p. 8.
4   S. Zweig, *Brazil: Land of the Future* (London, 1942).
5   *Brazil Builds: Architecture New and Old, 1652–1942,* exh. cat., Museum of Modern Art, New York (1943), pp. 81–9.
6   C. Lévi-Strauss, *Tristes Tropiques* [1936] (London, 1976).
7   Le Corbusier, for his part, seems to have been most taken with Leão. L. Cavalcanti, *Moderno e Brasileiro: A História de uma Nova Linguagem na Arquitetura, 1930–60* (Rio de Janeiro, 2006), p. 47.
8   Y. Bruand, *Arquitetura Contemporânea no Brasil* (São Paulo, 2002), p. 93.
9   *Brazil Builds*, p. 106.
10 *New York Times* (13 January 1943).
11 Bruand, *Arquitetura Contemporânea*, p. 93.
12 M. Bill, 'Report on Brazil', *Architectural Review*, cxvi/694 (October 1954), p. 238.
13 K. Frampton, *Modern Architecture: A Critical History* (London and New York, 1992).
14 C. Jencks, *The Language of Postmodern Architecture* (London, 1977).
15 Cavalcanti, *Moderno e Brasileiro*.
16 A. Nobre et al., eds, *Lúcio Costa: Um Modo de Ser Moderno* (São Paulo, 2004).
17 Holanda in H. Segawa, *Arquiteturas no Brasil, 1900–1990* (São Paulo, 1998), p. 46.
18 F. Alambert and P. Canhête, *Bienais de São Paulo: Da Era do Museu à Era do Curadores* (São Paulo, 2004).
19 R. V. Zein, *O Lugar da Critica* (São Paulo, 2003), p. 102.
20 Translated as J. Jacobs, *A Morte e Vida das Grandes Cidades* (São Paulo, 2000).
21 Bill, 'Report on Brazil', p. 238.
22 T. Coelho, *Arte no Brasil, 1911–1980: Estraégias para Entrar e Sair da Modernidade*, exh. guide, Museu de Arte de São Paulo (2008), unpaginated.
23 P. Wilcken, *Empire Adrift: The Portuguese Court in Rio de Janeiro, 1808–1821* (London, 2004).
24 A joint intelligence and security operation initiated in 1975 involving the governments of Argentina, Bolivia, Brazil, Colombia, Paraguay and Uruguay, with the assistance of Peru and Ecuador at a later stage. Known in Spanish-speaking South America as Operación Condor.
25 P. F. Arantes, *Arquitetura Nova: Sérgio Ferro, Flávio Império e Rodrigo Lefèvre de Artigas aos Mutirões* (São Paulo, 2002), pp. 35, 95–8.
26 Segawa, *Arquiteturas no Brasil*, p. 122.
27 http://www.economist.com/countries/Brazil/index.cfm (accessed May 2008).
28 See J. Garreau, *Edge City: Life on the New Frontier* (New York, 1992).
29 http://www.economist.com/countries/Brazil/index.cfm (accessed May 2008).

30 T. Caldeira, *City of Walls: Crime, Segregation and Citizenship in São Paulo* (Berkeley and Los Angeles, 2000).

31 There are great disparities between cities. Rio's murder rate remains among the world's highest, with approximately 45 murders per 100,000. But São Paulo has seen a dramatic fall in murders during the first decade of the twenty-first century, and in 2007 was, on paper at least, rather less dangerous than Glasgow.

32 T. Goertzel and T. Kahn, 'The Unsung Story of São Paulo's Murder Rate Drop', *Brazzil Magazine* (10 June 2007): http://news.ncmonline.com/news/view_article.html?article_id=0a7ee25d39a7d2b0737cef 8c76bc84b5 (accessed 6 April 2008).

33 Translated as G. Freyre, *The Masters and the Slaves: A Study in the Development of Brazilian Civilization* (New York and London, 1956).

34 Ibid., p. 264. Freyre quotes the German historian Heinrich von Treitschke here.

35 C. Veloso, *Verdade Tropical* (São Paulo, 1997), pp. 500–01.

36 A. Boal, *Teatro do Oprimido e Outras Poéticas Políticas* (Rio de Janeiro, 1991); G. Rocha, 'Uma Estética da Fome', *Resenha do Cinema Latino-Americano* [Genoa] (1965): http://www.dhnet.org.br/desejos/textos/glauber.htm (accessed 15 November 2005); P. Freire, *Pedagogy of the Oppressed* (London, 1996).

37 Zein, *O Lugar da Crítica* p. 102.

38 Lara, 'Arquitetura Brasileira', pp. 8–9.

39 'Oscar Niemeyer Opens RIBA Conference', *Building Design* (29 October 2007).

40 Norman Foster, presentation at Serpentine Gallery Pavilion, London, June 2003.

41 http://oica.net/category/production-statistics/ (figures updated April 2008).

42 http://www.flightglobal.com/articles/2004/10/19/189007/country-profile-brazil.html (accessed May 2008).

43 *Projeto Design*, 251 (January 2001), p. 46.

chapter one: **The Politics of the Past**

1 A. Forty and E. Andreoli, eds, *Brazil's Modern Architecture* (London, 2004), p. 12.

2 C. Lévi-Strauss, *Tristes Tropiques* [1936] (London, 1976), pp. 120–21.

3 L. Costa, 'Muita Construção: Alguma Arquitetura e um Milagre', *Correio da Manhã* (15 June 1951)

4 L. Cavalcanti, *Moderno e Brasileiro: A História de uma Nova Linguagem na Arquitetura, 1930–60* (Rio de Janeiro, 2006), p. 15.

5 See R. J. Williams, *The Anxious City: English Urbanism at the End of the Twentieth Century* (London, 2004); A. Powers, *Britain: Modern Architectures in History* (London, 2007). The best-known source for Pevsner's argument is *The Englishness of English Art* (London, 1956).

6 N. Evenson, *Two Brazilian Capitals: Architecture and Urbanism in Rio de Janeiro and Brasília* (New Haven, CT, 1973), p. 12.

7 H. Mindlin, *Modern Architecture in Brazil* (Rio de Janeiro and Amsterdam, 1956), p. 2.

8 K. Frampton, *Modern Architecture: A Critical History* (London, 1992).

9 Reproduced in A. Xavier, ed., *Depoimento de uma Geração* (São Paulo, 2003), pp. 39–52.

10 G. Wisnik, in *Lúcio Costa: Um Modo de Ser Moderno*, ed. A. L. Nobre et al. (São Paulo, 2004), p. 33.

11 Benzaquen de Araújo, in ibid., p. 62.

12 Ibid., p. 63.

13 Cavalcanti, *Moderno e Brasileiro*, p. 10.

14 G. Freyre, *The Masters and the Slaves: A Study in the Development of Brazilian Civilization* (London, 1946), p. xxxiii.

15 Ibid.

16 Ibid., p. xxxv.

17 Costa quoted in ibid., p. xliii.
18 G. Freyre, *Brasis, Brasil e Brasília* (Lisbon, 1960), p. 165.
19 Costa, in Cavalcanti, *Moderno e Brasileiro*, p. 14.
20 The *Rough Guide* is not complimentary: 'This is one of Oscar Niemeyer's earliest creations, though not one of his best. If you like airport lounges you'll love this three-star hotel' (D. Cleary, D. Jenkins and O. Marshall, *The Rough Guide to Brazil*, New York, London and Delhi, 2003, p. 189).
21 Cavalcanti, *Moderno e Brasileiro*, p. 116.
22 Ibid.
23 Ibid., p. 114.
24 Costa quoted by Cavalcanti in *Oscar Niemeyer: Eine Legende der Moderne*, ed. P. Andreas and I. Flagge (Frankfurt am Main, 2003), p. 5.
25 Bruand, *Arquitetura Contemporânea no Brasil*, p. 108.
26 Ibid.
27 Ibid., p. 109.
28 Ibid.
29 O. Niemeyer, *The Curves of Time: Memoirs* (London, 2000), p. 59.
30 Goodwin was also one of the architects of MOMA's strikingly Modernist premises.
31 Andrade quoted in H. Segawa, *Arquiteturas no Brasil, 1900–1990* (São Paulo, 1998), p. 96.
32 There is a good argument to say that it *is* in fact a work of architecture, if architecture's definition is expanded to include unbuilt projects and theories of architecture. Internationally, the impact of *Brazil Builds* is certainly no less than the highly material project of Brasília. For more on the status of architectural exhibitions, see F. Kossak, 'The Exhibition as a Laboratory for an Emerging Architecture', unpublished PHD thesis, Edinburgh College of Art (2008).
33 L. Cavalcanti, *Quando Brasil era Moderno: Guia de Arquitetura, 1928–1960* (Rio de Janeiro, 2001), p. 199.
34 *Brazil Builds*, exh. cat., Museum of Modern Art, New York (1943), p. 34.
35 Ibid., pp. 38–9.
36 Ibid., p 42.
37 *Cubism and Abstract Art*, exh. cat., Museum of Modern Art, New York (1936).
38 *Brazil Builds*, p. 42.
39 L. Cavalcanti, *Quando Brasil era Moderno*, p. 189.
40 Mindlin, *Modern Architecture*, p. 11.
41 Ibid., pp. 106–7.
42 Bruand, *Arquitetura Contemporânea no Brasil,* p. 132.
43 A. Da Costa Braga and F.A.R. Falcão, *Guia de Urbanismo: Arquitetura e Arte de Brasília* (Brasília, 1997)
44 Bruand, *Arquitetura Contemporânea no Brasil*, p. 135.
45 R. J. Williams, 'Paulo Mendes da Rocha', *Blueprint*, 251 (February 2007), pp. 36–42.

chapter two: The Politics of Eros

1 I mean Eros in the Freudian sense, that is, as a primary human drive that has expression in a constellation of bodily pleasures or activities, not just clearly sexual acts. This definition of sexuality is broadly accepted in the field of sociology. See also M. Foucault, *The History of Sexuality, vol 1: An Introduction* (New York, 1990) and J. Weeks, *Sexuality and Its Discontents* (London, 1955).
2 G. Freyre, *The Masters and the Slaves: A Study in the Development of Brazilian Civilization* (Lisbon, 1957).
3 They were there, tacked to the wall, in September 2001 when I interviewed Niemeyer. They were plainly still there in 2007 when the RIBA had him make a speech, by weblink

from his studio, to their annual conference. See image in 'Oscar Niemeyer Opens RIBA Conference', *Building Design* (29 October 2007).

4   In any case, almost all western cultures until the nineteenth century were deeply 'heliophobic'. See L. Lenðek and G. Bosker, *The Beach: The History of Paradise on Earth* (London, 1998), p. 200.

5   P. Robb, *A Death in Brazil* (London, 2003), p. 60.

6   S. Zweig, *Brazil: Land of the Future* (London, 1942), p. 170.

7   Ruy Castro, *Carnaval no Fogo* [2003]; as *Rio de Janeiro: Carnival Under Fire*, trans. John Gledson (London, 2004), pp. 56–7.

8   Zweig, *Brazil*, p. 186.

9   Castro, *Rio de Janeiro*, p. 212.

10 Ibid., pp. 120, 134.

11 R. Guerrero, 'La Religion du Corps', *Match du Monde* (February 2005), pp. 76–9.

12 K. Frampton, *Le Corbusier* (London, 2001), pp. 106–7, 115.

13 All Le Corbusier's Brazilian work is collected in C. Rodrigues dos Santos et al., *Le Corbusier e o Brasil* (São Paulo, 1987).

14 B. Colomina, ed., *Sexuality and Space* (Princeton, NJ, 1992), p. 119.

15 Ibid., p. 120.

16 L. Cavalcanti, *Moderno e Brasileiro: A História de uma Nova Linguagem na Arquitetura, 1930–60* (Rio de Janeiro, 2006), p. 184.

17 Ibid.

18 P. Goodwin, *Brazil Builds: Architecture New and Old, 1652–1942* (New York, 1943).

19 Max Bill's attack on Niemeyer in 1954 was provoked in large part by a visit to Pampulha. See also the complaints of an anonymous American architect in a letter to *Architectural Forum* in N. Evenson, *Two Brazilian Capitals* (New Haven, CT, and London, 1973), p. 90: 'The mass, grouping and fenestration of the entrance to the Pampulha casino is one of the finest things in the world today. And ten feet inside the casino is a ghastly sight. Two ordinary pieces of gas pipe – flues for the kitchen stove – stick up into the room like an obscenity. I asked about the pipes and found out an amazing thing. The building cost them $500,000 to build, but they forgot the kitchen. They installed it afterward, but didn't care about the look of it. This seemed typical to me of all that we have seen of the new architecture.'

20 R. Scruton, *The Classical Vernacular* (Manchester, 1989).

21 V. Fraser, *Building the New World* (London, 2000), p. 189.

22 Evenson, *Two Brazilian Capitals*, p. 90.

23 Fraser, *Building the New World*, p. 188.

24 L. Cavalcanti, *Quando Brasil era Moderno: Guia de Arquitetura, 1928–1960* (Rio de Janeiro, 2001), pp. 292–3.

25 D. Underwood, *Oscar Niemeyer and Brazilian Free-Form Modernism* (New York, 1994), p. 66.

26 Cavalcanti, *Moderno e Brasileiro*, p. 138.

27 Ibid., p. 140.

28 Ibid., p. 141.

29 J. G. Ballard, *High Rise* (London, 1977).

30 J. Holston, *The Modernist City: An Anthropological Critique of Brasília* (Chicago, 1989), pp. 182–7.

31 For an account of the controversy, see T. Phillips, 'Sex Museum Sparks Rio Row', *The Guardian* (20 July 2006): http://arts.guardian.co.uk/news/story/0,,1824812,00.html, accessed 20 July 2006.

32 http://www.cidadedosexo.arq.br/projeto.htm, accessed 20 July 2006.

33 See S. Freud, 'From the History of an Infantile Neurosis', in *The Penguin Freud Library Vol. 9: Case Histories II* (London, 1979), pp. 269–9.

34 'Rio de Janeiro estuda criar a Cidade do Sexo', *Gazeta do Povo Online* (2 July 2006): http://canais.ondarpc.com.br/noticias/brasil/conteudo.phtml?id=578646

35 http://arts.guardian.co.uk/news/story/0,,1824812,00.html

36 http://arts.guardian.co.uk/news/story/0,,1824812,00.html

chapter three: Brasília, or the Politics of Progress

1 Both Belo Horizonte and Goiânia deserve longer treatment, but in a different context. Their place, with the outstanding exception of Pampulha, a suburb of Belo Horizonte, is peripheral in the context of architectural Modernism.

2 A. Malraux, *Palavras no Brasil* (Rio de Janeiro, 1998).

3 Oscar Niemeyer, *A Minha Experiéncia em Brasília* (Rio de Janeiro, 1961).

4 Kenneth Frampton, *Modern Architecture: A Critical History* (London, 1992), pp. 256–7.

5 See account in Y. Tsiomis and J. Rolin, 'Brasília', *L'Architecture d'aujourd'hui*, 313 (October 1997), pp. 76–87.

6 J. Holston, *The Modernist City: An Anthropological Critique of Brasília* (Chicago, 1989), pp. 161–2.

7 L. Costa, 'Brasília Revisitada', *Correio Braziliense* (8 March 1987), p. 29.

8 Fr Vicente de Salvador, *Historia do Brasil* (Rio de Janeiro, 1889): http://purl.pt/154/1/P3.html (accessed May 2008).

9 P. Goodwin, *Brazil Builds: Architecture New and Old, 1652–1942* (New York, 1943).

10 O. C. Ferreira, 'O Sistema Elétrico Brasileiro', *Economia & Energia*, 32 (May–June 2002): http://ecen.com/eee32/sistelet.htm (accessed May 2008).

11 Holston, *The Modernist City*, p. 122; H. Segawa, *Arquiteturas no Brasil 1900–1990* (São Paulo, 1998), p. 122.

12 Marcel Gautherot, *Brasília* (Munich, 1966).

13 Information from the Instituto Brasileiro de Geografia e Estatística website: www.igbe.gov.br (accessed 22 April 2008).

14 Costa cited in F. de Holanda, *O Espaço de Exceção* (Brasília, 2002), p. 293.

15 Ibid., p. 294.

16 Segawa, *Arquitecturas no Brasil*, p. 164.

17 Ibid.

18 Holanda, *O Espaço de Exceção*, p. 284.

19 N. Evenson, *Two Brazilian Capitals* (New Haven, CT, and London, 1973), p. 113.

20 Ibid., p. 114.

21 *L'Architecture d'aujourd'hui*, 80 (1958), pp. 60–61.

22 P. Zimbres, 'A Study of Brasília: From Master Plan to Implementation', unpublished M.Phil. thesis, University of Edinburgh (1974), p. 43.

23 W. Holford, 'Brasília: A New Capital City For Brazil', *Architectural Review*, CXXII/731 (1957), pp. 395–402.

24 Costa in ibid.

25 Holston, *The Modernist City*; F. de Holanda, ed., *Arquitetura e Urbanidade* (São Paulo, 2004).

26 Holanda, *Arquitetura e Urbanidade*.

27 Costa in Holford, 'Brasília', pp. 395–402.

28 Holston, *The Modernist City*, p. 101.

29 Franciney Carreiro de França, 'A indisciplina que muda a arquitetura – a dinâmica do espaço doméstico no Distrito Federal', unpublished PhD thesis, Faculdade de Arquitetura da Universidade de Brasília (2008).

30 'Brasília Palace Hotel', *L'Architecture d'aujourd'hui*, 80 (1958), pp. 66–7.

31 A. da Costa Braga and F.A.R. Falcão, *Guia de Urbanismo: Arquitetura e Arte de Brasília* (Brasília, 1997).

32 For more on air space as a cultural idea, see David Pascoe, *Air Spaces* (London, 2001).

33 S. de Beauvoir, *La Force des choses* (Paris, 1963).

34 C. Buchanan, 'The Moon's Backside', *RIBA Journal*, LXXIV/7 (April 1967), pp. 159–60.

35 D. Epstein, *Brasília, Plan and Reality: A Study of Planned and Spontaneous Urban Development* (Berkeley and Los Angeles, 1973).
36 A. Paviani, ed., *Brasília: Ideologia e Realidade / Espacao Urbano em Questao* (São Paulo, 1985), and *Urbanização e Metropolização: A Gestão dos Conflitos em Brasília* (Brasília, 1987). For a commentary on the historiography of Brasília, see R. J. Williams, 'Brasília depois de Brasília', *Arquitextos* [Brazil] 83 (April 2007): http://www.vitruvius.com.br/arquitextos/arq083/arq083_00.asp, and R. J. Williams, 'Brasilia after Brasília', *Progress in Planning*, 67 (2007), pp. 301–66.
37 Gilberto Freyre, *Brasis, Brasil e Brasília* (Lisbon, 1960), p. 165.
38 A. Bellos, 'Tomorrow's World', *The Guardian* (14 August 1999).
39 www.brasiliashopping.com.br (accessed May 2006).
40 Ibid.
41 P. Zimbres, 'Águas Claras: Um Exercício de Urbanismo no Distrito Federal', unpublished masterplan (1991).
42 Zimbres, 'A Study of Brasília'.
43 http://www.mbengenharia.com.br/ (accessed 28 August 2006).
44 Sales brochure for Portal das Andorinhas, 2006.
45 G. Agamben, *Homo Sacer: Sovereign Power and Bare Life* (Stanford, CA, 1998).
46 Le Corbusier, *Towards a New Architecture* (Oxford, 1989), pp. 122–3.
47 Holston, *The Modernist City*, pp. 177–8.

chapter four: **The Aesthetics of Poverty**

1 National Security Archive, White House Audio Tape, President Lyndon B. Johnson discussing the impending coup in Brazil with Undersecretary of State George Ball, 31 March 1964: http://www.gwu.edu/~nsarchiv/NSAEBB/NSAEBB118/LBJ-Brazil.mp3 (accessed February 2008).
2 *Terra em Transe* was banned throughout Brazil on both political and religious grounds.
3 G. Rocha, 'Uma Estética da Fome', *Resehna do Cinema Latino-Americano* [Genoa] (1965): http://www.dhnet.org.br/desejos/textos/glauber.htm (accessed 15 November 2005).
4 Ibid., p. 2.
5 Ibid.
6 Niemeyer and Costa are the main figures implied here, along with Affonso Reidy, Carlos Leão and the Roberto brothers.
7 Lina Bo Bardi in Museu de Arte de São Paulo, exh. cat., *Lina Bo Bardi, 1957–1968* (1997), unpaginated.
8 K. Frampton, *Modern Architecture: A Critical History* (London, 1992), p. 262.
9 Banham in ibid., p. 265.
10 Museu de Arte de São Paulo, *Lina Bo Bardi*.
11 Wisnik, in *Brazil's Modern Architecture*, ed. A. Forty and E. Andreoli (London, 2004), p. 42.
12 H. Segawa, *Arquiteturas no Brasil, 1900–1990* (São Paulo, 1998), p. 150.
13 Roberto Conduru in *Brazil's Modern Architecture*, ed. Forty and Andreoli, p. 78.
14 V. Artigas, *Caminhos da Arquitetura* (São Paulo 2004), pp. 30–34.
15 Ibid., p. 33, 37, 38. The Engels he refers to is the work known as *A Situação da Clase Trabalhadora na Inglaterra*, then regarded by Brazilian Marxists as a live, not historical, text. For an English edition, see F. Engels, *The Condition of the Working Class in England*, ed. David McLellan (Oxford, 1993).
16 Artigas, *Caminhos da Arquitetura*, p. 47.
17 Ibid., p. 38. Author's translation.
18 Ibid., p. 28.
19 Segawa, *Arquiteturas no Brasil*, p. 145.

20 Ibid., p. 146.

21 Ibid., p. 151.

22 A. Farias, *La Arquitetura de Ruy Ohtake* (Madrid, 1994), p. 68: 'Compared to the Carioca faction, the language of the Paulista school, in particular that of Artigas, is based on the belief in the revolutionary role of architecture; it devalues artistic intention in favour of a more ascetic and barren aesthetic in which the amount of human labour used to build the project is explicit.'

23 P. F. Arantes, *Arquitetura Nova: Sérgio Ferro, Flávio Império e Rodrigo Lefèvre de Artigas aos Mutirões* (São Paulo, 2002), p. 39.

24 Ibid., p. 40.

25 Ibid. See also Forty and Andreoli, eds, *Brazil's Modern Architecture*, pp. 18–19.

26 Forty and Andreoli, eds, p. 19.

27 Max Bill cited *Habitat* as an example of the high quality of Brazil's architectural culture in his 1954 outburst against Niemeyer: 'Report on Brazil', *Architectural Review*, cxvi/694 (October 1954), p. 238. On the Salvador museum, see http://www.itaucultural.org.br/ AplicExternas/enciclopedia_IC/index.cfm?fuseaction=instituicoes_texto&cd_verbete= 4990 (accessed 19 January 2008).

28 Museu de Arte de São Paulo, *Lina Bo Bardi*.

29 Ibid.

30 A. Malraux, *La Musée imaginaire de la sculpture mondiale* (Paris, 1952).

31 O. de Oliveira, *Lina Bo Bardi: Sutis Substâncias da Arquitetura* (São Paulo and Barcelona, 2006), p. 281.

32 R.M.A. Lima Zueler, 'The Faces of Janus: Modernism and Hybridization in the Architecture of Lina Bo Bardi', *Journal of Architecture*, xi/2 (April 2006), p. 258. This view was entirely consistent with contemporary views on race, although it seems patronizing (and possibly racist) now.

33 Oliveira, *Lina Bo Bardi*, p. 203.

34 C. Rodriges de Santos, in Museu de Arte de São Paulo, *Lina Bo Bardi*.

35 Ibid.

36 E. Subirats, 'Arquitetura e Poesia: Dois Exemplos Latino-Americanos', *Projeto*, 143 (July 1991), p. 77.

37 Ibid.

38 Rodriges de Santos, in Museu de Arte de São Paulo, *Lina Bo Bardi*.

39 Forty and Andreoli, eds, *Brazil's Modern Architecture*.

40 For more commentary on the apertures see Ruth Verde Zein, *O Lugar da Critica* (São Paulo, 2003). They are a crucial image for Zein, and are illustrated on the book's cover.

41 Wisnik in Forty and Andreoli, eds, *Brazil's Modern Architecture*, p. 49.

chapter five: **The Politics of Liberation**

1 *Architecture without Architects*, exh. cat., Museum of Modern Art (New York, 1964).

2 O. de Oliveira, *Lina Bo Bardi: Sutis Substâncias da Arquitetura* (São Paulo, 2006), p. 254.

3 P. Zimbres, 'A Study of Brasília: From Master Plan to Implementation', unpublished m.phil. thesis, University of Edinburgh (1974), p. 103.

4 O. Niemeyer, *A Minha Experiéncia em Brasília* (Rio de Janeiro, 1961), pp. 18–19.

5 Ibid., pp. 9–10.

6 Ibid., p. 23.

7 See also R. J. Williams, 'Modernist Civic Space', *Journal of Urban History*, xxxii/1 (November 2005), p. 130. For an academic commentary on Brasília's social segregation, see A. Paviani, ed., *Brasília: Ideologia e Realidade / Espaço Urbano em Questão* (São Paulo, 1985), p. 56.

8 E. Silva, *História de Brasília: Um Sonho, Uma Esperança, Uma Realidade* (Brasília, 1971),

p. 231.

9   D. Caute, *Sixty-Eight: The Year of the Barricades* (London, 1988).

10 These letters appear in L. Figueiredo, ed., *Lygia Clark, Hélio Oiticica: Cartas, 1964–74* (Rio de Janeiro, 1998), p. 50.

11 See J. C. Soares, 'A Recepção das Ideias de Marcuse no Brasil': http://www.gseis.ucla.edu/faculty/kellner/Illumina%20Folder/marc1.htmI (accessed 14 April 2006). The journal *Revista da Civilisação Brasilieira* published Marcuse for the first time in Brazil in 1968. Oiticica's education in Marcusean thought, however, came from existing translations (probably French) of his work.

12 Figueiredo, ed., *Lygia Clark, Hélio Oiticica*, p. 44.

13 G. Freyre, *The Masters and the Slaves: A Study in the Development of Brazilian Civilization* (New York and London, 1956).

14 P. Freire, *Pedagogy of the Oppressed* (London, 1996), pp. 8–16.

15 Ibid., pp. 18, 106 ff.

16 A. Boal, *Teatro do Oprimido e Outras Poéticas Políticas* (Rio de Janeiro, 1991).

17 A. Gilbert, *The Latin American City* (London, 1994), p. 80.

18 P. Lloyd-Sherlock, 'The Recent Appearance of *Favelas* in São Paulo City: An Old Problem in a New Setting', *Bulletin of Latin American Research*, xvi/3 (1997), p. 292.

19 B. Diken, 'City of God', *City*, ix/3 (December 2005), pp. 307–20.

20 S. Philippou, 'The Primitive as an Instrument of Subversion in Twentieth Century Brazilian Cultural Practice', *Arq*, viii/3–4 (2006), pp. 285–98.

21 Ibid., p. 288.

22 Ibid.

23 An updated version of the Orpheus myth, with the *favela* standing in for the underworld. It is a place of uninhibited eroticism, in marked contrast to the formality of the central city.

24 J.F.C. Turner, 'Dwelling Resources in South America', *Architectural Design* (August 1963), pp. 360–93.

25 J.F.C. Turner, 'The Squatter Settlement: An Architecture that Works', *Architectural Design* (October 1968), pp. 355–60.

26 In a later work, Turner wonders 'how many admirers of Brasilia [*sic*], for example, stay longer than necessary'. Modernist architecture is, he continues in a later passage, 'aesthetically hideous, socially alienating, and technically incompetent', what happens 'when fossil-fuelled heteronomy takes over, or as Sigfried Giedeon puts it, when mechanisation takes command.' See J.F.C. Turner, *Housing By People: Towards Autonomy in Building Environments*, introduction by Colin Ward (London and New York, 1976), pp. 17, 49.

27 C. M. de Jesus, *Beyond All Pity* (London, 1962).

28 J. Perlman, *The Myth of Marginality: Urban Poverty and Politics in Rio de Janeiro* (Berkeley and Los Angeles, 1976), p. 243.

29 Figueiredo, ed., *Lygia Clark, Hélio Oiticica*, p. 103.

30 There is something of a bohemian quarter in Santa Teresa, a picturesque nineteenth-century suburb above the city proper.

31 C. Basualdo, ed., *Tropicália: A Revolution in Brazilian Culture, 1967–1972* (São Paulo, 2006).

32 Ibid., p. 17. Oiticica originally visited at the invitation of another artist, Jackson Ribeiro, to collaborate on costumes for Mangueira's Samba school.

33 Ibid., p. 348.

34 Whitechapel Art Gallery, *Hélio Oiticica*, exh. cat. (London, 1969).

35 L. Cavalcanti, *Quando Brasil era Moderno: Guia de Arquitetura, 1928–1960* (Rio de Janeiro, 2001), p. 46.

36 Basnaldo, *Tropicália*.

37 S. Ferro, *Arquitectura e Trabalho Livre* (São Paulo, 2006), pp. 47–58.

38 Ibid., pp. 105–202.

39 Ibid., p. 132.

40 Ibid., pp. 105–6.
41 Ibid., p. 314.
42 P. F. Arantes, *Arquitectura Nova: Sérgio Ferro, Flávio Império e Rodrigo Lefèvre de Artigas aos Mutirões* (São Paulo, 2002), pp. 20–21.
43 Temporary sheds built by the British army in the Second World War. The similarity is probably coincidental.
44 Arantes, *Arquitectura Nova*, p. 78.
45 Ibid., p. 79.
46 Ferro, *Arquitectura e Trabalho Livre*, pp. 315–16.
47 *Casa popular* refers to both housing types and social groups that do not have exact equivalents outside Brazil. It means housing built by and for the poor, using local materials, knowledge and skills.
48 Arantes, *Arquitectura Nova*, p. 83.
49 *Tropicália*, Barbican Arts Centre (13 February–22 May 2006); *Hélio Oiticica: The Body of Colour*, Tate Modern (6 June–23 September 2007); Whitechapel Art Gallery, *Hélio Oiticica: Quasi Cinemas* (3 May–23 June 2002).
50 N. Evenson, *Two Brazilian Capitals* (New Haven, CT, and London, 1973), p. 28.
51 R. Schwarz, 'City of God', *New Left Review*, 12 (November–December 2001): http://www.newleftreview.net/Issue12.asp?Article=06 (accessed 22 March 2006). Schwarz is referring to the novel here.
52 D. M. Goldstein, *Laughter Out of Place: Race, Class, Violence and Sexuality in a Rio Shantytown* (Berkeley and Los Angeles, 2003); D. Epstein, *Brasília, Plan and Reality: A Study of Planned and Spontaneous Urban Development* (Berkeley and Los Angeles, 1973).

chapter six: **The Politics of Spectacle**

1 L. Costa, 'Muita Construção, Alguma Arquitetura e um Milagre', *Correio da Manhã* (15 June 1951).
2 http://www.prefeitura.sp.gov.br/portal/a_cidade/historia/index.php?p=4827 (accessed 14 August 2007). São Paulo city proper has a population of 11 million.
3 A. C. Fernandes and R. Negreiros, 'Economic Developmentism and Change within the Brazilian Urban System', *Geoforum*, XXXII/4 (November 2001), pp. 415–35.
4 Brasília is only a qualified exception here. The metropolitan region has high-rises of a type found throughout Brazil. See chapter Three for more details.
5 *A Construção em São Paulo*, 1250 (January 1972); quoted in M.A.J. Bastos, *Pos-Brasília: Rumos da Arquitetura Brasileira* (São Paulo, 2003), pp. 24–7.
6 Ibid., p. 25.
7 For regularly updated information on this question, see www.emporis.com
8 A. Faiola, 'Brazil's Elites Fly Above Their Fears: Rich Try To Wall Off Urban Violence', *Washington Post* (1 June 2002), p. A1.
9 R. V. Zein, *O Lugar da Critica* (São Paulo, 2003), p. 19.
10 G. Debord, 'Society of the Spectacle', in www.marxists.org/reference/archive/debord/society/htm (accessed 10 October 2008).
11 L. Recamán, in *Brazil's Modern Architecture*, ed. E. Andreoli and A. Forty (London, 2004), p. 108.
12 Bastos, *Pós-Brasília*, p. 24.
13 L. Korawick, ed., *Social Struggles and the City: The Case of São Paulo* (New York, 1994), p. 127.
14 C. Gati, 'Perfil de Arquitecto – Franz Heep', *Projeto*, 97 (March 1987), pp. 97–104.
15 For an account of the conflicts between poverty and wealth involved in the creation of this new district, see M. Fix, *Parceiros da Exclusão* (São Paulo, 2001).
16 Engels's *The Condition of the Working Class in England* is well known in Brazil. For further discussion on this text, see chapter Four.

17 For more on this comparison, see J. D. Wirth and R. L. Jones, eds, *Manchester and São Paulo: Problems of Rapid Urban Growth* (Stanford, CA, 1978).

18 C. Lévi-Strauss, *Tristes Tropiques* (London, 1976), p. 120.

19 Ibid., pp. 120–21.

20 Ibid., p. 118.

21 C. Lévi-Strauss, *Saudades do Brasil: A Photographic Memoir* (Seattle, WA, and London, 1995), p. 30.

22 This and the earlier quotations from S. Zweig, *Brazil: Land of the Future* (London, 1942), pp. 211–17.

23 'Report on Brazil', *Architectural Review*, CXVI/694 (October 1954), pp. 236–7.

24 Ibid., pp. 238–9.

25 S. Giedeon, in H. Mindlin, *Modern Architecture in Brazil* (Rio de Janeiro and Amsterdam, 1956), pp. 155–6.

26 S. de Beauvoir, *La Force des choses* (Paris, 1963), pp. 564–5.

27 N. B. Peixoto, *Paisagens Urbanas* (São Paulo, 2003), p. 285.

28 Ibid., p. 289.

29 E. Subirats, 'Arquitetura e Poesia: Dois Exemplos Latino-Americanos', *Projeto*, 143 (July 1991), pp. 75–9.

30 L. Kowarick, *Social Struggles and the City: The Case of São Paulo* (New York, 1994), pp. 57–8.

31 Ibid., p. 13.

32 T. Caldeira, *City of Walls: Crime, Segregation and Citizenship in São Paulo* (Berkeley and Los Angeles, 2000), p. 19.

33 The Brazilians were represented in the exhibition *Espaço Aberto / Espaço Fechado* at the Henry Moore Institute, Leeds (5 February–16 April 2006). All showed works responding to Niemeyer's architecture for the Bienal pavilions.

34 Caldeira, *City of Walls*, pp. 225–6.

35 V. Artigas, interview of 1984 in *Depoimento de uma Geração*, ed. A. Xavier (São Paulo, 2003), p. 222.

36 N. Somekh, 'O Prédio Martinelli', unpublished MA dissertation, University of São Paulo, Faculty of Architecture and Urbanism (1976), pp. 15–17.

37 http://www.prediomartinelli.com.br/historia.php (accessed 14 August 2007).

38 The relative lack of literature on the Copan is perhaps a function of its status as a private development.

39 G. Wisnik, in *Brazil's Modern Architecture*, ed. Andreoli and Forty, p. 33.

40 D. Macedo, 'A Obra de Oscar Niemeyer em Belo Horizonte': http://www.mdc.arq.br/mdc/txt/mdc02-txt05.pdf, accessed June 2007.

41 Serapião, *São Paulo: Guia de Arquitetura Contemporânea*, pp. 44–5.

42 Fix, *Parceiros da Exclusão*.

43 M. Castells, *The Rise of the Network Society* (Oxford, 1996), pp. 404ff. See also discussion in R. J. Williams, *The Anxious City: English Urbanism at the End of the Twentieth Century* (London, 2004), pp. 184–91.

44 Zein quoted in Bastos, *Pos-Brasília*, p. 73.

45 Serapião, *São Paulo: Guia de Arquitetura Contemporânea*, pp. 90–91.

46 A. Farias, *La Arquitectura de Ruy Ohtake* (Madrid, 1994), p. 235.

47 A. Zapparoli, 'Cores, Curvas e Concreto', *Veja* (27 July 2005), p. 22.

48 Ibid., p. 24.

49 R. Segre, *Ruy Ohtake: Contemporaneidade da Arquitetura Brasileira* (São Paulo, 1999), p. 22, 44.

50 Hence the nickname, *prédio das carambolas*, or 'starfruit building'.

51 P. Goldberger, 'The Next Seven Wonders', *Condé Nast Traveler* (April 2004): http://www.concierge.com/cntraveler/articles/detail?articleId=5822&pageNumber=2 (accessed May 2006). The list also included the new Prada store in Tokyo, Frank Gehry's Walt Disney Concert Hall in Los Angeles, and Future Systems' Selfridges

building in Birmingham, UK.

52 Based on a visit by the author in July 2005.

53 J. Czajkowski, *Guia da Arquitetura Moderna no Rio de Janeiro* (Rio de Janeiro, 2000), p. 139.

chapter seven: The Politics of Public Space

1 T. Caldeira, *City of Walls: Crime, Segregation and Citizenship in São Paulo* (Berkeley and Los Angeles, 2000), pp. 320–21.

2 J. Rykwert, *The Idea of a Town: The Anthropology of Urban Form in Rome, Italy, and the Ancient World* (Cambridge, MA, 1988), preface, unpaginated.

3 L. Mumford, *The Culture of Cities* (London, 1938), p. 5 especially. In this context see also R. Sennett, *The Fall of Public Man* (London, 1986); P. G. Rowe, *Civic Realism* (Cambridge, MA, 1997); R. J. Williams, *The Anxious City: English Urbanism at the End of the Twentieth Century* (London, 2004).

4 J. Holston, *The Modernist City: An Anthropological Critique of Brasília* (Chicago, 1989), p. 105.

5 G. Freyre, *The Masters and the Slaves: A Study in the Development of Brazilian Civilization* (New York and London, 1956); S. B. de Holanda, *Raízes do Brasil* (São Paulo, 1995).

6 See P. G. Rowe, *Civic Realism* (Cambridge, MA, and London, 1996).

7 N. Evenson, *Two Brazilian Capitals* (New Haven, CT, and London, 1973), p. 32.

8 And also Washington, DC, at precisely the same time.

9 Evenson, *Two Brazilian Capitals*, p. 46.

10 For more on Le Corbusier's general conception of social life, see S. Richards, *Le Corbusier and the Concept of Self* (Cambridge, MA, 2003), p. 65.

11 Evenson, *Two Brazilian Capitals*, p. 13. The population has subsequently declined to fewer than 200,000. Many of the more wealthy residents have moved further south to the newer, and more secure, *bairro* of Barra da Tijuca.

12 Ibid., p. 13.

13 T. Richardson, 'Copacabana Pavements', *Architectural Review*, CLXXVII/1056 (February 1985), pp. 80–81.

14 A useful, short, introduction to Burle Marx can be found in J.-F. Lejeune, ed., *Cruelty and Utopia: Cities and Landscapes of Latin America* (New York, 2003), pp. 182–95.

15 In a car, with light traffic, the transition between the two projects can seem almost momentary, punctuated only by the Botafogo tunnel. The one is certainly conceptually a continuation of the other, a huge space for promenades.

16 J. Czajkowski, ed., *Guia da Arquitetura Moderna no Rio de Janeiro* (Rio de Janeiro, 2000), p. 74.

17 S. Eliovson, *The Gardens of Roberto Burle Marx* (London and New York, 1991), p. 18.

18 Ibid., p. 103.

19 Lejeune, ed., *Cruelty and Utopia*, p. 193.

20 Williams, *The Anxious City*, pp. 82–106.

21 Richardson, 'Copacabana Pavements'.

22 For a more detailed version of this argument, see Williams, *The Anxious City*, pp. 228–41.

23 R. V. Zein, 'Descubre os Sete Erros', *Projeto Design*, 120 (April 1989), pp. 72–3.

24 'Os limites de Sarney', *Folha de São Paulo* (19 March 1989), p. A2.

25 C. Rowe and F. Koetter, *Collage City* (Cambridge, MA, 1978), pp. 62–3.

26 D. Underwood, *Oscar Niemeyer and Brazilian Free-Form Modernism* (New York, 1994), p. 115.

27 M. Bastos, *Pos-Brasília: Rumos da Arquitetura Brasileira* (São Paulo, 2003), p. 223.

28 D. Ribeiro, *América Latina: A Pátria Grande* (Rio de Janeiro, 1986), p. 11.

29 Underwood, *Oscar Niemeyer*, p. 109.

30 'Entrevista com Darcy Ribeiro', *Arquitetura e Urbanismo*, V/24 (June–July 1989), p. 56.

31 *Folha de São Paulo* (18 March 1989).

32 *Estado de São Paulo* (18 March 1989), p. 10.

33 No public competition was held for the project's construction, contravening Brazilian law: *Folha de São Paulo* (19 March 1989).

34 'Inauguração do Memorial reúne só mil pessoas', *Folha de São Paulo* (19 March 1989), p. A9.

35 For an excellent alternative summary of the debate around the Memorial, see Bastos, *Pos-Brasília*, pp. 223–9. At the time of the inauguration, one of Niemeyer's allies, the art critic Ferreira Gullar, nevertheless still claimed that only 'mediocrities' would dare to criticize the master.

36 Zein, 'Descubre os Sete Erros', p. 72.

37 Ibid.

38 E. Mahfuz, 'Do Minimalismo e da Disperção como Método Projetual', *Arquitetura e Urbanismo*, v/24 (June–July 1989), p. 44.

39 Comas, cited in Bastos, *Pos-Brasília*, p. 228.

40 Maria Alice Junqueira Bastos, *Pos-Brasília: Rumos da Arquitetura Brasileira* (São Paulo, 2003), p. 236.

41 R. J. Williams, 'Paulo Mendes da Rocha', *Blueprint*, 251 (February 2007), pp. 36–43.

42 O. Bohigas, 'Ten Points for an Urban Methodology', *Architectural Review*, CCVI/1231 (September 1999), pp. 88–91.

43 F. Serapião, *São Paulo: Guia de Arquitetura Contemporânea* (Rio de Janeiro, 2005), pp. 56–7.

44 Wisnik, in *Brazil's Modern Architecture*, ed. A. Forty and E. Andreoli (London, 2004), p. 226.

45 The British architect Richard Rogers, for example, has been a keen supporter of Lerner. See R. Rogers, *Cities for a Small Planet* (London, 1997), pp. 59–61.

46 J. Lerner, *Acupunctura Urbana* (Rio de Janeiro and São Paulo, 2005).

47 For a critique of the touristic model of urban development, see Williams, *The Anxious City*, chapters 3 and 8.

48 *Projeto Design*, 239 (January 2000), pp. 42–3.

49 Ibid., p. 42.

50 'Marché de Rocinha, Rio de Janeiro (RJ)', *L'Architecture d'aujourd-hui*, 359 (July–August 2006), pp. 56–7.

51 C. Davidson, 'Behind Closed Doors', *Blueprint* (December 2004–January 2005), pp. 34–8.

52 M. Carvalho, R. George and K. Anthony, 'Residential Satisfaction in *Condomínios Exclusivos* (Gate-Guarded Neighbourhoods) in Brazil', *Environment and Behaviour*, XXIX/6 (November 1997), pp. 734–68.

53 See Caldeira, *City of Walls*, pp. 278–9.

chapter eight: Brazil's Legacies

1 Niemeyer was awarded the prize jointly with Gordon Bunshaft.

2 Norman Foster, panel discussion chaired by Ricky Burdett, Serpentine Pavilion, London (June 2003).

3 H. Harman, 'Big Mac and Prize To Go', *Building Design* (16 October 1998), p. 12.

4 R. V. Zein, *O Lugar da Critica* (São Paulo, 2003), pp. 181–5.

5 R. J. Williams, 'Paulo Mendes da Rocha', *Blueprint*, 251 (February 2007), pp. 36–43.

6 For the history of Minimalism's move towards site-specificity, see R. J. Williams, *After Modern Sculpture: Art in the United States and Europe, 1965–70* (Manchester, 2000).

7 The crucial case study here is *Tilted Arc*, a sculpture built by Serra in New York for Federal Plaza, commissioned, installed and then (after a long campaign) destroyed.

8 Segawa, in M.A.J. Bastos, *Pos-Brasília: Rumos da Arquitetura Brasileira* (São Paulo, 2003), p. 236.

9 S. Telles, quoted in ibid., p. 238.

10 J. M. Montaner, quoted in ibid., p. 236.

11 Arantes, quoted in ibid., p. 238.

12 Ibid., p. 240.

13 G. Wisnik, in *Brazil's Modern Architecture*, ed. A. Forty and E. Andreoli (London, 2004), pp. 51–5.

14 http://www.pritzkerprize.com/full_new_site/2006/pdf/mediakit.pdf (accessed November 2006).

15 O. Niemeyer, 'Més Experiences à Brasília', *L'Architecture d'aujourd'hui*, 90 (1960), p. 9.

16 O. Niemeyer, *Minha Arquitectura* (Rio de Janeiro, 2000), p. 43.

17 See R. J. Williams, 'Surreal City: The Case of Brasília', in *Architecture and Surrealism*, ed. T. Mical (London, 2005), pp. 234–48; D. Underwood, *Oscar Niemeyer and Brazilian Free-Form Modernism* (New York, 1994).

18 Bill quoted in N. Evenson, *Two Brazilian Capitals* (New Haven, CT, 1973), p. 92.

19 Ibid.

20 Harman, 'Big Mac and Prize To Go', p. 12.

21 M. Wajnberg (dir.), *An Architect Committed to his Century* (Belgium, 2000).

22 Harman, 'Big Mac and Prize To Go'.

23 Reported to the author by Teixeira Coelho, 2006.

24 J. Glancey, 'The Old Boy from Brazil', *The Guardian* (23 June 2003), www.guardian.co.uk, (accessed June 2003).

25 London, Serpentine Gallery, press release (2003): http://www.serpentinegallery.org/aac.html.

26 D. Sudjic, 'The Old Boy from Brazil', *Observer* (22 June 2003) (accessed June 2003).

27 Niemeyer's office on Copocabana is decorated with semi-pornographic nudes. When the author met him in 2001 he was still going out every day to watch (and draw) the girls on the beach.

28 See R. Cork, in *New Statesman* (30 June 2003); Glancey, 'The Old Boy from Brazil'.

29 O. Niemeyer, 'Brasília, hoje: uma cidade como outra cualquer', *Jornal do Brasil* (31 August 1983)

30 See K. Frampton, *Modern Architecture: A Critical History* (London and New York, 1992), pp. 256–7.

31 Glancey, 'The Old Boy from Brazil'.

32 H. Baldock, 'Brasília Was Built for Cars, not People', *Icon*, 004 (July–August 2003).

33 C. M. Teixeira, 'La Vraie Nature de Brasília: Photographies d'Emmanuel Pinard', *L'Architecture d'aujourd'hui*, 359 (July–August 2005), p. 103.

34 Y. Tsiomis and J. Rolin, 'Brasília', *L'Architecture d'aujourd'hui*, 313 (October 1997), p. 81.

35 Ibid., p. 87.

36 Governo do Distrito Federal (GDF), *Brasília: Capital do Século 21* (Brasília, 2001)

37 *Brasília: Une Metaphore de la Liberté. Photographies d'Alberto Ferreira et Jair Lanes*, exh. cat., Maison des Amériques Latines, Paris (2005).

38 *Espaço Aberto / Espaço Fechado: Sites for Sculpture in Modern Brazil*, exh. cat., Henry Moore Institute, Leeds (2006).

39 F. L. Lara, 'Arquitetura Brasileira Volta as Páginas das Publicações Internacionais na Decada do 90', *Projeto Design*, 251 (January 2001), pp. 8–9.

40 Ibid., p. 8.

41 Frampton, *Modern Architecture*, p. 343.

Select Bibliography

Agamben, G., *Homo Sacer: Sovereign Power and Bare Life* (Stanford, CA, 1998)

Agüero, F., and J. Stark, ed. *Fault Lines of Democracy in Post-Transition Latin America* (Coral Gables, FL, 1998)

Alambert, F., and P. Canhête, *Bienais de São Paulo: Da Era do Museu à Era do Curadores* (São Paulo, 2004)

Almandoz, A., 'Urban Planning and Historiography in Latin America', *Progress in Planning*, 65 (2006), pp. 81–123

Andreas, P., and I. Flagge, eds, *Oscar Niemeyer: Eine Legende der Moderne* (Frankfurt am Main, 2003)

Arantes, P. F., *Arquitetura Nova: Sérgio Ferro, Flávio Império e Rodrigo Lefèvre de Artigas aos Mutirões* (São Paulo, 2002)

L'Architecture d'aujourd'hui, 171 (1962) [special issue on Oscar Niemeyer]

L'Architecture d'aujourd'hui, 251 (June 1987), pp. 2–8 [special issue on Brazil]

'The Architecture of Democracy', *Architectural Design* (August 1968) [special issue]

Baiocchi, G. P., ed., *Radicals in Power: The Workers' Party (PT) and Experiments in Urban Democracy in Brazil* (London and New York, 2003)

Baldock, H., 'Brasília Was Built for Cars, not People', *Icon*, 004 (July–August 2003)

Bastos, M.A.J., *Pos-Brasília: Rumos da Arquitetura Brasileira* (São Paulo, 2003)

Basualdo, C., ed., *Tropicália: A Revolution in Brazilian Culture, 1967–1972* (São Paulo, 2006)

Beauvoir, S. de, *La Force des choses* (Paris, 1963)

Bellos, A., 'Tomorrow's World', *The Guardian* (14 August 1999): www.guardian.co.uk, accessed May 2006

Boal, A., *Teatro do Oprimido e Outras Poéticas Políticas* (Rio de Janeiro, 1991)

Bohigas, O., 'Ten Points for an Urban Methodology', *Architectural Review*, CCVI/1231 (September 1999), pp. 88–91

Barbosa, M. C., 'A Obra de Adolf Franz Heep no Brasil', PhD thesis, Universidade de São Paulo, Faculdade de Arquitetura e Urbanismo (2002)

'Brésil-France Architecture', *Les Cahiers de la recherche architecturale et urbaine*, 18–19 (May 2006)

Breugmann, R., *Sprawl: A Compact History* (Chicago, 2005)

Brillembourg, C., *Latin American Architecture, 1929–1960: Contemporary Reflections* (New York, 2004)

Bruand, Y., *Arquitetura Contemporâea no Brasil* (São Paulo, 1981)

Buchanan, C., 'The Moon's Backside', *RIBA Journal*, LXXIV/7 (April 1967), pp. 159–60

Bussell, D., 'Serpentine Gallery: Oscar Niemeyer: London', *Architecture*, XCII/8 (August 2003), p. 90

Caldeira, T., *City of Walls: Crime, Segregation and Citizenship in São Paulo* (Berkeley and Los Angeles, 2000)

Cardeman, D., and R. Cardeman, *O Rio de Janeiro nas Alturas* (Rio de Janeiro, 2004)

Cardoso, R., 'Brazilian Blend', *Architectural Review*, CLXXXVII/1125 (November 1990), pp. 90–92

Carvalho, M., R. George and K. Anthony, 'Residential Satisfaction in *Condomínios Exclusivos*

(Gate-Guarded Neighbourhoods) in Brazil', *Environment and Behaviour*, xxix/6 (November 1997), pp. 734–68

Casal, S. M., 'Architecture and Urbanism in South America: The Context of Latin American Architecture', *Journal of Architecture*, xi/2 (April 2006), pp. 205–8

Castells, M., *The Rise of the Network Society* (Oxford, 1996)

Cavalcanti, L., *Quando Brasil era Moderno: Guia de Arquitetura, 1928–1960* (Rio de Janeiro, 2001)

—, *Moderno e Brasileiro: A História de uma Nova Linguagem na Arquitetura, 1930–60* (Rio de Janeiro, 2006)

Chester, S., 'King of Curves', *Sunday Telegraph Magazine* (22 October 2006), pp. 54–60

Cleary, D., D. Jenkins and O. Marshall, *The Rough Guide to Brazil* (New York, London and Delhi, 2003)

Coley, N., *Urban / Wild* (London, 2004)

Costa, L., 'Muita Construção: Alguma Arquitetura e um Milagre', *Correio da Manhã* (15 June 1951)

—, 'O Relatório do Plano Piloto de Brasília', *Modulo*, 8 (1957)

—, 'Brasília Revisitada', *Correio Braziliense* (8 March 1987), p. 29

Costa Braga, A. da, and F.A.R. Falcão, *Guia de Urbanismo: Arquitetura e arte de Brasília* (Brasília, 1997)

Czajkowski, J., *Guia da Arquitetura Moderna no Rio de Janeiro* (Rio de Janeiro, 2000)

el-Dahdah, F., *Case: Lúcio Costa, Brasília's Superquadras* (Munich, 2005)

Davidson, C., 'Behind Closed Doors', *Blueprint* (December 2004–January 2005), pp. 34–8

Davis, M., *Planet of Slums* (London, 2006)

Deckker, T., *The Modern City Revisited* (London, 2000)

Deckker, Z. Q., *Brazil Built: The Architecture of the Modern Movement in Brazil* (London, 2000)

Dickenson, J., 'The Future of the Past in the Latin American City: The Case of Brazil', *Bulletin of Latin American Research*, xiii/1 (May 1994), pp. 13–25

Docomomo, 'The Modern City Facing the Future', *Docomomo*, 23 (August 2000), pp. 1–55

Eliovson, S., *The Gardens of Roberto Burle Marx* (London and New York, 1991)

Encarnación, O. G., *The Myth of Civil Society: Social Capital and Democratic Consolidation in Spain and Brazil* (New York and Basingstoke, 2003)

'Entrevista com Paulo Mendes da Rocha', *Projeto Design*, 220 (May 1998), pp. 46–7

Epstein, D., *Brasília, Plan and Reality: A Study of Planned and Spontaneous Urban Development* (Berkeley and Los Angeles, 1973)

Espaço Aberto / Espaço Fechado: Sites for Sculpture in Modern Brazil, exh. cat., Henry Moore Institute, Leeds (2006)

'Especial: Brasília 40 Anos', *Projeto Design*, 242 (April 2000), pp. 48–59

Evenson, N., *Two Brazilian Capitals* (New Haven, ct, and London, 1973)

Farias, A., *La Arquitetura de Ruy Ohtake* (Madrid, 1994)

—, 'O artista como viajante', *Espaço e Debates*, xxiii/43–4 (January–December 2003), pp. 120–28

Ferraz, I. G., ed., *Museu de Arte de São Paulo* (Lisbon, 1997)

Ferro, S., *Arquitetura e Trabalho Livre* (São Paulo, 2006)

Ficher, S., 'Lúcio Costa (1902–1998): Modernism and Brazilian Tradition', *Docomomo*, 23 (August 2000), pp. 16–27

Figueiredo, L., ed., *Lygia Clark, Hélio Oiticica: Cartas, 1964–74* (Rio de Janeiro, 1998), p. 50

Fix, M., *Parceiros da Exclusão* (São Paulo, 2001)

Forty, A. and E. Andreoli, eds, *Brazil's Modern Architecture* (London, 2004)

Frampton, K., *Modern Architecture: A Critical History* (London, 1992)

—, *Le Corbusier* (London and New York, 2001)

Fraser, V., *Building the New World: Studies in the Modern Architecture of Latin America, 1930–1960* (London, 2000)

Freire, P., *Pedagogy of the Oppressed* (London, 1996)

Freyre, G., *The Masters and the Slaves: A Study in the Development of Brazilian Civilization* (New York and London, 1956)

—, *Brasis, Brasil e Brasília: sugestões em tôrno de problemas brasileiros de unidade e diversidade e das relações de alguns dêles com problemas gerais de pluralismo étnico e cultural* (Lisbon, 1961)

Garnett, P., 'Brasília Revisited', *RIBA Journal* (July 1988), pp. 44–7

Gautherot, M., *Brasília* (New York, 1966)

Gilbert, A., *Latin American Cities* (London, 1995)

Glancey, J., 'The Old Boy from Brazil', *The Guardian* (23 June 2003)

—, 'I Pick Up My Pen: A Building Appears', *The Guardian* (1 August 2007)

Goertzel, T., and T. Kahn, 'The Unsung Story of São Paulo's Murder Rate Drop', *Brazzil Magazine* (10 June 2007): http://newamericamedia.org, accessed 6 April 2008

Goldberger, P., 'The Next Seven Wonders', *Condé Nast Traveler* (April 2004): www.concierge.com/cntraveler/articles/detail?articleId=5822&pageNumber=2 accessed May 2006

Goldstein, D. M., *Laughter Out of Place: Race, Class, Violence and Sexuality in a Rio Shantytown* (Berkeley and Los Angeles, 2003)

—, *Brazil Builds: Architecture New and Old, 1652–1942*, exh. cat., Museum of Modern Art (New York, 1943)

Gorelik, A., *Das Vanguardas a Brasília* (Belo Horizonte, 2005)

Gorowitz, M., *Brasília: uma Questâo de Escala* (São Paulo, 1985)

Gouvêa, L., *Brasília: A Capital de Segregação de do Controle Social: Uma Avialação da Ação Governamental na Area da Habitação* (São Paulo, 1995)

Governo do Distrito Federal (GDF), *Brasília: Capital do Século 21* (Brasília, 2001)

Habitat, XL/1 (March–April 1957) [Brasília special issue], pp. 1–29

Hall, P., '*La Ville Radieuse* Meets MK', *Town and Country Planning*, LXXIV/4 (April 2005), pp. 122–3

Hélio Oiticica, exh. cat., Whitechapel Art Gallery, London (1969)

Hemming, J., *Die If You Must: Brazilian Indians in the Twentieth Century* (London, 2003)

Hitchcock, H. R., *Latin American Architecture since 1945*, exh. cat., Museum of Modern Art (New York, 1955)

Holanda, F. de, ed., *Arquitetura e Urbanidade* (São Paulo, 2004)

—, *O Espaço de Exceção* (Brasília, 2002)

—, 'Cidade Moderna, Cidade Eterna' (unpublished conference paper, Barcelona, 2006)

Holanda, S. B. de, *Raízes do Brasil* (São Paulo, 1995)

Holford, W., 'Brasília: A New Capital City For Brazil', *Architectural Review*, CXXII/731 (1957), pp. 395–402

Holston, J., *The Modernist City: An Anthropological Critique of Brasília* (Chicago, 1989)

—, 'Spaces of Insurgent Citizenship', *Architectural Design*, LXVI/11–12 (1996), pp. 54–9

Homem, M., 'A Ascenção do Imigrante e a Verticalização de São Paulo', MA dissertation, University of São Paulo, Faculty of Architecture and Urbanism (1982)

ICOMOS (International Council on Monuments and Sites), *World Heritage List*, 445 (Brasília, October 1987): http,//whc.unesco.org/en/list/445, accessed June 2006

Jesus, C. M. de, *Quarto de Despejo* (São Paulo, 1960)

Kinzo, M., and J. Dunkerley, eds, *Brazil since 1985: Economy, Polity and Society* (London, 2003)

Kossak, F., 'The Exhibition as a Laboratory for an Emerging Architecture', PhD thesis, Edinburgh College of Art (2008)

Koury, A., *Grupo Arquitetura Nova: Flávio Império, Rodrigo Lefèvre, Sérgio Ferro* (São Paulo, 2003)

Kowarick, L., *Social Struggles and the City: The Case of São Paulo* (New York, 1994)

Kubitschek, J., *Meu Caminho Para Brasília*, 3 vols (Rio de Janeiro, 1974–8)

Lara, F., 'Arquitetura Brasileira Volta as Páginas das Publicações Internacionais na Decada do 90', *Projeto Design*, 251 (January 2001), pp. 8–9

—, 'Dissemination of Design Knowledge: Evidence from 1950s Brazil', *Journal of Architecture*, XI/2 (April 2006), pp. 241–56

Le Corbusier, *The City of Tomorrow and its Planning* (New York, 1987)

—, *Towards a New Architecture* (Oxford, 1989)

Lejeune, J.-F., ed., *Cruelty and Utopia: Cities and Landscapes of Latin America* (New York, 2003)

Leneček, L., and G. Bosker, *The Beach: A History of Paradise on Earth* (London, 1998)

Lerner, J., *Acupunctura Urbana* (Rio de Janeiro and São Paulo, 2005)

Lévi-Strauss, C., *Tristes Tropiques* (London, 1976)

—, *The Raw and the Cooked* (London, 1994)

—, *Saudades do Brasil: A Photographic Memoir* (Seattle, WA, and London, 1995)

Lewis, O., 'The Culture of Poverty', *Scientific American*, CCXV/4 (1966), pp. 19–25

Lind, D., 'A Grand Master Breaks New Ground at the Serpentine', *Architectural Record*, CXCI/8 (3 August 2003), pp. 71–2

Lloyd, P., *Slums of Hope? Shanty Towns of the Third World* (Manchester, 1979)

Lobo, M., 'Brasília: da Utopia à Distopia', PhD thesis, FAU-USP (2002)

—, 'Ensaio para uma história da arte construtiva no Brasil como história de Brasília', *Espaço e Debates*, XXIII/43–4 (January–December 2003), pp. 105–19

Lores, R., 'São Paulo', in *La Biennale di Venezia, 10 Mostra Internazionale di Architectura: Cities, Architecture and Society* (Venice, 2006), pp. 96–103

Lynch, K., *The Image of the City* (Cambridge, MA, 1962)

McGuire, P., 'Interior Design: Art Gallery, São Paulo, Brazil', *Architectural Review*, CCVII/1236 (February 2000), pp. 76–8

Madaleno, I., 'Brasília: The Frontier Capital', *Cities*, XIII/4 (1996), pp. 273–80

Mahfuz, E., 'Do Minimalismo e da Disperção como Método Projetual', *Arquitetura e Urbanismo*, V/24 (June–July 1989), pp. 42–7

'Marché de Rocinha, Rio de Janeiro (RJ)', *L'Architecture d'aujourd'hui*, 359 (July–August 2006), pp. 56–7

Melendez, A., 'Complexo Ohtake Cultural', *Projeto Design*, 259 (September 2001), pp. 72–6

Mical, T., ed., *Surrealism and Architecture* (London, 2005)

Mindlin, H., *Modern Architecture in Brazil* (Rio de Janeiro and Amsterdam, 1956)

Museu de Arte de São Paulo, *Pompéia Factory, Lina Bo Bardi, 1977–1986* (São Paulo, 1996)

Museu de Arte de São Paulo, *Lina Bo Bardi, 1957–1968* (São Paulo, 1997)

Needell, J. D., 'Identity, Race, Gender and Modernity in the Origins of Gilberto Freyre's Oeuvre', *American Historical Review*, 100/1 (February 1995), pp. 51–77

Negromonte, S., 'Águas Claras Atrai Clase Media do DF', *Correio Braziliense* (20 October 2001): www.correioweb.com.br, accessed June 2005

Niemeyer, O., *A Minha Experiéncia em Brasília* (Rio de Janeiro, 1961)

—, 'Brasília, hoje: uma cidade como outra cualquer', *Jornal do Brasil* (31 August 1983)

—, *Les Courbes du Temps: Mémoires* (Paris, 1999)

—, *Minha Arquitetura* (Rio de Janeiro, 2000)

Nobre, A., et al., eds, *Lúcio Costa: Um Modo de Ser Moderno* (São Paulo, 2004)

Ohtake, R., ed., *Vilanova Artigas* (São Paulo, 2003)

Oliveira, M. N. de, 'Architecture, Culture and Curves: The Residential Buildings of Architect Ruy Ohtake in São Paulo, Brazil' (1997): http,//www.geocities.com/capitolhill/3836/saoPaulo.html?200620, accessed February 2008

Oliveira, O. de, *Lina Bo Bardi: Sutis Substâncias da Arquitetura* (São Paulo and Barcelona, 2006)

'Oscar Niemeyer, Galeria, Londres', *Projeto Design*, 283 (September 2003), pp. 68–71

Owensby, B. P., *Intimate Ironies: Modernity and the Making of Middle Class Lives in Brazil* (Stanford, CA, 1999)

Papadaki, S., *The Work of Oscar Niemeyer* (New York, 1950)

Paviani, A., ed., *Brasília: Ideologia e Realidade / Espação Urbano em Questão* (São Paulo, 1985)

—, ed., *Urbanização e Metropolização: A Gestão dos Conflitos em Brasília* (Brasília, 1987)

—, ed., *A Conquista da Cidade: Movimentos Populares em Brasília* (Brasília, 1991)

—, ed., *Brasília: Moradia e Exclusão* (Brasília, 1996)

Pearson, C., 'Re-engaging Global Culture', *CAA News*, XXXI/5 (2006), pp. 13–14

Peixoto, N., *Paisagens Urbanas* (São Paulo, 2003)

Perlman, J., *The Myth of Marginality: Urban Poverty and Politics in Rio de Janeiro* (Berkeley and Los Angeles, 1976)

Pevsner, N., 'Modern Architecture and the Historian or the Return of Historicism', RIBA
    Journal, LXVIII/6 (April 1961), pp. 230–40
Process Architecture, 17 (August 1980), pp. 4–162 [special issue on Brazil]
'Report on Brazil', Architectural Review, CXVI/694 (October 1954), pp. 234–50
Richards, J. M., 'Brasília: Progress Report', Architectural Review, CXXV/745 (1959), pp. 94–104
Ribeiro, D., The Americas and Civilization (London, 1971)
—, The Civilizational Process (New York, 1971)
—, América Latina: A Pátria Grande (Rio de Janeiro, 1986)
Richards, S., Le Corbusier and the Concept of Self (Cambridge, MA, 2003)
Richardson, T., 'Copacabana Pavements', Architectural Review, CLXXVII/1056 (February 1985),
    pp. 80–81
Robb, P., A Death in Brazil (London, 2003)
Rocha, G., 'Uma Estética da Fome', Resehna do Cinema Latino-Americano (Genoa, 1965):
    http://www.dhnet.org.br/desejos/textos/glauber.htm (accessed 15 November 2005)
Rogers, R., Cities for a Small Planet (London, 1997)
Rykwert, J., 'Preface', Architectural Design, LXVI/11–12 (1996), p. 6
—, The Seduction of Place (London, 2000)
Sassen, S., Cities in a World Economy (Thousand Oaks, CA, London and New Delhi, 2000)
Schwarz, R., 'City of God', New Left Review, 12 (November–December 2001):
    http://www.newleftreview.net/Issue12.asp?Article=06, accessed 22 March 2006
Segawa, H., 'Arquiteturas Modelando a Paisagem', Projeto Design, 183 (March 1995), pp. 32–47
—, Arquiteturas no Brasil, 1900–1990 (São Paulo, 1998)
Segre, R., 'Oscar Niemeyer na Bahia de Guanabara', Projeto Design, 202 (November 1996),
    pp. 34–45
—, Ruy Ohtake: Contemporaneidade da Arquitetura Brasileira (São Paulo, 1999)
Serapião, F., São Paulo: Guia de Arquitetura Contemporânea (Rio de Janeiro, 2005)
—, 'Bastante Construção, Muita Arquitetura e Nunhum Milagre', Projeto Design, 251 (January
    2001), pp. 60–61
Somekh, N., 'O Predio Martinelli', MA dissertation, University of São Paulo, Faculty of
    Architecture and Urbanism (1976)
Staübli, W., Brasília (London, 1966)
Subirats, E., 'Arquitetura e Poesia: Dois Exemplos Latino-Americanos', Projeto Design, 143
    (July 1991), pp. 75–9
Teixeira, C. M., 'La Vraie Nature de Brasília: photographies d'Emmanuel Pinard',
    L'Architecture d'aujourd'hui, 359 (July–August 2005), pp. 100–05
Trigeiros, L., and M. Ferraz, eds, SESC Fabrica da Pompéia (Lisbon, 1996)
Tsiomis, Y., and J. Rolin, 'Brasília', L'Architecture d'aujourd'hui, 313 (October 1997), pp. 76–87
Turner, J., 'Dwelling Resources in South America', Architectural Design (August 1963), pp. 360–93
—, 'The Squatter Settlement: An Architecture that Works', Architectural Design (October
    1968), pp. 355–60
'Una Vela nel Parco', Domus, 862 (September 2003), p. 26
UNESCO World Heritage Centre (2006), Brasília: http,//whc.unesco.org/en/list/445, accessed
    June 2006
Underwood, D., Oscar Niemeyer and Brazilian Free-Form Modernism (New York, 1994)
Wilcken, P., Empire Adrift: The Portuguese Court in Rio de Janeiro, 1808–1821 (London, 2004)
Williams, R. J., The Anxious City: English Urbanism at the End of the Twentieth Century
    (London 2006)
—, 'Modernist Civic Space', Journal of Urban History, XXXII/1 (November 2005), pp. 120–37
—, 'New Town Neuroses', Map, 4 (Winter 2005–6), pp. 36–9
—, 'Brasília After Brasília', Progress in Planning, 67 (2007), pp. 301–66
—, 'Paulo Mendes da Rocha', Blueprint, 251 (February 2007), pp. 36–43
—, 'Niemeyer in Brasília', Blueprint, 263 (February 2008), pp. 34–9
Wirth, J. D., and R. L. Jones, eds, Manchester and São Paulo: Problems of Rapid Urban Growth
    (Stanford, CA, 1978)

Wright, C. L., and B. Turkienicz, 'Brasília and the Ageing of Modernism', *Cities*, 4 (1988), pp. 347–64

Xavier, A., ed., *Depoimento de uma Geração* (São Paulo, 2003)

Zapparoli, A., 'Cores, Curvas e Concreto', *Veja* (27 July 2005), pp. 20–26

Zein, R. V., 'Descubre os Sete Erros', *Projeto Design*, 120 (April 1989), pp. 72–3

—, *O Lugar da Critica* (São Paulo, 2003)

Zimbres, P., 'Águas Claras: Um Exercício de Urbanismo no Distrito Federal', unpublished masterplan (1991)

Zueler, R., 'The Faces of Janus: Modernism and Hybridization in the Architecture of Lina Bo Bardi', *Journal of Architecture*, XI/2 (April 2006), pp. 257–68

Zweig, S., *Brazil: Land of the Future* (London, 1942)

Acknowledgements

Vivian Constantinopoulos has been a marvellous editor. My thanks to her for picking up on the project in the first place, and giving it a proper shape. There would have been no book without her. During the researching and writing of *Brazil*, my dealings with the following were in various ways invaluable: Tim Abrahams, Michael Asbury, Alice Bain, Nick Barley, Regina Teixera de Barros, Guy Brett, Leslie Brettell, Michael Bury, Hugh Campbell, Teixeira Coelho, Nathan Coley, Richard Coyne, Stephen Cairns, Mark Crinson, Vivienne Dalmeyer, Alastair Donald, Alan Farlie, Stephen Feeke, Clive Fenton, Les Forsyth, Valerie Fraser, Miles Glendinning, Jonathan Harris, Michael Hebbert, David Hopkins, Andrew Hussey, Jane M. Jacobs, Paul Jenkins, Tiffany Jenkins, Geoffrey Kantaris, Douglas Kellner, Florian Kossak, Debby Kuypers, Penny Lewis, Christoph Lindner, Isi Metzstein, Thomas Mical, Bob Morris, Lúcia Nagib, Oscar Niemeyer, Fred Orton, Karl Posso, Alex Potts, Alan Powers, Karl Sharro, Florian Urban, Marcus Verhagen, Tony Vidler, Iain Boyd Whyte, Austin Williams, Ruth Verde Zein, Paulo Zimbres and Sharon Zukin. In Rio de Janeiro, Marcos and Rose Vieira Lucas and their family provided incomparable hospitality, as well as an education in Brazilian music. In São Paulo, the outstanding FAU-USP library became a home from home. At home in Edinburgh, Stacy Boldrick, Alex Williams and Abigail Williams put up heroically (again) with my frequent and mysterious absences. I owe a special debt to Fred de Holanda of the University of Brasília, who provided me with a marvellously offbeat introduction to Brasília and its surroundings in 2001. He was a constant source of advice, criticism and encouragement thereafter.

The project was generously supported the Arts and Humanities Research Council (AHRC), the British Academy, and the University of Edinburgh, who provided research leave and funding for travel in various combinations between 2001 and 2007.

Photo Acknowledgements

The author and publishers wish to express their thanks to the following sources of illustrative material and/or permission to reproduce it. Every effort has been made to contact the copyright holders for illustrations in this book; if there are any inadvertent omissions these will be corrected in a future reprint.

L'Architecture d'Aujourd'hui: pp. 106, 107, 116; Arquivo Carmen Portinho: p. 87 (foot); Bureau du Livre Français: pp. 193, 194; René Burri / Magnum Photos: p. 94; Maria Elisa Costa: pp. 16, 56, 70, 71, 96, 102; MB Engenharia: pp. 128, 129; FAU-USP: pp. 15 (top), 97, 104, 141, 142, 143, 157, 175, 178, 179, 180, 181; Fondation Le Corbusier / DACS: pp. 15 (foot), 66, 67, 68; Fundação Oscar Niemeyer: pp. 45, 64, 74, 75; Instituto Lina Bo e P.M. Bardi: pp. 78, 147, 148 (top), 150, 151; Instituto Moreira Salles: p. 177; Anselm Kiefer: pp. 197, 198; Nelson Kon: p. 114; Konigsberger Vannuchi Arquitectos: p. 208; Julia MacKenzie: p. 223; Paulo Mendes da Rocha: p. 159; Museum of Modern Art, New York: pp. 6, 13, 32, 50, 51, 53, 54, 87 (top); *O Globo* archive: p. 21; Projeto Lygia Pape: p. 173; *RIBA Journal*: p. 123; Serpentine Gallery, London: p. 244; University of Chicago Press: p. 24; Versátil Home Video: p. 135; Igor de Vetyemy: p. 92; Whitechapel Art Gallery, London: pp. 168, 170, 172; Richard J. Williams: pp. 9, 10, 11, 26, 36, 37, 38, 39, 41, 46, 47, 57, 58, 60, 61, 62, 72, 73, 76, 79, 80, 81, 83, 84, 85, 86, 87 (top), 89, 90, 98, 100, 101, 103, 108, 109, 110, 112, 113, 118, 119, 120, 121, 125, 126, 127, 132, 134, 144, 148 (foot), 149, 154, 155, 156, 158, 160, 171, 184, 186, 187, 189, 190, 191, 199, 201, 203, 205, 210, 211, 212, 213, 214, 215, 216, 218, 222, 225, 226, 227, 228, 231, 232, 234, 238, 239, 242, 247, 250, 251, 252, 253, 255, 258 and 259.

Index

Numerals in *italics* indicate figures